AMBER
GOLD &
BLACK

AMBER GOLD & BLACK

The History of Britain's Great Beers

MARTYN CORNELL

To Arthur Harry Cornell (1922–1990)
and Herbert Charles 'Bert' Cornell (1926–2000)

My mentors in beer

Many thanks to Fuller, Smith & Turner of Chiswick, London
and Harvey & Sons of Lewes, Sussex, without whose help
this book would not have appeared.

First published 2010

The History Press
The Mill, Brimscombe Port
Stroud, Gloucestershire, GL5 2QG
www.thehistorypress.co.uk

© Martyn Cornell, 2010

The right of Martyn Cornell to be identified as the Author
of this work has been asserted in accordance with the
Copyrights, Designs and Patents Act 1988.

British Library Cataloguing in Publication Data.
A catalogue record for this book is available from the British Library.

ISBN 978 0 7524 5567 9

Typesetting and origination by The History Press
Printed in Great Britain

CONTENTS

INTRODUCTION

Britain is one of the world's greatest brewing nations: a fact the British themselves often seem to be unaware of. We need to be much more proud of what we have given ourselves and the world: beautiful, refreshing hoppy bitters and IPAs, golden summer ales for hot days in the garden, heady, rich barley wines, unctuous winter warmers, cheering, sociable, conversation-encouraging milds, creamy, reviving black porters and hearty, filling stouts, barley wines and old ales for sipping and relaxing, beers that go with food of all sorts and beers that can be enjoyed on their own, beer styles born in these islands and now appreciated and brewed from San Francisco to Singapore, from St Petersburg to Sydney.

This book is a celebration of the depths of British beer, a look at the roots of the styles we enjoy today, as well as those ales and beers we have lost; a study into how the liquids that fill our beer glasses, amber, gold and black, developed over the years and a look forward to some of the new styles of beer being developed in Britain in the twenty-first century, such as ales aged in casks that once contained whisky or rum.

Astonishingly, despite a greatly increased interest in beer as a subject in Britain over the past thirty or so years, this is the first book devoted solely to looking at the unique history of the different styles of beer produced in Britain; more world-conquering styles, it might be suggested, than any other nation has managed.

It may be a good thing that Britons would rather be down the pub enjoying their beer with friends than sitting on their own at home reading about it. But I hope that learning more about, for example, how bitter grew and developed out of the Victorian middle class' desire for the then newly fashionable pale ales once exclusively enjoyed by the gentry; how the demand by the street and river porters of London for a filling, strength-giving beer to help them get through the working day eventually gave us a style that, in Irish arms, circled the globe; how a style developed for Baltic aristocrats became Burton Ale, one of the most popular beers in Britain until a couple of generations ago and now almost forgotten; how beers such as Broom Ale, Mum and West Country White Ale once thrived and then vanished; how the huge boom in brewery numbers in Britain in the past thirty years, with more than 700 microbreweries now in operation, has helped bring in new styles such as golden ale and wood-aged beers, and even how nineteenth-century British brewers helped inspire the development of modern lager, all may add to the enjoyment of your beer-drinking experience, wherever you are doing it and encourage you to appreciate the marvellous drink, beer, more and to explore further its many offerings.

In addition, detailing the long histories behind Britain's beers may go some way to restoring respect for the country's national drink. While Thomas Hardy could write in *The Trumpet Major* of Dorchester beer that 'The masses worshipped it; the minor gentry loved it more than wine, and by the most illustrious county families it was not despised', today beer is seldom given the position at the heart of British gastronomic life that it deserves. British food grew and developed alongside beer and the two complement each other, just as French or Italian food is complemented by wine. Roast beef is fantastic with pale ale, porter is terrific with steak or lamb, stout is great with pork and chicken or spicy foods and any British cheese has its companion beer, from Cheddar and bitter to Stilton and barley wine – and desserts go just as well with beer too, as anyone who has tried apricot clafoutis with IPA, strong ale with plum pudding or chocolate stout with good vanilla ice cream will affirm.

In short, this book is a celebration of British beer in all its many beautiful shades and inspiring flavours. Good drinking!

1

BITTER

I'm getting rather hoarse, I fear,
After so much reciting:
So, if you don't object, my dear,
We'll try a glass of bitter beer –
I think it looks inviting.

Phantasmagoria, Lewis Carroll, 1869

The pint is one of the icons of Britain – and to most people today the beer in that iconic pint must be bitter, the amber-brown, malty beer strongly flavoured with hops that everyone imagines in the hands of Britons as they drink at an old oak table in a thatched-roof country pub, or while they enjoy an evening song around a battered piano in a cheery street-corner boozer. Except that bitter, while undoubtedly one of Britain's greatest contributions to the world of beer, only became the country's favourite drink in the early 1960s.

The origins of bitter, especially considering its popularity, are surprisingly obscure. There does not appear to have been a beer called 'bitter' much before the time that Queen Victoria came to the throne in 1837. What seems to have happened is that the name 'bitter' came about because drinkers wanted to differentiate the well-hopped, matured pale ales, which were gaining a place in brewers' portfolios around the country by the start of the 1840s, from the sweeter, less-aged and generally less hopped mild ales that, until then, had been almost the only alternative to porter and stout for most drinkers for more than a century.

Porter, which was slowly losing its enormous popularity when William IV died, after 100 years as the nation's top seller, was always called 'beer'. Even in the 1930s if you ordered simply 'beer' in certain pubs in 'mean neighbourhoods' you were likely to be served porter, no further questions asked. If you didn't want porter you asked for 'ale'. What you got for 'ale' was young, mild, sweet and, at that time around 1840, pale as well, being made generally entirely from pale malt. What to call it, then, when a new type of beer, pale, but tart, aged and hoppy, began appearing in pubs?

Brewers named, and continued to name, the new hoppier drink 'pale ale'. The London brewer Whitbread listed 'pale ale, mild ale, stout and Burton' as the 'four chief types of beer today', and many of the beers we think of today as bitters are still called 'pale ales' by their makers. Truman, Hanbury and Buxton brewed beers at its Burton upon Trent brewery called PA1 and PA2 for pale ales one and two. The first was its strong Ben Truman bitter, the second its standard bitter. When Young & Co.'s Ram brewery in Wandsworth, South London, closed in 2006, it still sent its 'ordinary' bitter out in casks labelled PA for Pale Ale, exactly the same as when it was first brewed in 1864, while casks of its special bitter are marked 'SPA'. In 1952 Marston's of Burton gave its best pale ale the name Pedigree Pale Ale, while London Pride was originally advertised by its brewer, Fuller, Smith & Turner, as London Pride pale ale; today no drinker would call Pedigree or Pride anything except brands of bitter.

However, there were no pump-clips on the handles of the beer engines in Victorian pubs (pump-clips did not appear until the 1930s and did not come into wide use until the 1950s) and while brewers could dictate the nomenclature of the new drink on labels of the bottled versions (which is why we have bottled pale ale, not bottled bitter), drinkers themselves could decide what they were going to call the draught version when they ordered it. They kept the name 'ale' for the old, mild style of drink and called the new one by a name that defined and contrasted it – bitter beer, 'bitter' for short. The ale/bitter, rather than mild/bitter dichotomy lasted for at least 120 years on the customers' side of the bar in some areas: Tom Berkley, who was a trainee pub manager in the early 1950s in Poplar, East London, close to the docks, had to learn quickly that when the stevedores walked in and said simply 'ghissile', they wanted mild, while bitter was more specifically 'pinta bi'er'.

From the start, 'pale ale' and 'bitter' were synonyms. The very first mention of the term 'bitter beer' in *The Times* comes on 5 September 1842, in a small advertisement for 'Ashby's Australian Pale Ale', made by the Quaker-founded Ashby's brewery in Staines, Middlesex, a few miles up the Thames from London, which 'is the most pleasant of all the different sorts of bitter beer that we have ever tasted', according to a newspaper quoted in the ad.

The best evidence for the idea that brewers and the public regarded pale ale and bitter beer as interchangeable synonyms comes with the 'great strychnine libel' of 1852. In March that year, a French professor, Monsieur Payen, claimed that large amounts of strychnine were being exported from France to England for use instead of hops to give beer a bitter flavour. The libel was repeated in an English medical journal, the *Medical Times and Gazette*, which wrote:

> It is just now the fashion to believe that bitter beer is the best stomachic that was ever invented ... That the bitterness of the best kind of 'pale ale' is given simply by an excess of hops or camomile we firmly believe [but] large quantities of strychnine have been made in Paris ... to be intended for exportation to England, in order to fabricate bitter beer.

A letter appeared in *The Times* on 29 March under the heading 'Bitter Beer', calling the wider public's attention to the French claim. This was answered by a broadside from the brewers intended to bring down M. Payen's canard, including a letter the next day from Michael Thomas Bass, head of one of Burton upon Trent's biggest brewers and one of the biggest exporters of pale ale to India. Bass said:

> When a letter is admitted into *The Times*, warning the public that they may be imbibing the most subtle and deadly poison while they are only dreaming of the pleasures of 'bitter beer', I may, perhaps, be pardoned as one of the brewers of that favourite beverage if I ask your permission to notice what the *Spectator* in its last number called a 'Paris Fable of Pale Ale' ... Why, Sir, India would long ago have been depopulated of its European inhabitants had there been anything pernicious in pale ale.

Bass's letter makes no distinction between bitter beer and pale ale and neither did a follow-up story published in *The Times* on 12 May 1852 under the heading 'Alleged adulteration of pale ales by strychnine'. This was about a report commissioned from two professors of chemistry in England by Henry Allsopp, head of another big Burton upon Trent brewer, which said: '... the charge of adulteration is totally unfounded, and the bitter beer drinker may dismiss all fears of being poisoned some day while quietly enjoying his favourite beverage.'

In the mid-nineteenth century, the new pale bitter drink was particularly in vogue with young middle-class and upper middle-class consumers as something visibly different from the sweeter milds and black porters of the working classes. In the novel *The Adventures of Mr. Verdant Green, an Oxford Freshman*, by Cuthbert Bede (the pseudonym of an Oxford don, the Reverend Edward Bradley), written around 1853, the Oxford undergraduates who populate its pages all drink bitter beer, which one of the characters calls 'doing bitters'. Not everybody welcomed this new drink; in 1850 an editorial in *The Times* said that while 'among the wealthier classes beer has been much superseded by light wines', among 'the middle ranks the iniquitous compound termed "bitter beer" bids fair to drive out the old British drink as completely as the Hanoverian rat exterminated that indigenous breed which is now only visible in the Isle of Portland.' Two years later the newspaper, talking about 'the "pale ale" of upper-class drinkers' and allegations of under-sized pints, said: 'If we were forced to drink a pint of 'bitter beer' for dinner we candidly own that we shouldn't care how small the measure was.'

By 1855 *Punch* magazine was making jokes about the 'fast young gents' who drank 'bitter beer' living an 'embittered existence'. A few years later, in 1864, the music hall artist Tom Maclagan, dressed as a fashionable 'swell' in a top hat and monocle and with nine-inch-long 'Dundreary' sideburns, was performing a song in praise of 'Bass's Bitter Beer', with the sheet music advertising India Pale Ale on the back page. The growing popularity of pale bitter ales among 'fast young gents' and swells (probably because pale ales were expensive and visibly different in the newly untaxed beer glasses that were then replacing pewter and china mugs in saloon bars) was intimately connected with the growth of Burton upon Trent as a brewing centre.

Pale ale had been around probably since the 1640s, after the invention of coke (coal with its toxic volatile elements removed). Maltsters could not use ordinary coal to dry the green malt, it poisoned their product, but they could use coke instead of wood or straw. This meant, with a more reliable fuel, they could control the temperature of the malt kilns, and thus the colour of the finished malt, more easily. With the invention and increasing use of the saccharometer in the eighteenth century, brewers were able to discover that pale malt contains more fermentable material than darker malts, and it was often used in the eighteenth century to brew strong, pale, heavily hopped October or stock beers, which matured for twelve months or more. However, these were expensive, because coke was more expensive than wood to dry malt and they were generally drunk only by the wealthy.

The cover to the sheet music of Tom Maclagan's music hall song from 1864, 'Bitter Beer', with the singer sporting the Dundreary whiskers of a mid-Victorian 'swell'

At the end of the eighteenth century a market for these stock pale ales grew up in India, where they were very popular with the civil servants (clerks and bureaucrats) and military servants (officers in its private armies) of the East India Company, the giant trading concern that ended up running much of the sub-continent. Before the reign of George IV, the biggest supplier to the Indian market was a brewer called Hodgson from Bow, on the eastern edge of London, close to the East India Company's docks. But the brewers of Burton upon Trent in Staffordshire began brewing a version of pale bitter beer in the 1820s to compete with Hodgson in the India market. This beer was originally known under a variety of names, including 'pale ale as prepared for India', but by the late 1830s it had become known as 'India Pale Ale' or 'East India Pale Ale'.

Although the brewers of the time scarcely knew why, the well waters of Burton, naturally laden with calcium sulphate thanks to the beds of gypsum deep below the town, were perfect for brewing highly-hopped, sparkling pale ales. The gypseous brewing liquor used by the town's brewers assisted the coagulation of proteinaceous matter during boiling (the 'hot break'), which would otherwise cause cloudiness in the beer. It allowed a higher hop ratio without bringing out harshness from the hops in the way that the carbonate-high waters used by London brewers did; took less colour out of the malt, producing paler beers even from already pale malts and promoted yeast growth during fermentation.

The arrival of the railway in Burton upon Trent in 1839 enabled the Staffordshire town's brewers to start sending the pale, hopped beers of the kind they shipped to India to customers around Britain as well, without having to pay the huge charges and suffer the inevitable pilfering they faced when sending their beers by canal. Their trade leapt by 50 per cent in a year and continued to climb rapidly. Within a few years other brewers had to offer similar pale bitter beers themselves to compete.

Before the 1840s the few advertisements for brewers in local newspapers normally listed only ale (in three separate grades, X, XX and XXX) and porter. One of the first brewers outside London and Burton to offer a bitter beer in the style of IPA was Thomas Henry Wyatt of the Bridge Street brewery, Banbury in Oxfordshire, who was advertising 'Very Fine Pale Bitter Ale (India)' in July 1843 at the high price of 17*d* a gallon, the most expensive beer on his list. An advertisement from 1851 from Laws and Company of the Chevalier brewery in King's Lynn, Norfolk declared: 'Pale Bitter Beer! Laws and Company, Family Brewers, have succeeded in producing an excellent article, which they are selling to families at 1*s* a gallon', showing a cheaper version of bitter-flavoured pale ale was now available.

The same year Hall & Woodhouse, then still at the Anstey brewery near Blandford, Dorset, said pale ale had 'recently been added' to its brews. A year later, 1852, Nanson & Co. of the Lady's Bridge brewery in Sheffield was advertising 'Bitter Beer'. But these were rarities. Through the 1850s most brewers seem to have carried on advertising just ale and porter. From the 1860s, however, many brewers had started brewing pale ales and were selling both an IPA and a lower-priced 'bitter ale'. In 1875 Henry Earle of the Barnet brewery, Middlesex, listed three different grades of 'bitter ales', IPA, BA and LBA, in descending order of strength and price.

Other brewers followed a similar pattern, though not always with a beer called IPA in the range. Michael Bowyer of the Stoke brewery, Guildford, Surrey, for example, brewed three different bitter ales in 1887: PA light bitter at 15*s* a kilderkin (18 gallon cask), implying an OG (original gravity – See Glossary for explanation) of around 1040 and a retail price of 3*d* a (quart) pot, about the cheapest brew in any Victorian pub; BA bitter ale at 18*s* a kilderkin, 4*d* a pot, with an OG of around 1045 to 1050; and BBA strong stock bitter at 27*s* a kilderkin, an OG of around 1070 and a retail price of 7*d* a pot.

The term 'bitter' never crossed the Atlantic as the name of a local-brewed beer style, perhaps because it came into being after the time of maximum English immigration to North America, though plenty of brewers in Canada and the New England states brewed pale ales for their customers. It occurs, however, in South Africa, Australia and New Zealand, where emigration from Britain was strong during the 1840s and 1850s, a time when the word was coming into use in British pubs. In 1868, in the recently founded town of Newcastle, Natal, William Peel's Umlaas brewery, a direct ancestor of the later South African Breweries, was selling 'Pale Bitter Ale' at 2*s* a gallon. In Australia the style kept its full name, rather than being shortened to just 'bitter', so that the South Australian brewery in Adelaide produced West End XXX Bitter Beer and Southwark Bitter Beer, while Toohey's Standard brewery in Sydney sold Standard Bitter Ale, and its rival, Tooth's, made Sydney Bitter Ale. Australian brewers also called their bottled versions of the beer 'bitter ale' or 'bitter beer', rather than pale ale, as in Britain. By the 1920s in Australia, however, 'bitter' as a style meant simply a slightly darker type of beer compared to local lager, served cold and brewed with bottom-fermenting yeast: Castlemaine XXXX, for example, called a lager in the UK, is known as a 'bitter ale' in its Queensland home.

At least one author, writing anonymously in 1884, regarded the development of Burton IPA as the invention of bitter beer in general. However, there was a style of hopped pale ale that existed independently of the IPA tradition, which went by the name KK or AK. Although the K style of bitter pale ale was probably an old one, evidence is lacking: one of the first mentions in print is in 1855 in an advertisement for the Stafford brewery, which was selling 'Pale India Ale' at 18*d* a gallon, and AK Ale, 'a delicate bitter ale', at 14*d* a gallon. The Burton brewer James Herbert said of AK ale: 'This class of ale has come very much into use, mostly for private families, it being a light tonic ale, and sent out by most brewers at 1*s* per gallon. The gravity of this Ale is usually brewed at 20lb', which is 1056 OG.

Other evidence suggests that Herbert was wrong in his estimation of the strength of AK, though it was certainly a popular style. A single edition of the *Richmond and Twickenham Times*, dated 8 July 1893, carries advertisements from five different brewers in south and west London, four of whom offered a beer called AK or KK, all indeed priced at 1*s* a gallon, which suggests an OG of 1045 to 1050. Professor Charles Graham, in his talk to the Society of Chemical Industry in 1881, confirmed the original gravity of AK as 1045, with an alcohol-by-weight of 4.3 per cent (5.4 per cent abv, which seems rather high), while Burton bitter, he said, has an OG of 1064 and an abv of 5.4 per cent. AK was matured for slightly less time than other pale ales: In 1898 Dr Edmund Moritz, describing beer types to a parliamentary committee on beer, spoke of light pale ales, or AK, kept two to three weeks before delivery, while other pale ales were kept for up to a month.

Brewers seem to have maintained a deliberate difference between the two types of bitter beer: lower-gravity, lighter-coloured, less-hopped AK light bitters, served relatively soon after brewing; and slightly darker, hoppier, stronger 'pale ales', often designated PA, stored for some time before sending out. The brewing books of Garne & Sons of Burford, Oxfordshire, in 1912 show AK being brewed at an OG of 1040 and with a colour of 14, a reddish-brown hue, while PA was brewed to an OG of 1056 and with a colour of 18, a darker, medium brown. The difference is confirmed by contemporary comments on the two beers. Alfred Barnard, the late-Victorian drinks writer, sampled an AK brewed by Rogers of Bristol in 1889, which he described as 'a bright sparkling beverage of a rich golden colour and … a nice delicate hop flavour'. Of Whitbread's Pale Ale, on the other hand, a more standard bitter, he wrote that it tasted 'well of the hop', though it too looked 'both bright and sparkling'. Crowley's brewery in Croydon High Street, Surrey, in 1900 described its AK in one of its advertisements as 'a Bitter Ale of sound quality with a delicate Hop flavour' and the frequent description of AK in Victorian advertisements of 'for family use' suggests a not-too-bitter, not-too-strong beer.

Why a K was used in the name of these pale, lower-hopped beers is a mystery yet to be properly solved. It may be simply to contrast with the X normally used for milds and darker ales. It may go all the way back to a popular medieval Dutch and Flemish beer called *koyt*, or *coyt*, which came in two strengths, single and double. In Old Flemish, the word for 'single' was *ankel* (*enkel* in modern Dutch), making 'single koyt' *ankel koyt*, which could easily have been shortened to AK. Many Dutch and Flemish brewers immigrated to England in the fifteenth and sixteenth centuries, bringing with them a preference for brewing with hops and a large number of brewing terms, from gyle to kilderkin. Perhaps they brought '*Ankel Koyt*' with them too. What AK does not have anything to do with, despite mythology to the contrary, is a brewer called Arthur King. Nor is it short for 'Asquith's Knockout', since the beer easily pre-dates Herbert Asquith, the Edwardian politician notoriously fond of a drink and who was Prime Minister in 1914 when the First World War began and beer taxes leapt from 7s 9d to 23s a barrel.

There was certainly room for a lower-hopped bitter beer, since the first rush of popular pale ales used hops in substantial quantities. Michael Bass, the Burton brewer, revealed in 1857 that even 'common beer' used up to 2 or 2½lb of hops per barrel, while 'Pale Ale and every superior quality of beer' used a remarkable 18lb of hops per quarter of malt, around 3¼lb to 4½lb of hops to the barrel. These were beers that needed vatting for twelve months or more to be drinkable. As tastes changed towards what was called in 1890 a 'less intoxicating and less narcotising' beer, which was produced more quickly, without lengthy storing, hop rates dropped. By 1902, the average for all beers in the UK was 1.9lb of hops per barrel, with a survey in 1908 finding 'London pale ale' hopped at a rate of 2lb 2oz to 2lb 13oz per barrel. By 1935, the average hop rate for all beers had dropped by a third, to 1.29lb a barrel.

The 1908 study, from the *American Handy Book of the Brewing, Malting, and Auxiliary Trades*, found London pale bitter ale had a quoted gravity of 14 Balling, equal to an OG of 1057. While for porter and stout all hops were added at the beginning of the boil, for pale beers a quarter to a third of the total was added 15–20 minutes before kettle knock-out, to give hop aroma, not just bitterness to the final beer. The 'classic' hop for

bitter ales is Goldings, specifically East Kent Goldings, but excellent versions of English bitter are made with such hop varieties as Northdown,
Challenger and Styrian Goldings, which, despite its name, is a variety of
the other great English hop, Fuggles.

Today the general definition of bitter is that it is pale, drier than a brewer's other products and the most highly hopped. Even now, strengths can
vary considerably: Palmers of Bridport in Dorset once brewed a so-called
'boys' bitter', BB, with an OG of just 1030.4, less than 3 per cent alcohol,
while Fuller Smith & Turner at Chiswick in West London bottles Extra
Special Bitter, ESB, at an OG of 1059, giving nearly 6 per cent alcohol.
Colour can also show considerable variation, from the golden bitters of
Manchester to the ambers of the South East and the ruddy, almost cor-
nelian shades of some West Country pale ales. Most traditional brewers
still produce at least two different bitters, an 'ordinary', today around 1037
OG, and a more expensive 'best' of around 1045 to 1048 OG. When bottled beers were more popular, these were put into bottle as 'light ale' and
'pale ale' respectively, and it was the light ale that drinkers would add to
poor quality draught beer as a light-and-bitter or light-and-mild.

Any attempt to find regional styles in bitter is controversial, with
many observers insisting that there are more differences to be found in
neighbouring brewers' beers than similarities. Finding real regional variety is made more difficult by the disappearance of so many hundreds of
regional breweries. However, there are useful generalisations that can be
made. Andrew Campbell, writing in 1956, said that London bitters were
'a little lighter [in strength] and either sweeter or less strongly hopped
than many from the country'. Campbell found Watney's ordinary
bitter, for example, brewed at the time at the Mortlake brewery near
Richmond in Surrey, was 'not very highly hopped', while its Red Barrel
bottled pale ale (later to win notoriety as one of the most widely available keg beers) was 'not very bitter, yet not sweet'. London bitters also
frequently have loose, big-bubbled heads which soon disappear.

Bitters from the North West of England were (and are) often very pale
and extremely, sometimes mouth-puckeringly bitter. Bitters from the
South West were often (but not always) sweeter and less well attenuated
than bitters from other parts of the country. Midland bitters were again
often sweet, but thin. Bitters from Kent were often very hoppy.

There are regional biases to be found in production methods, which
can make for particular tastes. For example, the Yorkshire Square method
of fermentation, found mainly in Yorkshire and Nottinghamshire (but
also in the past, in Norfolk and even at Watney's brewery in London), in

which the excess yeast produced in the fermenting wort flows up from a lower chamber to a top 'barm deck'. The system produces full, malty, highly conditioned beers which are well-hopped and then served with a tight, creamy head through a 'sparkler' device on the handpump tap.

An analysis of the brewing books from 1903 at Hammonds' brewery in Bradford, Yorkshire, by Dr Keith Thomas of Brewlab, found that it was producing four different strength bitters from 1042 OG to 1055 OG, all light in colour, 'possibly gold or straw', and with limited malt flavour although moderated by caramel. Large amounts of hops were used, to give EBU (European Bitterness Unit) bitterness levels of from 34 units to 55, which, as Dr Thomas says, means 'even the low gravity beers seem to be considerably more bitter than accepted today'. Bitterness would have dominated the flavour, despite a good mouth feel, because of the unfermented sugars that are evident in the moderately high final gravities shown in the brewing books.

The best known regional brewing method used for pale ales was the Burton union system, found in Staffordshire but also, in the past, in Derbyshire, Nottinghamshire, Edinburgh and (again) London. It turns out fruitier bitters which are often, because of the calcium sulphate-imbued water found in Burton and replicated by brewers elsewhere, distinctly sulphury.

A rather less well-known, though formerly common method was the 'dropping' system, where the partially fermented wort is dropped into a new vessel on a lower floor to reinvigorate the yeast and leave behind the first lot of 'trub', or dead yeast, and coagulated protein. It was once found from Bristol to Newark via Oxfordshire and London (Whitbread's brewery in Chiswell Street was still using it in the 1950s and Young's brewery used it occasionally in the early twenty-first century). It is said to give a butterscotch flavour to the beers. By the end of the twentieth century only one brewer was still regularly using the 'dropping' system, Brakspear's of Henley, in Oxfordshire, though when that brewery closed in 2002 its equipment and the 'dropping' system, was recreated at the Wychwood brewery in Witney, Oxfordshire to carry on brewing Brakspear beers.

Although pale bitter ales were increasingly popular from the 1850s, especially among the middle classes, they were still a minority taste, in part because they were more expensive. Bitter was 6*d* a 'pot', or quart, in the pub and thus sometimes known as 'six-ale', while mild, 'four-ale', was a third cheaper at 4*d* a pot. In the 1890s at Steward and Patteson, the big Norwich brewer, pale and light bitter ales made up only 5 per cent

'Six-ale' – bitter at sixpence a 'pot' or quart – advertised in the window of the Bakers Arms, Euston Square, London just before the First World War

of production. The best-selling beer, the standard tipple in the public bar, was mild, which had replaced porter as the nation's favourite. For the next sixty years, through the 'great gravity drop' of the First World War, which saw light bitter, under the pressure of higher excise duty and restrictions on raw materials, plunge from an OG of 1047 to 1030, and pale ale from 1055 to 1047, bitter remained, to quote Maurice Gorham in 1949, 'the staple draught drink in the Saloon Bar' but not much ordered in the public bar. However, Gorham said, 'it quite often happens that a house is out of bitter, and has nothing to serve but mild'.

Bitter was still clearly the minority drink even after the Second World War (at Hyde's brewery, Manchester, for example, it made up only 15 per cent of total production). But in the 1950s, mild began to lose ground. Much of the reason was precisely bitter's image as a middle-class choice. A commentator in 1958 wrote: 'In many parts of the country, the drinking of bitter beers is on the increase. Traditionally bitter is looked on as the bosses' drink. Any man reckons today he's as good as his boss. So he chooses bitter.' In 1959 draught mild still outsold draught bitter nationally by two pints to one, and draught bitter represented only one pint in five of total beer consumption. Within six years, however, by 1965 bitter had overtaken mild to become the country's most popular beer style.

Ten years later bitter peaked at just over 60 per cent of draught beer sales. Soon after the first new microbrewers began in Britain and quickly there were more different makes of bitter available than there had been for decades. Unfortunately, none of these new brewers had the marketing power of the big lager manufacturers and sales of bitter began to decline. They lifted only briefly around 1991–93, when the UK government's 'guest beer' orders, designed to increase competition, forced the national brewers to open up the bar-tops in their then massive pub estates to other brewers' beers. Since 1995 draught bitter has been only the second-best selling beer in the country; though for all that, perhaps the most loved by those who drink it. The best bitter beers leave the drinker satisfied and yet still happy to have more. The harmony of complex flavours that the finest examples contain, even at comparatively low alcoholic strengths, is one of Britain's greatest contributions to bibulous pleasure.

Today drinkers still have hundreds of bitters to choose from, but there are some that stand out. One is Landlord, from Timothy Taylor & Co., Keighley, West Yorkshire, at 1042 OG 4.3 per cent abv, a tremendously 'moreish', satisfying special bitter. It is the avowed favourite of beer drinkers from Ted Tuppen, chief executive of Britain's biggest pub company, Enterprise Inns, to Madonna, who was introduced to it by her former husband, Guy Ritchie. Landlord is made with Styrian Goldings and the almost floral hop flavours mesh brilliantly with the round, not-too-full maltiness.

Southerners would probably vote for the ordinary or special bitters from Young's, which transferred from their original home in Wandsworth in 2006 to Wells' brewery in Bedford, or London Pride from Fuller Smith & Turner of the Griffin brewery, Chiswick, London, at 1041.5 OG. All three of Fuller's bitters, the others being Chiswick at 3.5 per cent abv and ESB at 5.5 per cent, are excellent examples of the style, but London Pride, now one of Britain's most widely available cask beers, noses ahead: flowery, honeyed, a touch of marmalade and a Goldilocks attitude to alcohol – not too weak, not too strong, just right.

In the West Country, Palmer's IPA from J.C. & R.H. Palmer of The Old Brewery, Bridport, Dorset, at 1040 OG, 4.2 per cent abv, is dryer than the typical West Country bitter, with a deep copper colour and, like all the best bitters, a marvellous balance between sweet malt and bitter hop, with a lingering bitter aftertaste that almost demands another pint to follow. This is a hard-to-find beer that is, as a result, nowhere near as well-known as it ought to be.

Many drinkers, however, would rate as their number one bitter Adnam's, from the Sole Bay brewery, Southwold, Suffolk. At 1036 OG it is fine example of the complex flavour-filled beers British brewers can produce at comparatively low alcoholic strengths. It combines the two best known English hops, Fuggles and Goldings, in a subtle symphony with sweet malt.

Some prefer the hoppier Best Bitter from another established family brewer, Harveys of Lewes in Sussex, with Fuggles and Goldings hops again, and also Bramling Cross and Progress, two hops with Goldings in their ancestry.

One of the best breed of 'new' bitters is also, like Adnams, from East Anglia: Wherry Best Bitter, brewed by Woodforde's Norfolk Ales at Woodbastwick, Norfolk. The 1037.4 OG bitter has been a classic since its introduction when the brewery started in 1981; amber coloured, with a remarkable length of flavour as biscuity malt holds up citrus-tinged hops. It is certainly a worthy addition to the many offerings available in Britain's favourite native beer style.

2

MILD

'You must have seen great changes since you were a young man,' said Winston tentatively. The old man's pale blue eyes moved from the darts board to the bar, and from the bar to the door of the Gents … 'The beer was better,' he said finally. 'And cheaper! When I was a young man, mild beer — wallop we used to call it — was fourpence a pint. That was before the war, of course.' 'Which war was that?' said Winston. 'It's all wars,' said the old man vaguely. He took up his glass, and his shoulders straightened again. 'Ere's wishing you the very best of 'ealth!'

Nineteen Eighty-Four, George Orwell, 1949

Mild is Britain's most misunderstood beer. Originally the main, indeed, the only standard for a beer called mild was that it should be fresh, not more than a couple of weeks old, and have the taste and aroma that come with freshness. Any older, past the point at which the beer starts exhibiting the flavours that come with maturity, and it isn't mild any more, at least not what brewers would have recognised as mild back in the nineteenth and early twentieth centuries. To quote one commentator from 1869: 'New ale and porter, which are free from acid, are named mild.' That was it. For Victorian brewers, and those who came before them, any beer, strong or weak, hoppy or not, dark or light, could be called mild if it was young enough.

All the other characteristics generally associated with mild today are secondary to the fact that it was meant to be delivered into the pub soon after it was brewed (just four to ten days after being casked, against maturation periods of twenty-one days or more even for the lighter draught pale ales, according to the brewing chemist Dr Edmund Moritz, speaking in 1898), and drunk soon after that. 'Mild ale', *The Brewer's Art* said, 'is a draught beer

HAMMONDS DARK MILD is now a better drink than ever!

Next time you order a pint of Hammonds Dark Mild, you'll get an even better, more full-bodied beer, and it costs 2d. less now—thanks to the Budget. Try it and see!

A budget tax cut in the 1950s spurred the Yorkshire brewer Hammonds to advertise its dark mild, pictured in the classic ten-sided English pint glass

brewed for quick consumption'. Milds were and are frequently lower-hopped than other beers, because their speedy turnover meant that they do not need high hop levels to repel bugs that would make them go sour. The 1908 edition of the *American Handy Book of the Brewing, Malting, and Auxiliary Trades* said 'London four ale', or mild, so called because of its price in the public bar of 4*d* a quart, was brewed at an OG of 1053 to 1057 and 13oz to 1lb 4oz of hops per (US) barrel, a maximum of 1lb 13oz an imperial barrel, less than half the quantity of hops compared to pale ale/bitter, where the rate was at least 2lb 3oz an imperial barrel.

However, it is very possible to have a well-hopped mild. Thomas Sydenham, the seventeenth-century English physician sometimes called the English Hippocrates, drank small beer, 'soft and mild' but 'well-hopped', at both dinner and supper on the grounds that it formed 'an excellent diluent with food', according to William Brande, and 'he justly considered its being well hopped as possessing an important advantage'. The anonymous *Publican, Innkeeper and Brewer's Guide* referred to 'mild hopped ale' with 40lb of hops to 60 bushels of malt, which, at an OG of 1060, would be around 1lb 8oz a barrel.

Milds are often sweetish, since it takes time for yeasts to convert the higher sugars into alcohol. Milds were and are frequently weaker than other beers, again because their rapid turnover meant they did not need alcohol to preserve them from infection. But it was common, in the nineteenth century, for milds to be much stronger than they were in the later parts of the twentieth century. Professor Charles Graham, speaking to the Society of Chemical Industry in 1881 about beer strengths, listed five types of mild which ranged in original gravity from 'Scotch mild' at 1053 up to Burton mild at 1080, with the standard X and XX milds at 1055 and 1061 respectively. In 1902, Brook & Co. of the Cubley Brook brewery, Penistone, Yorkshire, was advertising 'Wharncliffe' Extra Strong Mild at a price that suggested an OG of around 1075.

To a brewer, a strong mild ale was generally not something ready for immediate drinking, but the name given to freshly produced beer that, because of its strength, needed to be laid down for some months. It would then lose the mawkish flavours of immature strong beer and, over time, turn into stock ale. The *Brewers' Journal*, in an article from 1936 on the brewing of strong stock ales 'of 30lb gravity and upwards' (that is over 1080 OG), said: 'The successful production of strong mild ale required to mature during a period of from nine to twelve months in wood prior to bottling requires both skill and experience.'

As a type of beer, mild goes back to the pre-Norman period. Charters and laws from the seventh century onwards listing the food rents required from an estate mention two main types of ale, one being *lithes aloth*, which translates from the Old English as either mild ale or sweet ale. This would have been newly brewed and still unacid, and probably still rather cloudy as well, since the other main type of Old English ale was called *hlutres aloth* or clear ale. This had been left standing long enough to clear (hence its later name, stale ale, from the same word as stall, something that stands or has been stood). By the time this ale had cleared, even using herbs such as alehoof, which was meant to clear ale quickly, it would probably have acquired at least a touch of sharp, sour flavour. These were the original, unhopped ales and whatever herbs they may have been flavoured with, those herbs were not as efficient as hops at keeping the souring bugs at bay.

Mild ale goes largely unmentioned for ten centuries or so, though the occasional record suggests it was sold cheaper than more mature beer. In Coventry in 1421 the mayor commanded that 'no brewstere sell no derre a galon of good ale will hit is new under the here syve [that is, just finished fermenting and just strained through a hair sieve] but for 1¼d and when hit is good and stale for 1½d.' By the time of William III, around 1699, (and probably long before that, too) mild ale and stale ale were frequently drunk mixed together, depending on the customer's preference, a practice illustrated in a pamphlet published that year titled 'The Sot's Paradise, or Humours of a Derby Alehouse', which contains the lines:

> In comes a female tapstress pale and wan
> Sodd'n with fumes of what she'd drank and drawn
> Sir, do you please, I pray, to have your ale
> Drawn new or with a little dash of stale?

According to a brewery rep, or 'outdoor clerk', writing under the pseudonym Obadiah Poundage in 1760 about the drinking habits of Londoners fifty years earlier, stale beer was simply the mild beer kept 'some time'. It was matured by third-party entrepreneurs who would buy fresh, mild, brown beer, the staple drink of the capital's working class in the early eighteenth century, keep it until it was stale and then sell it to the publicans. This arrangement saved both brewers and publicans cash-flow difficulties, though it denied the brewers profits which went to the middlemen.

Some drinkers liked to order 'mild beer and stale mixed', others 'three-threads' (most likely a mixture of strong pale ale, mild beer and stale beer blended together) at 3*d* per quart, but 'many used all stale at fourpence per pot,' Poundage said.

His account is corroborated by two anonymous rhyming 'good pub guides' to London published around 1716 to 1720, the *Vade Mecum for Malt Worms* (malt worm being an old slang expression for a drinker) and the *Guide for Malt Worms*. Almost thirty different types of beer were mentioned in the guides, the most common being twopenny pale ale (the most expensive regular beer in London), mild, stale and stout. Mild and stale were frequently mentioned together in the two guides, suggesting they were indeed drunk mixed or half-and-half, in the same way that mid-twentieth century drinkers drank mild-and-bitter.

Since mild was originally a description rather than a style, it was possible to find mild or freshly brewed, immature versions of any sort of beer: mild bitter (Sherwood brewery in Caerleon was advertising Mild Bitter at 1*s* a gallon in the nineteenth century, and McMullen's AK, a lightly hopped low-gravity pale brew, was being sold as Mild Bitter in the 1950s, while Toohey's brewery in Sydney, Australia, also sold a Mild Bitter Ale), mild porter, even mild stout (Ed Alexander of the Springfield brewery, Sydenham, was selling bottled Mild Stout in 1874, for example, while the Van Steemberge brewery in Ettvelde, East Flanders, still sells Wilson Mild Stout, a sweet, quite strong brown ale.) Public taste for mild stout eventually led to the invention of milk stout, using lactic sugars that would not ferment, so that the drink stayed sweet.

Wahl and Henius said of the style as brewed in that time in the United Kingdom: 'Mild beers, *whether ale, porter, or stout* [my italics], are called such as undergo no secondary fermentation, but are marketed about seven days after the principal fermentation is finished.' They added: 'The mild beers are distinguished from the stock beers by a more sweetish (mild) taste, containing more unfermented maltodextrin and less acid, the old beers, on the other hand, becoming more alcoholic and tart.' Stout has 'a sweetish taste if mild, and a more or less tart taste, according to age and circumstances'.

Through the nineteenth century, however, 'mild' as a term on its own gradually began to be restricted to the malt liquors of the kind brewed by London's specialist ale brewers, rivals to the porter brewers, who included names such as Goding of Knightsbridge (and later Lambeth), Stretton of Golden Square, Charrington and Mann of Mile End, Courage of Horsleydown, and Wyatt of Portpool Lane, Clerkenwell.

Their ale was sold mild, that is young, and 'ale', at least in London, became a synonym for 'mild'. To quote *Back to the Local*, 'In London pubs ale stands for mild ale.'

The ale brewers' drink seems to be descended from the original unhopped ale of the fourteenth century and before, as opposed to the porter brewers, whose product was a type of beer; the drink with a Dutch/German name made with hops that was brought to Britain from mainland Europe by immigrant brewers from the Low Countries early in the fifteenth century. By the end of the seventeenth century, ale in Britain, like beer, also contained hops, albeit fewer of them, but the two drinks continued to be regarded as separate; in the eighteenth century ale was still sold in the old 32 gallon ale barrel, not the 36 gallon beer barrel (a difference between the two put into law in the reign of Henry VIII, two centuries earlier, when ale was completely unhopped) at 16s a barrel, according to William Ellis in the *London and Country Brewer*. However, as early as the sixteenth century, the ale brewers' operations, in London at least, had been overtaken in scale by the beer brewers. The porter boom reinforced this. In 1814 even the twelfth largest London porter brewer made 50 per cent more beer in a year than the largest London ale brewer.

Writers on beer in the eighteenth century, such as Ellis, and Michael Combrune, continued to be careful to maintain a difference between ale, lightly hopped, and beer, more heavily hopped, and to talk about 'malt liquors' if they meant both types of drink. Both writers also confirm that ale was drunk 'mild', or young, as it probably would have been originally, since unhopped or lightly hopped malt liquor will not keep too long. Ellis wrote that ale 'to preserve in its mild Aley Taste, will not admit of any great Quantity of Hops'. Combrune said ales 'are not required to keep a long time'. While less hopped, they were strong, in order to try to keep bacterial infection away that would make them go sour and ropey. John Tuck's *Private Brewer's Guide to the Art of Brewing Ale and Porter* of 1822 says London ale in 1759 was brewed at 1½ to 1¾ barrels to the quarter of malt, around 1080 OG, while porter, which fell into the 'beer' category, was brewed at 2¼ to 2¾ barrels to the quarter, around 1065 OG. Even in 1819, Tuck's figures suggest that London ale was still 1070 OG, perhaps 7 per cent abv, while porter was weaker at 1060.

What was this 'ale' like? The *Cyclopaedia of Several Thousand Practical Receipts, and Collateral Information in the Arts, Manufactures and Trades*, gives a recipe for 'Ale, London' that uses all pale malt, at just under 2½ barrels of ale to the quarter of malt, which would give an OG of around

1070 or 1080, and 3lb 5oz of hops to the barrel, 8lb to the quarter of malt (6lb to the quarter if the ale was 'for immediate use'). This would be a lot of hops today, for a standard beer, but even now about right for ale of 1070 OG, according to Hough, Briggs and Stevens' *Malting and Brewing Science*.

The surprise is that while in the twentieth century, and certainly the second half of the twentieth century, most beers sold as 'mild' were dark – an analysis of the 1976 Campaign for Real Ale's *Good Beer Guide* shows that of 130 milds being brewed by 106 brewers, 101, or 77.7 per cent, were coloured mid-brown through to black, while just 29, or 22.3 per cent, were pale or light – in the nineteenth century milds were evidently not dark at all. Ron Pattinson, an historian of brewing methods, has made a study of old brewers' records and found that the malt used to make the standard X mild ale in the nineteenth century was almost always pale, which meant that these beers were 'usually pale in colour', albeit 'with fewer hops and a lesser degree of attenuation than pale ale', that is, less bitter and sweeter.

London's semi-hard water extracted more colour from malt than the permanently hard waters of Burton upon Trent, the iron mash tuns used by many brewers were reckoned to darken the worts obtained from them, and these milds were stronger liquors than most of the pale ales, with a higher percentage of everything from fermentables to colouring materials in the wort, than Victorian bitter beers. So even if they were brewed with pale malt, London ales, in the first seventy-five or so years of the nineteenth century, were very likely darker than the pale ales of Burton. But they were not the dark brown to almost black brews that made up the bulk of mild ales in the later twentieth century.

Gradually, mild ale began to take sales away in the capital from porter. The twelve principal porter brewers still provided 75 per cent of London's beer in the first decade of the nineteenth century, but the ale brewers in London were gradually gaining ground, and with a product that appears to have been mild rather than mature. The movement was being led by London's more up-market beer drinkers. John Martineau, a partner in Whitbread's brewery, told a parliamentary committee in 1817 that 'generally speaking, at the West End of the town [where the 'better class' of people lived] they drink their beer very mild.' Gourvish and Wilson, in *The British Brewing Industry 1830–1980*, quote a witness to the 1833 House of Commons select committee on the sale of beer who said that the London drinker:

GRIFFIN BREWERY, CHISWICK.

FULLER, SMITH, AND TURNER'S
WELL KNOWN BEERS

ARE NOW SUPPLIED IN 4½ GALLON CASKS (PINS).

PRICE LIST.

	Kils.	Firks.	Pins.		Kils.	Firks.	Pins.
AK Light Bitter Ale	18s. 0d.	9s. 0d.	4s. 9d.	P Porter	18s. 0d.	9s. 0d.	4s. 9d.
XK Bitter Pale Ale	22s. 0d.	11s. 0d.	6s. 0d.	S Single Stout	22s. 0d.	11s. 0d.	5s. 9d.
X Amber Ale (mild)	20s. 0d.	10s. 0d.	5s. 3d.	DS Double Stout	27s. 0d.	13s. 6d.	7s. 0d.

A Cash Discount of 1s. per Kilderkin 6d. per Firkin, and 3d. per Pin allowed.

Frequent Deliveries in the Neighbourhood.

AGENTS—FOSTER AND CO., Surbiton Hill; STOUT & CO., High Street, Brentford; EDWARD MARCH Barnes, S.W.R.; W. EVANS, Hampton Court and East Molesey; S. BARDRICK, Family Grocer, Kew Green; F. P. MEASOR, Family Grocer, 16, King Street, Twickenham.

CHARLES ASHBY & CO., LIMITED,
BREWERS OF PALE AND MILD ALES FOR FAMILY USE,
STAINES.

LONDON STORES :—WATERLOO STATION.

PRICE LIST.

MILD AND STOCK ALES

	18 galls.	9 galls.		18 galls.	9 galls.
Table Ale	15s.	7s. 6d.	Mild Ale, XXX	30s.	15s. 0d.
Harvest Ale	15s.	7s. 6d.	Christmas Ale, XA	30s.	15s. 0d.
Mild Ale KX	18s.	9s. 0d.			

PALE ALES.

	18 galls.	9 galls.		18 galls.	9 galls.
Family Table Ale, FTA	15s.	7s. 6d.	Pale Ale I	21s.	10s. 6d.
Family Pale Ale, FA	17s.	8s. 6d.	India Pale Ale	23s.	11s. 6d.
Pale Ale, BFA	18s.	9s. 0d.			
Porter				18s.	9s. 0d.
Double Stout				29s.	14s. 6d

These Ales can be had in 4½ gallon casks at proportionate prices. A discount of 6d. per nine gallons will be allowed for flash, paid strictly on delivery. Discount allowed on 4½ gallon casks.

Two newspaper advertisements from 1893 showing the range of draught beers sold by Victorian brewers, including milds called X, KX and XXX

will have nothing but what is mild, and that has caused a considerable revolution in the trade, so much so that Barclay and Perkins, and other great houses, finding that there is a decrease in the consumption of porter, and an increase in the consumption of ale, have gone into the ale trade; nearly all the new trade is composed of mild ale.

One cautionary point: this was the London market, and different things were undoubtedly happening outside the capital. There is, for example, a small ad in *The Times* from November 1845 which reads: 'WANTED to HIRE, a COUNTRY BREWERY, of about an eight-quarter plant, with public-houses and trade attached. It must be in a mild beer country. A distance from 30 to 50 miles from Cambridge would be preferred.' What this suggests is that parts of regional England, at least, were already given over to drinking mild beer. Thirty to fifty miles round Cambridge would take in a chunk of East Anglia, which was certainly 'a mild beer country' later in the century; at Steward & Patteson of Norwich the XX mild made up 45–50 per cent of production in the 1890s.

Before the Beer House Act of 1830 removed the 10s a barrel duty on beer (leaving taxed only the raw materials, malt and hops), regional brewers seem to have produced just one strength of beer in each style. The evidence is scarce, since local newspapers were rare before 1855, when the newspaper tax was abolished in Britain, and thus advertisements by brewers are hard to find from before the 1850s. James Durham of the Spread Eagle brewery in Northampton in 1800 advertised only Old Ale at 1s 10d a gallon, Mild Ale at 1s 8d and Porter at 1s 6d a gallon. Parsons & Co. of the St Clement's brewery in Oxford in 1826 sold one grade of strong ale at 1s 9d a gallon, one grade of mild at 1s 2d a gallon, porter and brown stout.

After 1830, when the duty came off beer, beer ranges seem to explode. Samuel Allsopp and Sons of Burton upon Trent, for example, sold nine different types of beer in 1861, of which four were milds, XX at 48s a barrel, XXX at 54s, F at 60s and A at 66s; their prices suggesting they ranged in strength from 1055 OG to 1090 or so. The Edinburgh brewer William Younger in 1862–63 sold its London customers four types of 'Scotch Mild Ale' from X at 38s a barrel to a thundering XXXX at 68s.

The X system was used mostly for milds in the Victorian era, or at least malt liquors made in the 'ale' tradition rather than the 'pale ale' or 'bitter ale' style, although Xs were not exclusive to milds, and before around 1860 the adjective 'mild' was rarely seen in price lists. The Stafford brewery in 1855, for example, only listed four types of 'ale' among its ten products, from 'X Ale' at 30s a barrel to 'XXXX Ale' at 54s. Gradually the descriptions became fuller, so that by 1893 A. Gordon & Co. of the Peckham brewery in South East London would be selling XXXX 'Strong Mild Ale' at 60s a barrel (around 1080 OG) and XXX 'Rich Mild Ale' at 48s (1055 to 1060 OG), as well as XX and X milds, while Henry Lovibond's Cannon brewery in Fulham, South West London, called its XXXX 'Best Quality Mild' and its XXX 'Extra Strength Mild'. (The opposite of 'mild' was, by the 1860s, 'hard' rather than 'stale', but this word never appears in brewers' advertising.)

The taste for mild was taken to Britain's colonies in the nineteenth century. Collison's brewery in Cape Town, South Africa, was selling 'Mild Scotch Ale' in 1837. Molson, the Canadian brewer, was brewing mild ale for one shilling (sic) a gallon at its Montreal brewery in 1859, and an XX mild in 1869. Several Australian brewers made milds, including Carlton in Melbourne, which was selling XXX mild in the 1880s.

However, the only colonial country where mild became a big seller was New Zealand, perhaps because it was settled at a time in the nineteenth century, the 1850s, when mild was becoming the dominant style among the young beer drinkers who were most likely to be emigrants. There it was probably the ancestor of the sweet, amber-coloured beer style now known as 'Kiwi Brown' or 'Draught', hugely popular in New Zealand for decades.

Back home, there seem to have been few specifically regional styles of mild. In Scotland the perceived position of mild as a low-gravity beer was filled by the style known as 'light', in opposition to the stronger 'heavy', 'light' being, paradoxically, usually dark in colour. About the only real example of a regional mild came from the North East of England around Durham and Northumberland. The local miners went for a very sweet, dark mild ale, known as Newcastle Mild or Newcastle sweet ale, with what Victorian observers called a 'sub-acid' flavour, hovering on the edge of tart.

The beer was sweet and dark because that was the sort the local 'indifferent' water supply made best, and in 1890 the journalist Alfred Barnard was told the Durham and Northumberland pit-men held it in high repute and 'prefer it to any other'. Brewers, such as John Barras (later a cornerstone of Newcastle Breweries) and Reid & Co., advertised themselves as brewers of the 'celebrated' Newcastle Mild Ales. However, although Newcastle Mild was said to be the only beer brewed in the town in 1863, by 1890 it was disappearing from Newcastle itself and the larger towns of the region, its place taken by more bitter ales from the brewers of Edinburgh and Burton. The North East was ahead of the rest of England in its tastes: Julian Baker, writing in 1905, declared that 'mild or four-ale … is still the beverage of the working classes'. This had only been true in the capital for the previous twenty years or so, however. Whitbread, then the third or fourth biggest brewer in London, whose production was entirely porter up to 1834, started brewing mild ale in 1835.

Output in thousand barrels of selected London brewers

Primarily porter brewers	1830	1850	1880
Barclay Perkins	320	460	480
Truman	230	420	580
Whitbread	190	207.2	250
Primarily ale brewers			
Mann	7	96	220
Charrington	15	84	470
Courage	10	56	250

Gradually the other big porter brewers followed, although it took almost forty years until the last porter-only brewer in London, Meux & Co., on Tottenham Court Road, began brewing ale as well, in 1872. Although the capital's original ale brewers began growing swiftly from the start of William IV's reign as tastes shifted towards their product, it was half a century before porter completely lost its pre-eminence and the ale brewers grew to be on equal terms with the former porter giants, and the important growth came after the Great Exhibition of 1851. It should also be said that over the years, not only did the porter brewers start brewing ale, but the ale brewers started brewing porter and stout, while both had to deal with new competition from the Burton upon Trent pale ale brewers. Tackling these rivals saw, for example, Truman, Mann and Charrington all open their own branch breweries in Burton to brew pale ale at the 'orignal source'.

Only in September 1887, the year of Victoria's Golden Jubilee, did the *Brewers' Journal* complain that 'There will be few to challenge the correctness of the assertion that there is a marked and increasing diminution in the amount of porter sold by London brewers.' The writer of this piece was surprisingly certain that '... the decline in the porter trade has little, if anything, to do with the public taste. Porter has long been esteemed by the British workman, and there is no doubt that his affections are as traditionally conservative in this respect as in most others.' The *Journal* then went on to assert that the British workman was changing from porter to mild solely because of price:

> Porter has found favour with him because ... above all he has hitherto been enabled to obtain a long draught at a cheap rate. It is the latter inducement that has secured its ready demand, rather than any preference for it over good, sparkling mild ale. It has not only been a cheaper beverage than ale, but a very much cheaper one, and it is in the main due to an alteration of the relative prices of ale and porter that the falling off in the sale of the latter is to be attributed ... As retail rates now rule, there is but a difference of one halfpenny a 'pot' between ale and porter, and this being insignificant the choice is given to the ale.

The *Journal* added that publicans were also less inclined to promote porter because the habit of illegally diluting it to increase retailers' profits – 'black beer told no tales, at least to the unsuspecting artisan' – had been made too dangerous as the authorities wielded the provisions of the

A public bar price list issued by Young's of Wandsworth in April 1942 showing two grades of draught mild on sale, one a penny a pint cheaper

Inland Revenue Act 1885 against those who watered down their porter. It urged the brewers to adjust the wholesale price of porter downwards so that it could compete again against mild ale, warning them:

> Many brewers who are now prospering will have cause to regret the change if the demand for porter should be allowed to expire for want of a slight readjustment in its wholesale price. It is of great importance to the industry that porter should continue to be brewed in large quantity.

Not everybody agreed that price was the only determinant in working men choosing between ale and porter. A few months earlier, in the *Journal*'s January 1887 issue, the brewing scientist Frank Faulkner, writing about London well waters, commented that their high sodium carbonate content, which meant high colour extraction and 'a certain roughness or rawness in flavour', meant that they 'could not well be employed in producing pale ales ... London brewers for years allowed their tenants freedom in reference to pale ale requirements, Burton firms supplying the London publican with his pale beer.' However, Faulkner said:

> Within the last few years a practical revolution has taken place. Public taste has changed in favour of a perfectly mild as compared with a matured beer, while the London brewer has discovered that by manipulating the [water] company supply he could, with a suitable blend of malt, produce a mild pale ale, not requiring, and indeed not suited for long storage, but still one that enabled him to satisfy the requirements in pale as well as in black beers, while, as a result of this, we shall, sooner or later, see London pale ale gradually driving out the Burton production, although it may not exactly equal it in general quality.

Even as the *Journal* was urging London's brewers to preserve porter brewing, those brewers were ripping out their porter vats to make more room for storing casks of ale. When Alfred Barnard visited Mann's brewery in the East End in 1889, he found large numbers of huge vats had been dismantled 'because the fickle public has got tired of the vinous-flavoured vatted porter and transferred its affections to the new and luscious "mild ale".'

As Faulkner's comment confirms, the beer that was driving out porter was 'a mild pale ale'. So when and why did darker milds start to arrive? The date of the change seems to be around the 1890s, since dark milds appear to be firmly established at the start of the twentieth century – about the time, which may be significant, that Mann's was developing the modern sweet brown ale. In 1893 Johnson's Saccharum Co. of Stratford, East London was advertising in the *Brewer's Journal* its 'Amber Malt Sugar for Mild Ales & Porter', strong support for the idea that some mild ales were now being brewed darker. By 1902, Wahl and Henius could write: 'Sometimes black beers and mild ales receive an addition of caramel solution in the fermenting vessel just prior to the close of the principal fermentation.' Caramel would be used to darken the colour of the mild, as well as sweeten it.

Wahl and Henius also said of the grain bill for mild ales: 'pale malt is used with a little black malt', suggesting again that a darker mild ale was now being made, A few years later we get the first mention of a specific 'mild malt' in *The Brewer's Analyst: A Systematic Handbook of Analysis Relating to Brewing*, by R. Douglas Bailey, which said: 'A diastatic power for a pale-ale malt ought not to be below 35° or more than 44°, a mild-ale malt from 23° to 30°, and a high-dried malt from 15° to 23°.' The reduced diastatic power (a measure of its ability to convert starch into sugar) for the mild ale malt would be matched by a darker colour, clearly midway between pale ale malt and high-dried malt, and the darker malt would, of course, give a darker colour to the beer.

In confirmation of the use of darker malts and sugars in mild, the *Encyclopedia Britannica* of 1911 reported: 'pale ales are made either from pale malt ... only, or from pale malt and a little flaked maize, rice, invert sugar or glucose. Running beers (mild ale) are made from a mixture of pale and amber malts, sugar and flaked goods.' It added that 'good mild ale waters should contain a certain quantity of sodium chloride' which, as we have seen, would have increased the colour extraction from the malt. Brewers were now adding sugar to the brew to ensure a sweeter taste: the *Encyclopedia Britannica* also wrote: 'Cane sugar is mostly used for the preparation of heavy mild ales and stouts, as it gives a peculiarly sweet and full flavour to the beer, to which, no doubt, the popularity of this class of beverage is largely due.'

An analysis of English beers conducted for the *Encyclopedia Britannica* found that milds contained less alcohol for a given OG than pale ales, stock ales and porter: one mild with an OG of 1055, for example, contained the same amount of alcohol, 4.2 per cent, as a bitter ale with an OG of 1047. The mild also contained two thirds more solids in the final beer than the bitter – 6.7 per cent against 4 per cent – suggesting a beer with a much fuller mouth-feel, and a sweeter one as well. A.C. Chapman's book, *Brewing*, called mild 'a lightly hopped beer of medium gravity and of full sweet flavour which in London is usually drunk when quite new, but which in the country is occasionally kept on draught for one or two months.' Judging by the gravities given by Steward & Patteson, the Norwich brewer, for its different strengths of mild in 1914, the average XXXX would be around 1065 OG, an XXX would be 1055 or so and an XX 1047. However, these may have been 'country' strengths. Courage, one of London's biggest mild ale brewers, brewed its XX 'fourpenny ale', the standard public bar brew, in 1891 to a gravity of 1060.

In the twentieth century the different strengths of mild could also be different colours, though for many this would range only from 'dark' to 'very, very dark'. Garne's brewery of Burford in 1912 gave the colours of its X beers as 25 for the XX, probably an old-oak brown, 30 for the XXX and 35, a very dark brown, for the XXXX (which, with oat malt in the grain bill, was probably regarded as a stout).

The Burton brewers always liked to be different: Bass, for example, sold five strengths of mild and numbered them from No 3 (the strongest) to No 7 (the weakest). Worthington had a completely illogical system, with the most expensive mild called B and the cheaper second grade called A:

Beer	Name
Best mild	B
Second-quality mild	A
Third-quality mild (Dash)	D
Fifth-quality mild	J
Sixth-quality mild	T

The First World War had the same disastrous effect on the strength of mild as it did on every other beer in Britain. At Steward & Patteson the standard XX mild crashed from 1047 OG in 1914 to 1029 in 1920. The XXX disappeared completely and the XXXX fell from 1065 OG to the former strength of XX, 1047. Elsewhere the falls were even worse: at Young & Co. of Wandsworth the fourpenny mild ale hit an OG of 1027 in 1919, though by the early 1930s the mild had recovered to a respectable 1038.

By the second half of the twentieth century, mild was certainly established as, mostly, a darker beer than pale ale or bitter. Maurice Gorham said in 1949 that mild ale was 'reddish-brown in colour, not unlike Burton to look at', while light mild 'is a mild ale lighter in colour than the ordinary mild: more the colour of bitter. This is not often met with in London pubs.' Whitbread's *The Brewer's Art*, in 1948, described mild ale as:

> the X or XX of the public bar. It is brewed from malt which has been heated on the kiln to a higher temperature than the pale ale malts, thereby acquiring a characteristic, slightly burnt flavour [that is, mild malt or mild-ale malt]. The beer usually has a sugar syrup known as 'priming' added in cask. Priming promotes a further fermentation in cask, giving the beer 'life' and at the same time guarantees the slightly sweet palate demanded by the drinker of this type of beer.

By now drinkers in different parts of the country often favoured a particular shade of mild: deep oak-brown in East Anglia and London (where the chloride-rich well water was good for dark mild ales); pale in Manchester and Staffordshire; dark again in the West Midlands and Wales. But many brewers around the country produced both dark and light milds. The Northants & Leicestershire Clubs brewery in 1935 brewed two grades of mild, XX and XXX, in three varieties, light, medium and dark.

The popularity of mild with the labouring classes meant that 'four-ale bar' as a synonym for public bar lasted long after mild ale stopped being 4*d* a quart (during the 1920s and 1930s, in fact, it was generally 5*d* a pint, a couple of pence less than bitter, with best mild at 6*d* a pint). Whether it was its cheapness or the sweeter, less bitter flavour, in many parts of Britain mild stayed extremely popular. Offilers' brewery of Derby, for example, still gave over around 95 per cent of production to draught mild in the years up to 1939. Joshua Tetley and Sons in Leeds in 1920 brewed four grades of mild, against just one of bitter ale, with the strongest 'Special Mild Ale' more expensive than the bitter.

However, tastes were altering in some surprising places; in and around Newcastle upon Tyne, once home to its own style of mild ale, Scotch brewed bitter ale now ruled. The newly formed Northern Clubs Federation brewery in Newcastle brewed only bitter for the first four years of its existence. It introduced a Burton Mild around the end of 1924, but by 1930 mild made up less than 6 per cent of production.

The North East of England seems to have been an exception. Bass actually introduced two new milds, No 8 and No 9, in the 1930s, to answer demand from the agricultural counties and the hotel industry for a lower-gravity mild beer. In London, Watney Combe and Reid gave over its Stag brewery in Victoria to the production of mild ales, with all the bitter for the London trade brewed on the Surrey side of the Thames at Mortlake, near Richmond. Frederic Robinson of Stockport devoted most of its advertising in the 1930s to its pale Best Mild, featuring two mismatched characters consuming the beer in various 'amusing' situations.

Andrew Campbell, writing in 1956, said mild beer grists 'may be of up to two thirds pale ale malt, and the balance a blend, in almost equal proportions, of amber malt and sugar'. Hough, Briggs and Stevens in 1971 gave a grain bill for mild ale of 10 per cent wheat flour (for head retention), 15 per cent invert sugar, 73 per cent mild-ale malt and 2 per cent black malt. The invert sugars used for milds were the Nos 2 and 3 grades, both dark in colour. Hough, Briggs and Stevens also suggested using two pints of primings per barrel, with the primings at an OG of 1150. The difference in hop levels was now much lower than seventy years earlier: 11oz of hops per barrel, against 13oz (18 per cent more) for bitter.

The continuing popularity of mild meant that even after the Second World War it made up close to 70 per cent of draught beer sales, though its reputation as a working class drink (and its cheapness) meant some pubs refused to sell it in their saloon bars, where beer was a penny or two a pint more, reserving it for the public bar. Campbell forgave this snobbishness, saying that 'it is an unquestionable fact that there is not a great demand for mild beer in the saloon bars of some public houses. A barrel of mild must be consumed within a few days and slow sales mean sour and spoiled beer.' Most mild now was low-gravity 'wallop' (an expression for mild, dating from at least the 1930s, and supposedly popular among darts players, which may be rhyming slang – 'wallop the child').

Campbell gave the gravity of the majority of mild ales as between 1030 and 1033, about 3 per cent abv, 'though some are very much weaker'. Mild beers, he said, 'are usually rather lightly hopped and in some districts, including London, rather sweet', the implication being that some other milds were more heavily hopped and not so sweet. London milds, Campbell said 'are dark in colour; in the country the colour varies and some breweries produce both a dark and a light mild'. Not all London milds were dark. Truman brewery in Brick Lane, in the East End of London, for example, brewed a light mild called LK, as well as a dark mild, both at OGs of 1032. Just north of London, Benskin's of Watford brewed KK light mild at 1033 OG and a Lovibond colour of 16, a light oak (for comparison the brewery's draught bitter had a colour of 11.5, light amber), and dark XX mild at 1032 OG with a colour of 38, a very dark brown.

Stronger, best milds, with gravities of 1033 to 1040 were still around: Taylor Walker of the Limehouse brewery, also in the East End of London, made a famous 'strong' sweet dark mild called Main Line (which drew the unkind joke in the 1930s that its name derived from its similarity to a mainline train: 'no sooner in than out'), though its OG seems to have been not much more than that of a best bitter. Whitbread's best mild was called Treble X. Watney's XX mild was still, until the 1950s, referred to simply as 'ale' – Watney's earliest keg mild, for example, was called 'Container Ale', while the bitter was 'Container Bitter'.

Mild was also drunk mixed with other beers: mild-and-bitter was a public bar favourite; brown-and-mild, bottled brown ale mixed with a half pint of draught mild, was drunk for those who wanted a more carbonated drink, or where the draught mild was poor in quality; old-and-mild (Burton and mild together) was drunk in the winter; while black-and-tan, according to *Lilliput* magazine's beer supplement in 1956, was stout and mild mixed: this, presumably, was only in areas where mild were light, rather than dark.

But mild was getting a reputation as the beer licensees with no scruples recycled all the slops back into it. The problem was that because mild was generally meant to be drunk soon after it arrived in the pub, and was not supposed to undergo any real secondary fermentation, it was often sent out from the brewery 'bright', that is without any yeast in the cask. Draught bitter, in contrast, which was meant to mature in the cellar, still contained yeast, which settled to the bottom of the cask when it was in the pub cellar. If licensees put overflow beer back into the bitter, they would stir up the yeast and the beer would go cloudy. With no yeast in the mild, this problem did not exist. Many pubs poured all the beer from the drip trays under the beer pumps into the mild casks. There was even a machine called a 'utiliser' which automated the system, draining all the waste beer from the different bars into a china bucket in the cellar, where it was added to the mild in the public bar by a little auxiliary pump at the rate of around a spoonful per glass.

This contempt for the public brought public contempt for the product. At the same time, mild drinkers were dying out. Bitter was seen as a drink to aspire to by the post-war generation; mild was looked down on as a beer drunk only by ageing, flat-capped working class types. Beer sales, after hitting a UK low of 24.6 million barrels in 1959, began to rise rapidly as affluence spread through the 1960s, but all the new volume was bitter and the now fashionable lager.

Sales of mild, both in absolute terms and as a proportion of the total amount of beer drunk in Britain, began to fall sharply. In 1959, mild (at a shilling a pint) still outsold bitter (at 1s 4d a pint, 33 per cent more expensive) two pints to one and made up six pints out of ten served on draught, at 10.3 million barrels a year. Five years later, in 1964, mild sales were down by a fifth, though it was still 50 per cent of all draught beer drunk. In 1968, sales of bitter had more than doubled over 1959 and bitter (including the new keg bitter, sold in pressurised metal containers) had finally overtaken mild in popularity. Into the 1970s and with beer sales still climbing, mild sales were still falling: down to 5.7 million barrels in 1972, a little over a fifth of all draught beer sales. They dropped to 5.1 million barrels in 1976, half the total fifteen years earlier, and were now just one pint in six of all draught beer sales.

All the same, in the mid-1970s there were still more than a hundred breweries in the UK producing milds, with at least eighteen brewing two different milds, and one – Border in Wrexham – selling three, one light and two dark. (By now, the proportion of dark mild sales to light was roughly around four to one.) Even in 1979, Robinson's brewery in Stockport, Manchester was selling more mild than bitter, while its near-neighbours Holts, Hydes and Oldham sold about the same amounts of each type, and the West Midlands brewery Banks of Wolverhampton still had 70 per cent of its output as mild. But outside these fortresses, sales were often tiny. At Ridley's brewery in Essex mild made up only 2 per cent of turnover. The decline continued; mild sales were down nationally to 3.7 million barrels in 1982, only one in eight pints of draught beer. Sales fell below 2 million barrels in 1990, an 80 per cent fall in three decades; topped barely one million barrels in 1997, and dropped to fewer than 800,000 barrels the following year, making mild just three pints in one hundred of all draught beer sales. Dozens of regional brewers' milds, many greatly loved by those who still drank them, had disappeared from bar-tops as they became uneconomical to brew, while few of the hundreds of new breweries that had opened since 1976 bothered to brew a beer for such a small and declining market as Britain's remaining mild drinkers.

One exception was the Sarah Hughes brewery, a revival of a former own-brew operation at the Beacon Hotel, Sedgley, in the Black Country. John Hughes started the brewery up again in 1987, naming it after his grandmother who had run it until her death in 1951. The first beer he produced was a strong dark mild made to one of his grandmother's old recipes, with an authentically pre-First World War OG of 1058 and an abv of 6 per cent. Dark ruby mild was made with 90 per cent pale malt and 10 per cent crystal, with Fuggles and Golding hops, a typical English dark mild recipe.

Other 'mild revivalists' include B&T of Shefford, Bedfordshire, which brews two, Shefford Dark Mild at 3.8 per cent abv and Black Dragon mild, at 4.3 per cent abv; Moorhouse's of Burnley with the 3.8 per cent abv Black Cat mild; Hanby in Wem, Shropshire, with Black Magic mild; Cain's of Liverpool, maintaining the tradition of Merseyside dark milds; Bartram's of Suffolk, doing the same for East Anglian dark milds with Marld (the local pronunciation of the word); and Hogs Back in Surrey, which brews an occasional dark mild. Others, however, have tried the beer and given up, including Goose Eye in Yorkshire and Burton Bridge in Burton upon Trent. Around the beginning of the 1990s mild seems to have stabilised and a survey in 2001 found that nationally a quarter of all pubs still stocked the beer, with one in three rural pubs selling mild, though much of that was in keg (pressurised container) form. By now 'mild' meant, and means, to most drinkers a much more specific sort of drink than brewers would once have recognised: generally dark (though the country's biggest-selling remaining mild, Banks' Original, is pale), and thus with roast and chocolate flavours from the dark malts used and generally with some sweetness. Mild malt has disappeared and modern recipes for mild use standard pale malt, with crystal malt, chocolate malt and/or caramel for colour.

London still has a dark mild, Hock, an occasional brew from Fuller, Smith & Turner at Chiswick. At least one brewer, Hydes of Manchester, is still brewing three milds, including the light mild it first introduced in 1942 and together they make up 20 per cent of production. But only 1 in 10 of the 500 or so post-1976 breweries running today make a beer they call a mild. The beer still seems to have the image problem it had fifty years ago: the beer writer Jeff Evans was told in 2004 of a brewer who found his mild just would not sell on the bar of a popular country pub. Then the barman put a sticker covering the world 'mild' on the pump clip; the cask was drained in a couple of hours.

3

BURTON ALE

The Rat, meanwhile, was busy examining the label on one of the beer-bottles. 'I perceive this to be Old Burton,' he remarked approvingly. 'Sensible Mole! The very thing!'

The Wind in the Willows, Kenneth Grahame, 1908

When Arthur Rackham illustrated the Christmas homecoming scene from Kenneth Grahame's classic children's tale *The Wind in the Willows*, the bottles of beer that Ratty found in Mole's cellar clearly bore on their labels the red diamond trademark of Bass Burton Ale. Parents reading the book to their children would have recognised the visual reference and smiled at the connoisseurship of Grahame's water-rat. Bass Burton Ale was one of the best-known brands in a popular style,

Today, however, Burton Ale is almost forgotten as a type of beer; a style famous for a century and a half that became obsolete within a couple of decades after the Second World War. Even in Britain, just a handful of beers are still brewed regularly in the Old Burton mode, and none of those bears the name Burton.

The Burton style has become so lost – 'gone for a Burton' – that where Burton ales survive today, they are called old ales, winter warmers or barley wine rather than by their correct designation. 'Gone for a Burton' is British slang for 'dead', supposedly because RAF pilots in the Second World War would rather say a colleague had 'gone for a Burton', slipped out for a beer, than say he was not coming back after being shot down. (The expression is sometimes said to have come from an advertisement for Burton Ale, though no such ad is known.) However, although Burton ale is forgotten, it is not yet completely gone.

Burton ale, it must be made clear, is not India Pale Ale, or IPA, the beer for which Burton upon Trent is most known today. Proper Burton ale is

the rather darker, slightly sweeter style Burton's brewers had made before
they became famous for brewing bitter IPA. In the nineteenth and early
twentieth centuries, whenever the big Burton upon Trent brewers advertised their brews, the posters and engraved mirrors declared the merits of
Bass's or Allsopp's or Salt's 'Pale and Burton Ales', not pale ale alone.

The book on *The Brewer's Art*, published by the London brewer
Whitbread, just after the Second World War, could declare confidently
that in Britain 'there are four chief types of beer: pale ale, mild ale, stout
and Burton'. It went on to say:

> Burton is a strong ale of the pale ale type, but made with a proportion
> of highly dried or slightly roasted malts; it is consequently darker in
> colour and with a fuller flavour than the pale ales. Essentially a draught
> beer, it is usually given a prolonged cellar treatment, in the course of
> which those special flavours develop which are associated with matu-
> rity in beer.

Although Burton ale was not necessarily made in Burton, the book said,
'it is based on the types of strong beer made famous by that centre of
pale ale brewing.' Burton ales were dry-hopped at racking, and stored
'for some weeks' in cool cellars before finings were added and they were
sent out to the pub, it said.

A year later, in 1949, the journalist Maurice Gorham was agreeing
that 'the drinks kept on draught in the ordinary London pub are bitter,
Burton and mild ale'. Gorham said Burton was:

> a draught beer darker and sweeter than bitter, named originally after
> the great brewing town of Burton-on-Trent [sic] but now common
> to all breweries wherever they are. Burton is also known as 'old' …
> some pubs used to keep a special Burton which was more of a strong
> ale and made an excellent mixture with mild … many pubs do not
> keep Burton during the hot weather, counting it a winter drink

Before the Second World War, 'several' brewers had stopped brewing
Burton in the summer months, and during the war it had disappeared
entirely, Gorham said. But there was now 'more of it about in the winter,
and Barclays [the big London brewer later taken over by Courage] for
one brews it all the year round.'

In London, Gorham said, 'old' and 'Burton' were used as synonyms
'quite arbitrarily. For instance, Burton (or old) mixed with mild ale is

usually asked for as old-and-mild, not mild-and-Burton … but if you want to mix Burton with bitter you ask for bitter-and-Burton (or BB).' The beer writer T.E.B. Clarke, writing in 1938, documented the less-than-PC nickname given to this mixture: 'mother-in-law', because it was 'old and bitter'. Clarke told novice drinkers that 'you might try a Burton (alias "old")' if they wanted something 'a little less acrid' than bitter. However, he warned his readers that 'beginners' often found Burton had 'a slightly metallic flavour' (it still can have), in which case they should order 'BB'.

In the years Gorham drank it, ordinary Burton was 'not particularly strong'. But this had not always been true. An analysis from 1843 by Jonathan Pereira gave 'Burton ale, first sort' an OG of 1111 to 1120, 'Burton ale, second sort' an OG of 1097 to 1111 and 'third sort' an OG of 1077 to 1092. For comparison, Pereira found porter had an OG of 1050 and 'good table beer' 1033 to 1039, while IPA was generally around 1065.

What Gorham did not say was that Burton was generally comparatively expensive. A price list from the Chiswick brewer Fuller, Smith and Turner in the 1950s showed mild at 1s 3d a pint, best bitter at 1s 8d a pint and Burton at 2s a pint, 60 per cent more than mild. In Edwardian pubs the difference was even greater; while mild was 4d a quart, Burton was twice as much, at 8d (and a quart of old-and-mild, which cost 6d, was known as an 'Old Six').

The roots of Burton ale were in the beers originally exported in the eighteenth century from Burton upon Trent to Russia, Poland and other Northern European countries. This very strong beer was brewed by men such as Michael Bass and Benjamin Wilson (and Wilson's nephew and successor, Samuel Allsopp) in Burton and shipped to the cities of St Petersburg, Riga, Danzig and Hamburg from the 1740s or so up to the early 1820s. It was nut-brown or darker (Wilson's was particularly dark) and fairly sweet, but its high strength seems to have been its special selling point.

In 1822, the Russian government suddenly and unexpectedly imposed a deliberately prohibitive tariff on beer imports and Allsopp, for one, found himself with large amounts of newly-brewed but unexportable beer. He tried selling it to customers in England, with some success. But 'those who admired its flavour and its purity, and who wished to drink more of it,' according to the journalist John Stevenson Bushnan, writing in 1853, 'found it too heady, too sweet, and too glutinous, if not too strong. Indeed it was so rich and luscious that if a little were spilled on a table the glass would stick to it.' The original Burton, as described by Bushnan, must have been very similar to the recipe for a Burton ale in an anonymously written book from 1824, *The Young Brewer's Monitor.* This gave a beer with an OG of a thumping 1140, using pale malt and 4½lb of hops to the barrel; only a little less hops than a good IPA. This beer needed maturing for at least eighteen months. But this sticky brew was already being superseded by a new style of Burton ale. When the October 1822 brewing season opened, Bushnan wrote, Allsopp brewed 'the first specimen of the improved Burton ale now so universally drank and admired', making it less sweet and more bitter than the original Russian version. The first casks of the new beer were sold to customers in Liverpool. They were not an instant success; after complaints, Allsopp had to visit each publican to persuade them to let the beer mature, promising to take back any that was unsellable. The beer was found to improve considerably with age and eventually none of that first brew was returned unsold. It was a busy time for Allsopp; the following year he sent his new pale ale out east in an endeavour to find another overseas market to replace the Baltic trade. But while pale ale for India, or IPA, also succeeded eventually in the British market, it always sold alongside Burton ale, the beer based on the Baltic export original.

The Victorian brewer George M. Amsinck recorded a recipe for Burton ale which used hard Burton water, pale malt and Kentish hops at a rate of around four and a half pounds to the barrel, not as much as would be used in a Burton IPA, but still a fair amount, to produce a beer with 6 per cent alcohol by volume. Amsinck used the same recipe, with slightly different mash temperatures and soft water, to make a 'London XXXX' of the same strength. Both were to be stored for six weeks to mature before being tapped, much less time than the early nineteenth century Burtons required to mature.

As with IPA, the other Burton brewers seem to have quickly adopted this new style of Burton ale (if, indeed, they were not already supplying it; Bushnan's story probably makes Samuel Allsopp too much of a 'heroic pioneer'). Bass used a red diamond trademark for its Burton ales, to distinguished them from the famous red triangle used on Bass India Pale Ale (the diamond mark was used for Burton ale from 1857, two years after the firm first put the red triangle on its pale ale labels). The firm brewed four different strengths of Burton ale for the on-trade in the second half of the nineteenth century. They ranged from the powerful No 1, at over 1110 OG, down through Nos 2 and 3 to No 4 at around 1070 OG. There were also two more grades for the private family trade, Nos 5 and 6, at around 1060 and 1055 OG.

The Bass Brewery in Burton upon Trent in 1856, still home to one of the best-known strong Burton ales, No 1

By the 1950s Nos 2, 3 and 4 had disappeared, and 5 and 6, now much weaker, were sold in pubs as draught milds; the underlying sweetness of Burton ale meant a blurry boundary between it and mild ale, as shown in a late nineteenth-century advertisement from Arnold, Perrett & Co. of Wickwar, Gloucestershire, which listed six beers under the category 'mild ale', numbered 3 to 8, of which number 5, at 21s a kilderkin, around 1052 OG, was called 'Burton Ale'. Another company with a brewery in Burton, Truman's, also sold a No 6 Burton Mild Ale, doubtless in competition with Bass.

Allsopp's brewery in Burton had a naming system involving letters, from A (the weakest) to C (the strongest) for its Burton ales, while the rival Burton brewer, Worthington, had, as usual, a completely illogical lettering system which saw its best strong Burton ale called G, its second best F and its third best C or CK. Mann, Crossman & Paulin, the London brewer, which had a branch brewery in Burton until 1897 (later occupied by Marston, Thompson & Evershed) numbered its own Burton ales in descending strength, 3, around 1080 OG, 4 (both these called 'Strong Burton Ale') and 5 ('Light Burton Ale', though even this, judging by its price, had an OG of around 1052). Marston's brewery later bottled a 'House of Lords' brand Burton ale, though Lord Burton was a Bass.

Elsewhere in Britain, just as other brewers copied Burton's pale ales, so they reproduced Burton Ale. By the early 1890s brewers far outside Staffordshire were producing a beer called Burton. Alfred Barnard, the Victorian journalist, found Burton ales being brewed at the Tyne brewery in Newcastle in the North East; by John Smith's in Tadcaster, Yorkshire; and by Eldridge Pope in Dorchester in the South West. At Eldridge Pope's brewery the XXX Burton sold for 54s a barrel, imply-ing an OG of around 1065 to 1075 and a retail price of 7d a quart. Page & Overton's Shirley brewery in Croydon, Surrey, was brewing XXX Burton at 13s 6d a firkin in 1898, while its rival Croydon brewery, Crowley's, sold Burton ale at 15s a firkin.

The beer won a reputation as a comforting brew. Charles Knight wrote in 1851 of 'the Burton which, like Sancho's sleep, "wraps one round like a blanket".' Burton Ale also found a home across the Atlantic, in New England, where at least three pre-Prohibition brewers in New York State, Amsdell Brothers of Albany and C.H. Evans & Sons and Grainger & Gregg, both of Hudson, advertised a Burton ale among their beers. In Newark, New Jersey, P. Ballantine & Sons' brewery (founded in 1840 by a Scot, Peter Ballantine, who had originally been a brewer in Albany) also brewed a Burton ale, with an abv of 10 or 11 per cent. In its last incarnation in the mid-twentieth century, Ballantine's Burton Ale was aged for up to twenty years in oak vats before bottling and not sold to the public, but given to valued customers every autumn. Ballantine's Burton Ale was said, by the beer writer Michael Jackson, to be one of the inspirations in the creation of Old Foghorn Barley Wine at the Anchor brewery, in San Francisco. Burton ale also seems to have been the stimu-lus behind Toohey's Old and Tooth's Old (now Kent Old Brown), two dark, sweetish, fruity top-fermented beers brewed in Sydney, Australia.

In London, where Burton became a winter favourite with many drinkers, the Chiswick brewer, Fuller, Smith and Turner, sold Old Burton Extra, or OBE. George Izzard, landlord of the Dove at Hammersmith, in west London, described its pre-Second World War manifestation in his memoirs as 'a strong Burton … a very strong beer which … didn't strike you as powerful at first sip. It had a winey, rather sweet taste. All the same, three pints of it were enough for the heaviest drinker, if he wanted to go out of the pub on his feet.' After the Second World War, OBE was brewed to a considerably reduced gravity of 1049, rather than the 1090 or more it must have been earlier. However, British drinkers' tastes moved away from sweeter, darker beers and towards the lighter, sharper and more bitter. By 1969 sales of OBE were so poor that the brewery decided it had to go and it was replaced with a strong, pale bitter called, at first, Winter Bitter. Later the name of Winter was changed to Extra Special Bitter, or ESB, which became famous for being, at the time, the strongest bitter in Britain.

The disappearance of Burton ale was astonishingly swift. In the 1930s and 1940s it was still being made in Burton, and by breweries in Suffolk, Kent, Essex, Hertfordshire, Bedfordshire and Oxfordshire, as well as by most or all of London's brewers. Even in 1956 the beer writer Andrew Campbell found Burton being brewed by Charrington ('medium sweet and of considerable body', Campbell said); Courage at the Horsleydown brewery alongside Tower Bridge, which would send out show cards to its pubs saying: 'Courage Burton is now on sale for the winter season'; Taylor Walker of Limehouse, which sold draught 'KKK Burton' ('a bitter-sweet quality and a definite substance' – Campbell); and Watney Combe Reid of Pimlico, which went one better with KKKK Burton. (Before the Second World War it had made KKKK 'strong ale' and KKK 'Burton'.) Watney's Burton was 'a good solid drink, but with a gentle bitter-sweet flavour that makes it pleasant drinking and one of the most suitable beers for mulling and for mixing', according to Campbell.

One London brewer could offer its drinkers a real Burton upon Trent-brewed Burton; Truman, Hanbury & Buxton of the Black Eagle brewery in Brick Lane owned a branch brewery in Derby Street, Burton from 1873 until it closed in 1971. They made several beers for shipping south, including a dark 5 per cent abv draught Burton ale sold (like several other Burtons) in the winter months, and No 1 Burton, at the barley wine end of the spectrum, 'a really strong old English ale, Burton brewed and matured … especially recommended during cold weather'. In Great Yarmouth, on the Suffolk coast, the local brewery, Lacon's, which had a good 'export' trade to London by ship, brewed its Burton under the name Winter Brew, available from October to March. Lovibond of Greenwich, which closed in 1962, had XXXX Burton, as did Friary Holroyd and Healy of Guildford in Surrey.

However, by the end of the 1960s the decline in demand for dark, sweet beers meant the style was being forgotten and debased. (Even in 1949 Maurice Gorham said that he had met lifelong bitter drinkers 'who thought that Burton was a brand rather than a brew'.) Greene King's bottled 'Burton ale' from Bury St Edmunds was actually its dark mild, which, at a gravity of only 1032, was a travesty of the original style (though Greene King also brewed, and still brews, a beer called Burton Pale Ale, or BPA, in the authentic Burton style of a sweet, darkish beer

The Two Brewers, Tottenham, North London, just before the First World War, advertising Bass Burton Ale with the red diamond trademark, and Bass Pale Ale with the red triangle (and also Reid's Stout from London)

made with dark sugars and crystal malt, which is blended with aged 5X stock beer to make its Strong Suffolk barley wine). Rayment's, a little country brewery in Furneux Pelham, Hertfordshire, brewed a draught BBA, which originally stood for 'Best Burton Ale', but which had lost the sugar that normally went into Burtons and so had become a standard bitter.

The cruellest blow came in 1976 when Ind Coope launched a new cask beer called Burton Ale, which was actually an IPA-style drink rather than a real Burton ale as older drinkers would have understood the term (my father, for one, a drinker of genuine dark Burton, was furious at this betrayal of the tradition). Ind Coope had brewed a 'proper' Burton ale (described by Andrew Campbell as 'rather light, not sweet at all') at Burton upon Trent until at least the mid-1950s, and the pump clips for the new draught pale ale copied the typeface and general style of the Edwardian Ind Coope Burton Ale bottle labels.

There are, still, Burton ales being brewed. At the former Bass plant in Burton, the White Shield brewery, owned by Coors, still brews Number 1, with an abv of 10.5 per cent. It still carries the red diamond trademark of Bass's nineteenth-century Burton ales, but No 1 is now regarded as a barley wine rather than an extra-strong member of the family of Burton ales (its earliest description was 'No 1 Strong Ale', which it kept until at least the 1890s, but by 1914 it was being advertised as 'No 1 Barley Wine'). Nor, today, is it allowed to carry the Bass name, since that is now owned by another brewer, Anheuser-Busch InBev.

Marston's Owd Rodger, first brewed in 1908, with its bitter-sweet finish, is another 'barley wine' that is really a Burton ale, this time at 7.6 per cent abv, in the middle of the range. Lower down the ladder of strengths, Theakston's Old Peculier, from Masham in Yorkshire, is an old ale with all the hallmarks of a Burton: fruity, underlying sweetness that matures well. Another Yorkshire brewer, Timothy Taylor, makes an old ale called Ram Tam with an OG of 1043 that has the characteristics of a lower-gravity Burton: dark brown in colour, a caramel sweetness with fruity undertones.

Young's, once of Wandsworth in South London and now of Bedford, brews the only other surviving draught version of a lower-strength London Burton, which it first produced in 1932. It was a winter-only brew, certainly by the mid-1950s, and until the early 1970s it was still officially sold as Burton ale. But in 1971 the decision was taken to change the name of the beer from Burton to Winter Warmer.

Nobody at Young's can remember why the name Burton was dropped, but probably drinkers were already expecting that anything called Burton would be a pale ale. Young's Winter Warmer is a classic of the Burton ale type, however, well-rounded, mellow, on the sombre side of amber, 1055 OG, but only 5 per cent abv and with a dark sugar tang from the use of 'YSM', Young's special, proprietorial mixture of brewing sugars, offset by a hint of bitter undercurrent, alongside malted barley.

A small revival has taken place in the brewing of proper Burton-style ales in recent years. Smiles brewery in Bristol, founded in 1977 but closed in 2004, made a beer it called Heritage with a recognisably Burton ale profile: red-brown, bitter-sweet, fruity and full-bodied, with a roast malt aroma. Heritage is still being brewed at the Highgate brewery, in the West Midlands. Scottish & Newcastle also began producing a couple of bottled beers that fit the style, in McEwan's Champion, a version of Gordon Highland Scotch (strictly this is a Scotch Ale), a beer brewed for the Belgian market; and Newcastle Star. Sadly, the latter seems to have disappeared.

Fuller, Smith & Turner, the London brewer, brought out a bottle-conditioned beer in 1995 called 1845, to celebrate the 150th anniversary of its partnership, which is firmly in the Burton style, fruity and slightly sweet, and which is always given the ageing that Samuel Allsopp had found necessary for a Burton ale. In October 2005, Young's, as part of its seasonal beer range, brewed a version of Burton under the Burton name, slightly lighter in colour than Winter Warmer (but still dark), slightly stronger at 5.5 per cent abv, and still using the 'YSM' brewing sugars mixture in the mash tun. The flavour was deeper than Winter Warmer, with caramel and baked apples apparent, and it went particularly well mixed half and half with Young's bitter – the traditional 'mother-in-law'.

4

PORTER

It was this day a twelvemonth since we left England, in consequence of which a peice [sic] of cheshire cheese was taken from a locker where it had been reservd for this occasion and a cask of Porter tappd which provd excellently good, so that we livd like English men and drank the hea[l]ths of our freinds in England.

The *Endeavour*, Journal of Joseph Banks, 25 August 1769

Porter, developed in London early in the eighteenth century, was the first truly global beer, brewed and enjoyed right around the planet. The *Gentleman's Magazine* in October 1788 published a short poem in praise of the favourite beer style of London's labouring classes. It included the line: 'Porter, which spreads its fame half the world o'er.' This was, even then, the literal truth. Seven months earlier, when the First Fleet had arrived in Sydney Cove, on the east coast of Australia, to set up a pioneering penal colony, the new arrivals drank toasts to the success of the settlement in glasses of porter brought 11,000 miles from England. Nearly twenty years earlier, when Joseph Banks and James Cook sailed to the Pacific to observe the transit of Venus, they had taken casks of porter with them.

By the time it reached Australia, porter had been the dominant style of beer in London for decades, and was drunk in enormous quantities. The leading London porter brewers, such as Sir Benjamin Truman, Samuel Whitbread, Henry Thrale of Southwark and the Calvert family (who owned two breweries, one near the Barbican and the other by the Thames near Charing Cross) had become, as Dr Samuel Johnson, a friend of Thrale, said, 'rich beyond the dreams of avarice'. They bought big country estates in Hertfordshire and Surrey, acquired knighthoods and seats in Parliament and some married into the aristocracy.

Porter was also popular in the newly independent American former colonies, in Ireland, where several big brewers had become porter specialists, and in the lands around the Baltic, while casks of porter were being shipped to India in the 1780s to satisfy homesick employees of the East India Company in their trading stations in Bombay, Madras and Calcutta.

The beer had developed in or soon after the reign of Queen Anne as a stronger, more hopped, more aged version of the heavy, sweet brown beer that was the staple product of most London's brewers in the late seventeenth and early eighteenth century. Unfortunately, as with most commercial developments, the people involved were too busy trying to make a living to write down an account of what they were doing and the earliest record of the start of porter comes some forty years or more after in 1760, in an account by an anonymous writer using the name 'Obadiah Poundage' ('poundage' being a synonym for tax – the original article, in the *London Chronicle*, was an argument for higher beer prices). 'Poundage' claimed to be eighty-six years old, to have spent seventy years in the business (taking us back to 1690), and to be 'the oldest acting [that is, still active] outdoor Clerk [brewer's rep or abroad cooper] in the brewery' (that is, the brewing industry).

Poundage said the beer that became known as porter was first brewed to combat the growing popularity of highly hopped pale beer, both strong and 'small', a taste for which had been brought from the country to London by the gentry, who were spending time in town much more than they used to. It was one of a class of strong beers, matured for some months in butts – casks holding 108 gallons, equal to three 36-gallon barrels or two hogsheads – that were known as butt-beers or butt-keeping-beers. Normally, strong beers were made from the first, most powerful mashing of the malt, but porter was made from four or five mashings of the same malt which were blended together. Such beers were called 'entire' or, in eighteenth-century spelling, 'intire'. So this beer made from a combination of all the mashes and stored in butts was 'entire butt-beer', entire butt or entire for short, and it continued to be referred to by brewers as entire for more than a hundred years.

It also used highly dried brown malt, which gave a roast flavour to the beer. Henry Stopes, a nineteenth-century malting expert (and father, incidentally, of the contraception pioneer Marie Stopes), wrote in *Malt and Malting*, of the making of 'brown, blown, snap or porter malt', talking about how the porter malthouses of Bishop's Stortford, on the Hertfordshire-Essex border, and elsewhere (including Ware and Stansted

Abbots, also in East Hertfordshire) burnt faggots of beech-wood or oak under the wet malt to dry it, going slowly at first until almost all the moisture has been driven from the malt, then building up the fire so that the sudden violent heat makes the malt grains burst like popcorn, growing 25 per cent in volume, and 'the nature of the fuel employed communicates, very agreeably, the empyreumatic [that is, roast or burnt, and probably smoky as well] properties that distinguish this class of malt.' Incidentally, the fierce heat needed to make blown or porter malt, and the consequent risk of setting the grain, and the whole maltings, on fire meant the makers had to pay high insurance rates, which was another reason, apart from the skill needed to get the heat and the timing just right, why the manufacture of porter malt was restricted to only a few place.

Brewers quickly discovered that the new version of London brown beer could be made at higher fermenting vessel temperatures than ales or the older-style brown beers. This meant that, in a time before artificial cooling was available, it could be brewed for more weeks during the year, when the weather was too hot to make other beers, and in larger fermenting vessels, which also created higher temperatures at which other types of beer suffered. These two important developments, bigger breweries brewing for longer, helped the leading porter brewers to brew more cheaply and outgrow their smaller ale-brewing rivals.

The new beer (as a well-hopped brew, porter was always called a beer, never an ale), which was fermented out as far as possible and therefore comparatively unsweet, was also aged, originally to ensure that over the months of storage it eventually lost the flavour of smoke picked up from the wood-dried malt used to make it. As it aged the beer began to acquire tart, vinous flavours of the kind found today in Belgian 'oud bruin' brown ales. The smokiness of wood-dried malt is mentioned by William Ellis in his *London and Country Brewer* of 1736, who says this type of malt was used by the London brewers of butt beer because of its cheapness and because the smoky taste eventually went away:

> Brown Malts are dried with Straw, Wood and Fern ... the Wood sort has a most unnatural Taste, that few can bear with, but the necessitous, and those that are accustomed to its strong smoaky tang ... many thousand Quarters of this Malt has been formerly used in *London* for brewing the Butt-keeping-beers with, and that because it sold for two Shillings *per* Quarter cheaper than the Straw-dryed Malt, nor was this Quality of the Wood-dryed Malt much regarded by some of its Brewers, for that its ill Taste is lost in nine or twelve Months, by the

The White Hart in Knightsbridge, London, on the edge of Hyde Park, in the early 1840s, with porters resting and enjoying a pot. The pub was the tap of Goding's Cannon ale brewery just up the road and sold the 'entire', or porter, made by Henry Meux's Horseshoe Brewery in Tottenham Court Road

Age of the Beer, and the strength of the great Quantity of Hops that were used in its Preservation.

Ellis's use of the phrase 'formerly used' suggests that by the time he was writing, smoke-flavoured malt was no longer an ingredient. However, even in the 1890s maltsters were advertising malt dried with oak faggots 'which gives the Malt the flavour of the wood', suggesting that a taste for woodsmoke-flavoured beer lasted for some centuries.

Entire-butt quickly became extremely popular with the thousands of men who unloaded ships on the river, known as 'fellowship' porters, and those who carried goods of all kinds around the streets of London – 'ticket' porters, so called because they wore a pewter 'ticket' or badge bearing the arms of the City of London to show they were officially registered and regulated porters. As a result, the drink soon took their name, being referred to as 'porter' by 1721, when it is mentioned as an accompaniment to beef and cabbage. As they worked, the ticket or street porters, would stop outside pubs, put down their loads on special benches and call for a pot of their eponymous drink to keep them energised. A ticket porter can be seen in the right-hand corner of Hogarth's famous illustration of 'Beer Street', wearing his pewter 'ticket', and with his load — in this case a basket of old books — beside him as his finishes off a quart of what must, surely, be porter before completing his journey. There was a pub in Arthur Street, near London Bridge, called the Ticket Porter until around 1970. (Market porters in Billingsgate, Smithfield or Covent Garden, incidentally, have nothing to do with the name of the beer, being only a tiny proportion of the many porters working in eighteenth-century London: probably because they represent working class history, the important role of the street and river porters is very rarely mentioned in histories of the city.)

The name porter, since it started as a slang word for the beer, does not appear to be used by London brewers officially much before about 1760 (when Samuel Whitbread opened the 'new porter tun room' at his brewery in Chiswell Street): they just spoke of 'beer', mild (fresh) or stale (aged). Even in 1768 the anonymous author of a book called *Every Man his Own Brewer* talked about 'The Method of Brewing London Brown Beer under the name of Porter'.

In 1802, a writer called John Feltham wrote three pages on porter brewing in a guidebook called *The Picture of London*. Feltham's version of the history of porter, which includes the claim that it was invented by a brewer called Harwood, has been repeated hundreds of times over the past two centuries as the allegedly authentic story of porter's origins. Unfortunately, very little of it is backed up by independent evidence and much of it is demonstrably wrong.

Feltham said that porter 'obtained its name about the year 1730 [sic]'. The malt liquors drunk in London before porter were 'ale [sweet, heavy and lightly hopped], beer [more hopped and more bitter than ale and brown] and twopenny [strong pale ale]', and it 'became the practice to call for a pint or tankard of three-threads, meaning a third of ale, beer and twopenny; and thus the publican had the trouble to go to three casks and turn three cocks for a pint of liquor'. Feltham claimed that Harwood, in an attempt to make serving customers easier for busy publicans, thought up the idea of brewing a single liquor 'which should partake of the united flavours of ale, beer and twopenny. He did so and called it Entire or Entire-butt, meaning that it was served entirely from one cask.' As it was 'a very hearty nourishing liquor it was very suitable for porters and other working people,' Feltham said, 'Hence it obtained the name porter.'

However, as we have seen, porter appeared earlier than 1730 and the name 'entire-butt' had a very different origin from the one Feltham claimed. There was a drink called 'three-threads', but there is no evidence to say it was mixed in the way Feltham describes and some contemporary evidence suggests it was served from one cask, not out of three. According to John Tuck, writing in 1822, a century after the event, three-threads was a mixture of 'stale, mild and pale'. Obadiah Poundage, in the letter published in the *London Chronicle*, did not define 'three-threads', though there is an unpublished version of his letter that suggests it was made up of ale, that is, the lightly hopped rival brew to brown beer, 'mild' beer (newly brewed brown beer) and 'stale' beer (the same brew aged for a while, using 'stale' in its original sense of something that has stood, the same root as the word stall). This mixture sold for 3*d* a pot, or quart. In addition, Poundage said, while some drank just the mild and stale mixed together at 'twopence halfpenny and twopence three farthings the quart', 'many used all stale at fourpence per pot'.

Feltham was right in saying there was a porter brewer called Harwood, who brewed in Shoreditch, East London, from at least the early decades of the eighteenth century and Harwood is claimed as the originator of porter in the article in *The Gentleman's Magazine* in 1788. This quoted the little verse about the drink, written by a man called Thomas Gutteridge, described by the historian James Sumner as an 'obscure Shoreditch elegist and shorthand instructor'. His poem began: 'Harwood my townsman, he invented first/Porter to rival wine, and quench the thirst.' The article itself does not give Harwood a first name, but the index to the 1788 volume of the magazine refers to 'Harwood, Ralph, the first Porterbrewer in London'.

At some time – certainly by 1855 – the Blue Last pub in Curtain Road, Shoreditch, began to be claimed as the public house where 'porter was first sold, about 1730'. The Blue Last, which was rebuilt in 1876 when Great Eastern Street was cut through Curtain Road, was certainly a tied house owned, in 1816, by the then occupiers of Harwood's old brewery, two Quakers called Thomas and Robert Pryor, when they merged their operations with their fellow Quakers at Truman's brewery in Brick Lane nearby. But Harwood's brewery appears much too small to have been the inventor of such an important development as porter – it did not even make the top twenty London breweries in the 1790s. Nor was it particularly successful. In 1747 Ralph Harwood, brewer of Shoreditch, and his partner James Harwood were declared bankrupt.

Against this must be set the fact that when James Harwood died in 1762, his obituary in the *London Gazette* described him as 'an eminent brewer in Shoreditch, and the first that brought porter to perfection'. But the first man in fact to bring porter production to perfection appears to have been Sir Humphrey Parsons, owner of the much larger Red Lion brewhouse by the Thames at St Katharine's in Lower East Smithfield, just to the east of the Tower of London. Parsons was reputedly the first porter brewer to store the maturing beer in huge vats rather than casks, building vats at his brewery in 1736 that would hold 1,500 barrels each, (54,000 gallons, equal to 500 butts) at a cost of £562 each time. They were repaired in 1766 for £124 and were still being used in 1774, after nearly forty years, so that the initial considerable capital outlay proved far cheaper long term than the equivalent capacity in casks, which would have a maximum life of fifteen years.

Parsons' career – his brewery was the fourth biggest in London in 1748, seven years after his death – certainly suggests he is a more likely candidate to have perfected porter than Harwood. His beer, described by Oliver Goldsmith in a poem from 1759 as 'Parsons' black champagne', had boosted the wealth that his brewer father, Sir John Parsons, had already made. Sir Humphrey was Lord Mayor of London twice, in 1730 and 1740, and Tory MP for Harwich from 1722 and for London from 1728. When he was elected Lord Mayor in 1730, on Lord Mayor's Day 'Four and Fifty Draymen with White Aprons and Truncheons' marched before him in the procession. He lived at Reigate Priory, a Tudor mansion bought in 1681 by his father, who was also Lord Mayor in 1703.

His favourite pastime was riding with staghounds at a time when every Lord Mayor had his own hounds for hunting in the fields of Middlesex and Parsons had a reputation as an intrepid rider that 'extended to every part of Europe wherever hunting men might chance to congregate'. On one apocryphal occasion, Parsons was stag hunting in France with a party which included the French king, Louis XV. Parsons's mount was so good that, ignoring royal etiquette, he beat the rest of the company in the cross-country chase and was first in at the death of the stag, ahead of the king. The king asked who this stranger was and was told by an indignant courtier, angered by the breach of protocol, that he was '*un chevalier de malte*'.

Louis XV began talking with Parsons and asked the price of his horse. Bowing, the brewer declared that his horse was 'beyond any price other than His Majesty's acceptance'. The king agreed to take the gift and in return Parsons was given the monopoly of, depending on which version

GREAT VAT

One of the giant vats used for maturing porter at Barclay and Perkins's brewery in Southwark around 1889

of the story you plump for, supplying the French court with porter or supplying the whole of France with porter duty-free.

Before Parsons, it seems, judging by what Obadiah Poundage told the *Chronicle's* readers, when 'Porter or Entire Butt' was first brewed, 'it was far from being in the perfection which since we have had it. I well remember for many years it was not expected, nor was it thought possible, for it to be made fine and bright, and four and five months was deemed to be sufficient age for it to be drunk at.' Maturing porter in butts was expensive in both money and space: in the late 1740s Whitbread's brewery, for example, was hiring cellars in fifty-four different locations around London for its porter butts to mature in, at a cost of £100 a year, while Thrale's Anchor brewery in Southwark, consistently one of the biggest two or three porter brewers, had almost 19,000 butts in 1748, worth more than £8,500, or around 11 per cent of the brewery's total capital.

It could also be dangerous. In 1758 it was recorded that the 'abroad cooper' employed by Mrs Hucks's brewery (the eighth-largest in London and probably the one in Brewer Street, Bloomsbury) to look after beer stored off-site had died when he went down into a cellar in Pall Mall to check on forty butts of unstoppered beer. Contemporary reports blamed the 'steam' off the beer, but the abroad cooper and the sedan chair man who went down after him in an attempt at rescue and also died, were undoubtedly suffocated by the carbon dioxide being given off by the beer as it underwent a secondary fermentation in the butts.

Storing beer in vats also had dangers. As other brewers realised the advantage of maturing porter in greater quantities (a smaller percentage of the total exposed to the air, for a start), the vats grew bigger, until they began to burst. The biggest collapse was at Henry Meux's brewery at the Oxford Street end of Tottenham Court Road in London in October 1814. A twenty-odd feet high vat, filled with some thirty-two tons in weight of ten-months-old porter, burst apart and a wave of beer smashed through the east wall of the brewery and out into the crowded residential area behind. Four houses were partially demolished, and eight people, all women and children living in the houses (it was the very early evening and the men were still at work) were killed.

Ageing porter in huge vats was the last of the series of technical developments that enabled the earliest porter brewers to perfect a stable, cheap to produce, clear, tasty beer capable of being brewed in vast quantities for a growing and thirsty population. But only a few brewers could afford the cost of the big vats that helped produce the best porter and few could afford to tie money up for so long in maturing beer. It meant the growth of a small aristocracy of brewers. By the mid-1740s the twelve biggest porter houses in London produced 42 per cent of the strong beer brewed in the capital, leaving the rest of the market to another 145 or so much smaller concerns.

The drink was now being brewed outside London, despite a popular belief that only Thames water could make good porter. In 1799, for example, a news item appeared in *The Times* which said: 'A Porter brewery is about to be established at Portsmouth, by a number of opulent Gentlemen, who have subscribed £5,000 each. The Thames water for this undertaking is to be conveyed by shipping.' (In fact, some of the biggest porter brewers, such as Whitbread, used water from the New River, built to supply London from a source in Hertfordshire and others used water from wells on their brewery sites).

Thomas Elliott declared in an advertisement in a Sheffield newspaper in 1744 that he was now able to supply 'the very best sort of brown Strong Beer, commonly called London Porter' and his brewer was:

> regularly Bred a Common Brewer, being served seven years apprenticeship to that trade in London, so that there is no difference between the London Brew'd Porter and his but the water of this place, which is far superior to the New River in London for the Purpose, and he does venture to say that in the brewing season it is equal to the Thames for the brewing of the brown Beer.

By the 1760s, George Watkins revealed that the great brewers were keeping their porter in large casks 'two years and more', before putting it on sale. This storage 'in a large body' for such a long time was the reason why 'the public brewed porter will always be superior'. The secret of this long-aged porter was almost certainly its infection with wild *Brettanomyces* yeasts and bacteria such as lactobacilli and *Pediococcus damnosus*, the same organisms found in two or three-year-old Belgian lambic beers. Researchers in the Centre for Malting and Brewery Science at the Catholic University of Leuven in Belgium have found that this combination of micro-organisms prevents the oxidation of chemicals in the beer, in part because they often form a skin on top of the beer like the 'flor' on maturing sherry so that the reactions which produce the aldehydes that make 'off' beer taste bad do not take place. The beer is thus able to age gracefully, like a fine wine.

However, the great porter brewers had also learnt another trick, how to blend in older beer to bring forward younger, less mature brews.

Watkins said: 'If a butt of porter be too mild, they will throw into it a small quantity of some that is very strong and too stale; first dissolving in it a little isinglass. This produces a new tho' slight fermentation; and this liquor, in eighteen or twenty days, fines down and has the expected flavour.' This practice was known as 'breaking in', in the 1820s, at least.

By now porter brewing had spread across the British Isles: to Glasgow by 1763; Dublin by 1764 (though without great success, since in 1776 John Purser, a brewer at Reid's brewery in Liquorpond Street, London, one of the big twelve London porter brewers, was persuaded to move to Ireland to teach Irish brewers the secrets of making porter); Bristol by 1780; Norwich by at least 1791; Leith by 1793; Liverpool by 1799.

However, London porter continued to be the beer with the best reputation. In 1806, when the Edinburgh brewers A.C. and W. Younger announced in the city's evening newspaper that they had 'commenced brewers of Porter', they took care to say that 'a London brewer of great professional ability' had been engaged to make it, and that he had 'succeeded in producing porter that will vie in every respect with the best that can be imported from London'.

The first reliable evidence for the strength of Georgian porter appeared in 1784, when John Richardson, a writer on brewing, published a book called *Statical* [sic] *Estimates of the Materials for Brewing*. Richardson found porter had an average original gravity (before fermentation) of 1071 and a final gravity (after fermentation) of 1018. The approximate alcohol content would have been 7.1 per cent for porter, against 7.8 per cent for strong ale, 6.7 per cent for common ale and 4.8 per cent for table beer.

If Richardson's samples were typical, porter was thus strong and, compared with both strong ale and common ale, dry, with more of the sugar turned to alcohol. However, eighteenth-century terminology was still in flux and what he may have been measuring was 'stout porter', the stronger variety, which later generations would simply call stout. One late eighteenth-century recipe 'To brew Porter or Brown Beer, with Table Beer after from the same malt and hops' said that with a mash of half pale and half brown malt, running liquor through it twice, 'the first wort fermented by itself will be stout porter ... the second will be the table beer ... but if you mix the first and second worts together ... it will be good common porter.' The recipe also recommended three quarters of a pound of hops per bushel of malt, about two pounds a barrel, 'if the beer is for present draught' (that is, for drinking right away), but one pound of hops per bushel of malt, about 2⅔ pounds a barrel, 'if intended for store beer'.

The reference in the recipe above to brewing porter from a mixture of brown and pale malt, against the all-brown malt porters of the early eighteenth century, reflects the discovery by Richardson, using the saccharometer, that brown malt, which gave porter its colour and flavour, also gave much less fermentable material than pale malt did, meaning that, although brown malt was cheaper, you needed more of it to make a strong drink. A good pale malt produced an extract of eighty-two 'brewer's pounds' (of fermentable sugars) per quarter. But brown malt from the great malting centre of Ware in Hertfordshire, the sort used by London porter brewers, might give only fifty-six pounds of extract per quarter, nearly a third less. The next big development in porter's history was thus the move to including pale and amber malts in the grist to help keep the cost of the final product down.

The problem then was to keep the dark colour that porter drinkers demanded while using enough pale malt to keep the overall cost down. Various tricks were used, including liquorice, either 'straight' or in the form of 'Spanish juice', or 'Spanish liquorice', liquorice boiled in water and then evaporated, for example; or burnt sugar, known as 'essentia binae', made by boiling muscovado sugar in an iron pot and then briefly setting fire to it. Essentia binae, however, and other colouring methods such as boiling down wort until it was sticky as treacle, were eventually ruled illegal by the excise authorities, who were always worried about material going into beer that no tax had been paid on. But in 1817 a man called Daniel Wheeler patented a method of roasting malt at 400 degrees Fahrenheit or more to make a deep brown malt, or 'patent malt', which was both legal (since tax had been paid on the malt) and powerful enough to allow brewers to make the darkest porter using almost all pale malt.

The invention of this new form of beer colouring was hailed in *Dr Thompson's Annals of Philosophy* for December 1817: 'There are few patents that promise to be of such great national importance as one lately obtained by D. Wheeler and Co. for a new and improved method of preparing brown malt.' The magazine went on to give a detailed description of porter brewing as it stood at the end of the Napoleonic Wars and how Wheeler's invention altered the game:

> The essential difference between ale and porter is that the latter liquor is of much deeper colour than the former, and has besides a peculiar empyreumatic flavour, not easily defined, though universally known. This colour and this flavour were originally obtained

by mixing with the pale malt commonly used for brewing a certain proportion of malt dried at a somewhat higher temperature, and, in consequence of being thus slightly scorched, capable of communicating to the water in which it is infused a deep tan-brown colour, and a peculiar flavour.

In the composition of the best genuine porter two parts of brown malt are required to three parts of pale malt. The price of the former is generally about seven-eighths of the latter; but the proportion of saccharine matter which it contains does not, according to the highest estimate, exceed one-half that afforded by the pale malt, and probably on an average scarcely amounts to one-fifth. Taking, however, the proportion of sugar in brown malt even at one half, it follows that the brewers are paying for the colour and flavour of their liquor one-fifth of the entire cost of their malt. The price of this latter article has of late years increased enormously, and the mutual competition of the manufacturers has become so active, as to offer temptations, not easily resisted, either of supplying the colour and flavour of porter by the use of Spanish liquorice, burned sugar, and other similar ingredients which, however innocent in themselves, are prohibited by the Legislation, or of diminishing the strength of the liquor, thus rendering it more likely to become sour or vapid by keeping, and hence bringing on the necessity of using alkaline substances to correct the first; and deleterious narcotics, such as coculus indicus, to supply the deficiency of alcohol.

It appears that the patentees have discovered that, by exposing common malt to about 430 deg. Fah. in close vessels, it acquires a dark chocolate-brown colour, and is rendered so soluble in water, either hot or cold, that, when mixed with pale malt in the proportion of one-eightieth, it communicates to the liquor the perfect colour and flavour of porter.

From this it follows that the brewer, by employing four parts of pale malt, and one twentieth of a part of porter malt, may obtain a stronger liquor than from his usual proportions of three parts of pale and two part of brown malt. The savings thus occasioned out in equity to be divided between the patentee, the brewer and the public. The revenue will be benefited by the increased consumption which will necessarily result from an improvement in the quality of the porter; and both the revenue and public morals will derive advantage from the greatly diminished temptation to fraudulent practices.

Dr Thompson's description of porter before Wheeler, made from 40 per cent brown malt and 60 per cent pale, as 'deep tan-brown', and how this colour could be reproduced perfectly by a mash that was under 1.25 per cent black malt, indicates that late eighteenth and early nineteenth-century porters were far from the completely black colour we associate with the style today. Dr Thompson also asserts that this tiny proportion of black malt also gave the 'perfect … flavour of porter'. But in 1822, five years after Wheeler's invention, the brewer John Tuck complained that 'the real taste of porter, as originally drank, is completely lost … Our ancestors brewed porter entirely with high dried malt; while in the present day, in many houses, high dried or blown malts are entirely omitted.' However, Tuck conceded that while 'to say the truth, there is little of porter left but the name … the taste of the public is so changed, that very few would be found to fancy its original flavour.'

Long storage in wooden vats, with the inevitable infection by wild *Brettanomyces* yeasts and lactobacillus bacteria, would have produced a 'stale' porter that was vinous, tart and almost still. For drinkers who wanted something livelier with a good head on it, the porter brewers sent out fresher, milder, newer-brewed, more carbon dioxide-impregnated beer alongside the matured, flat, stale porter. The mild and stale porters were then mixed at the time of serving, or drawing, in the pub to the customer's taste, a practice referred to in the *Ingoldsby Legends* by Richard Barham, published in 1842: 'I said, "A pint of double X, and please to draw it mild!"' By the end of the eighteenth century most porter was being sent out by the London brewers 'mild', that is, freshly brewed. Only a small proportion was sent out 'stale', or aged in vats. The stale beer was still known, to brewers at least, by the old name for porter, 'entire', or 'entire butt'.

A description of how porter was served at the start of the nineteenth century was given in *Rees's Cyclopaedia*, which said that what was served in pubs was:

> very generally compounded of two kinds, or rather the same liquor in two different stages, the due admixture of which is palatable, though neither is good alone. One is mild and the other stale porter; the former is that which has a slightly bitter flavour from having lately been brewed; the latter has been kept longer. This mixture the publican adapts to the palates of his several customers and effects the mixture very readily by means of a machine containing small pumps worked by handle.

The 'machine' contained four beer pumps and only three spouts, one pump and spout for pure 'mild', or fresh porter, one pump and stout for pure stale, or old porter, and the other two pumps drawing up mild and stale respectively to be thrown out mixed together via the third spout. An illustration of a beer cellar pump made by the inventor Joseph Bramah just like the one described in the *Cyclopaedia* appeared in *The Repertory of Arts and Manufactures*, published around 1790. The illustration shows casks of stale porter and mild porter standing alongside each other, their contents running through taps into the same pipe for drawing up together into the bar; the cocks on the separate taps would have enabled the landlord to set the percentage of stale drawn up with the mild.

The 'stale' or 'entire' beer was not just aged 'mild' porter, but all sorts of leftovers thrown in as well. Charles Barclay, one of the partners in Barclay Perkins, then easily the largest of the London porter brewers, told a House of Commons committee investigating the alleged adulteration of beer in the capital in 1818 that stale porter included returns from publicans, beer collected from brewery pipes and the bottoms of vats, and unsold strong brown stout, all recycled into the maturation vats. This saved money; Barclay told the House of Commons Committee that his own brewery recycled 20,000 barrels a year in this way, around 5 or 6 per cent of total production, and 'the price of beer must be considerably higher' if all that beer had to be thrown away. Adding recycled old beer also helped the raw beer mature quicker, easing the brewers' cashflow.

While all the porter brewers eventually used Wheeler's patent malt, the London brewers continued to use brown malt in their porter mashes, with Whitbread, for example, in 1850, brewing to a recipe that was 80 per cent pale malt, 15 per cent brown malt and 5 per cent black malt. But in Ireland, within a few years of the invention of patent malt, brewers were abandoning brown malt entirely. Guinness, for example, which had been using between 25 per cent and 47 per cent brown malt in its porter up to 1815, was probably using only pale malt and patent malt by 1824 and certainly by 1828. The result was a divergence in flavour between Irish porter (and stout) and London porter (and stout), with the former now drier, less sweet (because the pale malt fermented out more fully than the brown and amber malts that the English brewers used) and, because of the burnt flavours from the patent malt, more bitter.

In Ireland, as well, the practice was to add two gallons of unfermented or partially fermented wort into barrels of porter as it left the brewery. This was called 'gyling', from the original meaning of the word gyle, wort in process of fermentation. It caused a second fermentation in the cask which meant that by the time it reached the publican the beer was lively and sparkling. In the pub, the casks containing this highly conditioned beer were known as 'high', while casks containing maturer, less lively beer were known as 'low'. Publicans would fill glasses three quarters full from the 'low cask' and then top them up with foaming beer from the 'high cask'. The 'high' and 'low' cask system was in use for Irish stout and porter until at least the 1960s.

The evolution of porter thus looked probably like this:

'Palaeoporter' (*c.*1720–*c.*1740) Brewed entirely from highly-dried brown malt; matured for a relatively short time in butts; strong and cloudy and quite likely with at least some smoky tang when young. Colour: dark brown

'Early mesoporter' (*c.*1740–*c.*1790) Brewed entirely from brown malt; matured for a long time (up to two years) in vats; fine, clear and strong; some may have been sent out as new, or mild porter for mixing in the pot with stale, or matured porter. Colour: dark brown

'Late mesoporter' (*c.*1790–*c.*1820) Generally brewed from a mixture of pale and brown malts, or pale, amber and brown malts; most sent out mild, the remainder vatted for up to two years before sending out to publicans as 'stale' or 'entire' for mixing with the mild porter. Colour: variable but dark brown

'London neoporter' (*c.*1820 onwards) Brewed from a mixture of pale malt, brown malt and black malt; still sent out as mild and stale, and mixed to the customer's taste by the publican. Colour: brown to black

'Irish neoporter' (*c.*1824 onwards) Brewed from a mixture of pale malt and black malt. Sent out as 'low' (mature and nearly flat) or 'high' (freshly refermented and lively). Colour: black

Ireland had been one of the most enthusiastic markets for porter, with English brewers selling so much of the drink in Dublin that by 1764 local brewers had begun making it themselves, encouraged by a prize from the Dublin Society for the person brewing the most porter Irish (though, as we have seen, they needed help from an English brewer in the 1770s). Eventually, many Irish brewers became porter specialists, including Beamish & Crawford, merchants in Cork who acquired a brewery in South Main Street in 1792 and grew it into Ireland's largest – there were five large porter breweries and around a dozen smaller ones in Cork city alone by 1810 – and one Arthur Guinness at the St James's

Gate brewery in Dublin, who stopped brewing any other sort of beer except porter in 1799.

Other countries also took up porter brewing. George Washington, who was ordering porter from England around 1760, later bought his porter from a brewer in Philadelphia, Robert Hare. He was the emigrant son of a partner in a porter brewery in Stepney, East London, Salmon and Hare, which eventually became Taylor Walker. Philadelphia had at least two porter brewers in the late eighteenth century, though one English commentator in 1786 said the local version was 'vastly inferior even to Bristol or Bath [porter]', apparently because it was not aged long enough.

Porter was being brewed in Detroit in 1846 and continued to be an American tradition in the late nineteenth century, when even the great Milwaukee lager brewer, Joseph Schlitz, was also producing a Schlitz Porter. American porter survived the Prohibition, with brewers still making the beer while English porter brewers were giving up. The Chester brewery in Chester, Pennsylvania, for example, was making porter alongside pilsner and ale in the 1930s, while the Standard Brewing Company of Rochester, New York State, was making bottled Old Foghorn porter in the 1940s and also bottled Half and Half, ale and porter mixed (a popular drink in London in the 1830s). The style has survived into the twenty-first century, with Yuengling's brewery of Pottsville, Pennsylvania, the oldest in the United States, producing a bottom-fermented variety and Stegmaier, another Pennsylvania brewer, still making the beer.

Canadians also brewed porter. Robert Arkell opened the 'Kensington Ale and Porter brewery' in London, Ontario around the beginning of 1873 to make East India Pale Ale, Amber Ale and XXX Porter. Carling, another London, Ontario brewer, sold bottled 'half and half', the popular mixture of half porter and half strong ale, and was still selling porter in the 1930s after its merger with another Canadian brewer, Kuntz, while its rival, Labatt's, in 1881 was advertising 'Stout, Porter and Pale Ales, in Wood and Bottle'. Labatt's porter was still being brewed in 2005, albeit only, apparently, for the Quebec market. Molson's was brewing porter in Quebec in 1876 and making two different kinds of the beer just before the First World War, ordinary and its own XXX. Even in the early 1930s, Molson's was selling Cream Porter as one of its four main brands and the beer was still being made in the 1980s, although it had disappeared by 1991. Other Canadian porter brewers included Boswell's of Montreal, until its demise the oldest brewery in the country, which was making the beer in the 1920s.

Porter was being brewed in South Africa by 1830, when J. Letterstedt's brewery at Rondebosch, near Cape Town, was advertising 'Ale and Porter in Cask or Bottle warranted to keep in any climate'. Naturally, brewers in Australia made it. An advertisement in the *Sydney Gazette* of 23 December 1804 for Larken's brewery included 'London Porter ... prepared after the system of the British breweries' among the beers being made. Tooth's Kent brewery in Sydney was making porter from the moment it opened in 1835. In New Zealand, Paolo and Pelham's Nelson Ale and Porter brewery in Nelson was operating in October 1843, soon after the town was founded.

The first porter brewery in Sweden was founded by a man called William Knox (who must have been a Scot) in Gothenburg in 1791. In Russia, porter was on sale in 'porter shops', which were restricted by the authorities in 1814–30 in St Petersburg and four in Moscow. A porter brewery was set up in St Petersburg in 1822. But the feeling among local porter drinkers, who included some very influential people, was that although proper ale could be brewed in Russia, proper porter could not. Porter, therefore, escaped the high tariff placed on English ale exports to Russia from 1822, tariffs that wrecked the Burton upon Trent brewers' former Russian export business (and forced them to turn instead to India, by producing what became known as India Pale Ale).

The London porter brewer Barclay Perkins moved into the Russian trade, gaining a near-monopoly of English beer exports to Russia. The very strongest stout porter brewed by Barclay Perkins was sold to the Imperial Court of the Russian Tsar, so that the style became known as Imperial stout. As the nineteenth century wore on, dark beers were ousted by paler lagers and it was not until the fall of communism at the end of the twentieth century that porter made a comeback in Russia, albeit at strengths more like stouts. One of the most popular is from the country's biggest brewer, Baltika, with its Number 6 Porter at 1068 OG. The St Petersburg brewery Stepan Razin makes a 'porter' at Imperial Stout levels, 1080 OG and very bitter. Half a dozen other strong porters are made in modern Russia in cities such as Moscow and Tomsk, and a host of smaller Russian brewers make porters at around the 1052 mark.

Porter also became a tradition in Poland, where several brewers, including Okocim and Zywiec, still make a strong (7 per cent abv-plus), bottom-fermented version of the style, with an aroma that hints of ageing in wooden vats just like the original porters. It also took root in Denmark, while in Finland a Russian, Nikolai Sinebrychoff, founded a brewery to make ale and porter in 1819. Other Baltic countries still brew porter today, including Latvia and Lithuania.

There was an early porter brewery in Hamburg and 'Deutsche Porter' – German porter – eventually developed into two different styles by 1900, one sweet and the other dry. Both were around 1071 to 1075 OG and they came in both top-fermented and lagered versions. The now closed Dressler brewery in Bremen made a porter using *Brettanomyces* yeast, to give it a proper 'English' taste, until at least the late 1960s. A sweet Deutsche porter is still brewed by the Hoepfner brewery in Karlsruhe, Baden-Württemberg, while the Schwerter ('Sword') brewery in Meissen, Saxony, also brewers a beer called Deutsche porter, which is more in the Schwarzbier tradition. The Czechs also developed a porter tradition, with several porters still being brewed by Czech brewers.

Porter and its bigger brother, brown stout, found markets in the West Indies (where it stimulated a demand for black malt drinks that is still strong) and the East Indies, where it competed with pale ale. In the Indian sub-continent the black beer had a good market until at least the early 1860s; Whitbread was winning contracts for up to 38,000 barrels at a time, mostly porter, to cities such as Calcutta and Karachi in the years 1854–63. Porter eventually lost to pale ale and then lager in India, but in Indo-China (and Sri Lanka) black stouts are still brewed.

In the nineteenth century the world was fascinated by England's black beer. A writer in 1838 said that although porter was 'imitated by most of the countries of Europe', 'in the manufacture of this liquor the English have not been excelled by any other nation'. The large numbers of foreign visitors who came to London for the Great Exhibition in 1851 took the opportunity to try genuine English porter 'in enormous quantities', according to Benjamin Disraeli, then Chancellor of the Exchequer.

However, by the year of the Great Exhibition, porter had been seeing its domination in London slide away for twenty years The middle classes preferred Burton-style pale ales, now more widely available and being imitated by brewers around the country, which were seen as having more cachet, while the manual classes were gradually turning completely away from the aged, stale beer their fathers drank and moved towards mild ales. Whitbread, then the third or fourth biggest brewer in London, whose production was entirely porter up to 1834, started brewing mild ale in 1835. Ale quickly rose from nowhere to more than 10 per cent of Whitbread's production by 1839, and more than 20 per cent by 1859, when Whitbread's porter sales had dropped by almost 30 per cent compared to twenty-five years earlier. At Truman's, then fighting with

Barclay Perkins to be London's biggest brewer, the swing from porter
was stronger still, with ale making up 30 per cent of production by 1859.

In the rest of Britain, meanwhile, porter brewing had never been so
widespread. Almost every small brewer described himself in directory and
newspaper advertisements from the 1840s as 'ale and porter brewer'. Some
country brewers seem to have specialised in the style; in 1829 Pigot's trade
directory for Hertfordshire wrote that '... a brewery on a most extensive
scale has been for a considerable time been carried on here [Baldock]
by Mr Pryor; the beer made at it resembles London porter'. However,
Pryor's relatives were partners in Truman, Hanbury and Buxton, the big
London porter brewer, and they may have taught him black beer brewing. J.W. Baker of the Castle brewery, Leamington, Warwickshire was
more typical. He offered his customers in 1846 three grades of porter, XP,
XXP and XXXP, on draught at prices from 1s a gallon to 1s 8d a gallon
and in quart and pint bottles as well. But these were just three out of ten
different kinds and grades of beer made by Baker, the rest being pale ales
and milds, a typical range for a country brewer.

The strength of ordinary porter by now was rather less than it had
been in the eighteenth century, with an analyst in 1843 giving 'porter,
common sort' an OG of 1050. The stronger class of porter was now generally sold under the name stout, specifically 'brown stout' if it was made
with a good proportion of high-dried brown malt, rather than black
malt. Stout could be anything from 1055 to 1072 OG.

The brewer William Loftus described 'the qualities which characterise
what would be termed good porter or stout' as far as public taste was
concerned in 1863 as 'a light brown colour, fullness on the palate, pure
and moderate bitterness, with a mixture of sweetness, a certain sharp-
ness or acerbity without sourness or burnt flavour, and a close creamy
head instantly closing in when blown aside, a tart and astringent flavour.'
Porter and stout 'are now prepared almost entirely from pale and roasted
malts, the use of brown and amber malt being confined to a few of the
most extensive and best known porter breweries.' But 'although on the
score of economy and simplicity there is an advantage in brewing from
pale and black malt only,' he said, 'it cannot be doubted, judging from
the practice of the great porter brewers, that to obtain the true porter
flavour, a certain proportion of amber or slightly scorched malt should
enter into the composition of the grist.'

Loftus gave a recipe for export porter, which sounds more like an
export stout (the line between dark stout and porter was never clear,
given that the original name for the former was 'stout porter'), at ten

or eleven pounds of hops to the quarter of malt and an OG of between 1069 and 1089. It should be vatted for ten to twelve months before shipping, Loftus said, and made completely flat before final racking by leaving the vat's manhole cover off for three weeks.

Thomas Beames, in *The Rookeries of London*, in 1852 was still able to say that for the working classes 'porter is the common beverage with them, just as *vin ordinaire* is in France'. Porter still made up three quarters of London beer sales even in 1863. But the pace against it and towards milds and pale bitter ales was increasing. In 1872 the last porter-only brewery in London, Meux & Co., gave up its exclusive dedication to black beer and began brewing ales as well. Around the middle of the 1870s both Whitbread and Truman (and, undoubtedly, the other historically big London porter brewers too) began selling more ale than porter. By 1887 porter was down to only 30 per cent of the London trade.

For smaller brewers the fall was even greater; at Young & Co. of Wandsworth, on the Surrey side of the Thames, porter had been 70 per cent of production in 1835 and was down to just 16 per cent in 1880. The result was the disappearance from big breweries of the huge porter vats that had been the fascination of visitors. The journalist Alfred Barnard wrote in 1889 that Mann's brewery in the East End of London had removed scores of vats of up to 500 barrels capacity, made from 22-foot staves of best British oak and once used for ageing the drink of the masses, 'have all been removed within the last five years ... Our old friend porter, with its sombre hue and foaming head, is no longer the pet of fashion, but a bright and sparkling bitter, the colour of sherry and the condition of champagne, carries off the palm.'

One problem was that as sales of porter fell, brewers began to abandon proper porter brewing methods. The *Scottish Wine, Spirits and Beer Trades' Review* complained in September 1887 that:

> far too much of the stout brewed in ale brewings might well be described as coloured mild ale; indeed, we know of a case where porter is made from the same mash as mild ale, adding to the last copper a large quantity of sugar to raise the gravity, and enough black malt to impart the requisite colour. Little surprise can be felt that the article thus produced did not give satisfaction to the customer.

The wood-dried malt used in the original porters, where the malt-maker had rapidly raised the temperature of the kiln towards the end of the drying period and the malt grains had popped like corn, was becoming rare. *The Brewer's Journal* wrote in February 1890 that brown malt was now:

> no longer used by the majority of brewers in the production of black beers to anything like the original extent ... [original, here, meaning twenty or thirty years earlier rather than the 1720s] the brown malt of the present day neither corresponds in physical appearance or value to the 'blown' material that was manufactured with the greatest possible care fifteen or twenty years ago. In fact crystal and candied forms of coloured malt have latterly been taking the place of the brown, while dextrinous forms of caramelized sugar are now frequently used ...

Although in 1869 it could still be said that 'in general porter is more highly hopped than ale', by now porter's hopping rate was now much the same as for 'running' mild ale, that is beer brewed for speedy consumption. *The American Handy Book of the Brewing, Malting, and Auxiliary Trades* in 1908, said porter brewed at an OG of 1053 to 1061 used four fifths to 1½lb of hops per (US) barrel, a minimum of 1.2lb per imperial barrel, the same as for 'London four ale', or mild. All the hops were added at the beginning of the boil, which would have maximised bitterness over hop flavour, against pale ale, where up to a third of the hops was held back for the last twenty minutes of the boil, to give hop character. The emphasis on bitterness over taste is confirmed by a book on brewing published in 1912, where the author, the chemist A.C. Chapman, said that porter was 'devoid of any pronounced hop flavour'.

Wahl and Henius emphasised the difference between Irish and English porter recipes, declaring:

> Porter and stout are brewed in Dublin from high-dried pale malt [probably the same as mild malt] and black malt only, while London brewers generally prefer a grist containing all three qualities of colored malt, viz amber, brown, and black, in addition to the pale malt. When black malt only is used in brewing porter and stout, one [part] of black, by measure, to seven of pale is sufficient for the blackest beers, and one [part] of black to twelve of pale is the smallest that is used even in Ireland, where the black beers are generally far less highly colored than in London.

The beer generally remained as strong as it had been late in the nineteenth century. The *Licensed Victuallers' Year Book* of 1915 said London porter had an average alcohol content of 5.5 per cent, though Watney's porter at, now, just 1045 OG, was weaker than its mild. Another big London brewer, Courage, also brewed its porter weaker than its best-selling XX mild and, in 1891, sold it for only 3*d* a quart, a penny a quart less than the 'four-ale'. Porter's declining popularity left it vulnerable in the draconian limits on the amount of raw materials that could be used in beer production that were brought in as the First World War progressed. To keep up volumes, brewers dropped the strength of their beer. The result for porter was that its average gravity fell from around 1054 or so to 1036 or less.

When the restrictions ended after the war, gravities did not rise again because taxes on higher-gravity beers were still so great and former porter drinkers who wanted something like the pre-war version now switched to stout. This had also plummeted in strength, from around 1074 to 1047 OG, but it still had some kick to it and it was generally only a penny a pint dearer than the weakened porter. Across Britain, brewers stopped making porter altogether. The Norfolk firm of Steward and Patteson, for example, ended porter production in May 1918. In 1920, for the first time, Watney Combe Reid, the London brewer, sent no porter to the Brewer's Exhibition for sampling.

Even in Ireland the style was under threat. In 1921 the chairman of Murphy's brewery in Cork declared that 'porter is now practically dead in the south of Ireland'. Murphy's stopped selling porter in Cork city in 1926 and finally ended brewings of porter for sale in country districts in 1943. (Small brewings of porter continued at Murphy's Lady's Well brewery for some years in August and September for harvest workers – a sign of how weak it had become, since harvest beer was always a weak refresher for men needing to replace fluid sweated away in hot summer fields.)

In London, porter limped on, sustained only by its continuing popularity among older drinkers. My father, Arthur, remembered being sent aged eleven, around 1933, to the bottle-and-jug department of the local pub in north London to bring back a quart jug of porter for his grandfather, who would then have been around seventy; on the way home the young boy would take a sly mouthful of beer. Truman's, once one of the three great porter brewers, stopped making the beer in 1930. Porter was fading away, just as London's porters were. There were only fifty former fellowship porters still alive in 1924 and just sixteen in 1932. The writer T.E.B. Clarke in 1938 called porter 'a lowly brand of draught stout [sic] selling in the Public [bar] at fourpence a pint', making it again one of the cheapest (and presumably weakest) beers available.

The East London brewer Taylor Walker was still selling draught porter in 1936 at a wholesale price of 28s a firkin (nine gallons), the same price as the cheapest mild. But the Second World War, which brought another severe restriction on brewing materials, effectively killed the style in Britain. Whitbread 'brewed its last gyle of porter in 1941', exactly 199 years after Samuel Whitbread started in business, according to the beer writer Andrew Campbell. A book published in 1948 by Whitbread, which had been the world's biggest brewer of the style in the eighteenth century, said, sadly: 'Once the pride of the great London breweries, porter is today an almost obsolete term.' The journalist Maurice Gorham wrote a year later: 'Porter is obsolete in the London pubs, though its name survives on the beerpulls of some unmodernised houses and the name is used in some off-licences.' Though bottled porter seems to have continued for a few years after 1945, by 1958 *The Times* survey *Beer in Britain* stated: 'Porter, the strong dark staple beer of eighteenth century England, is no longer brewed in Great Britain. In Ireland it means a light stout, usually sold on draught; in Scandinavia it is a strong dark bottled beer.'

Irish porter continued to have patches of strong support long after its decline to insignificance in Britain. Porter (known as 'plain') outsold stout by as much as eleven to one in some Dublin pubs serving railway men and dockers in the 1930s. Only a drinker up from the country, where porter never sold, would order a pint of stout in a Dublin pub. But by the 1960s, stout had taken over as the black beer of choice even in Dublin. The last stand of porter drinking in the British Isles was Belfast, where Guinness porter, at an OG of 1036, was popular with shipyard workers looking to rehydrate. (Porter was also blended with Guinness Extra Stout, at a ratio of three parts porter to four stout, to make keg draught Guinness in Ireland.) But in 1973 Guinness decided the few pockets of porter drinkers in Belfast were too small to continue satisfying and pulled the plug. For the first time in more than 250 years, no one in these islands was brewing porter.

In England, however, new interest in porter was being stimulated by the rise of the Campaign for Real Ale (CAMRA), which encouraged huge numbers of beer drinkers to look at the country's brewing heritage; and also by the writings of authors such as the late Michael Jackson. His *World Guide to Beer* had a section given over to what Jackson called 'a lost, though not forgotten, beer', and it quoted the nineteenth-century beer writer John Bickerdyke who, quoting another anonymous author, had called porter 'the most universally favourite liquor the world has ever known'.

The next year, 1978, two English brewers brought out the first draught porters to be seen in English pubs for around forty years. One was a small family brewer, Timothy Taylor and Co. of Keighley, West Yorkshire, whose porter was a 1920s style 1042 OG. The other was one of the first wave of new breweries started since CAMRA was founded, Penrhos, based near Kington in Herefordshire. Its Penrhos Porter had a more authentically nineteenth-century OG of 1050.

Six years later, in 1984, a handful of porters were being brewed in Britain, when Grand Metropolitan, owner of Watney's, a former London porter brewer that had swelled into a national concern, brought out a cask-conditioned 1038 OG porter. It was called Hammerton's, after a south London brewer bought by Watney's in 1951 and it was rumoured to be an attempt to steal sales from draught Guinness. But although it was a delicious beer it was only on sale in a small number of pubs in the London area and it was withdrawn after a brief life. That a national brewer should produce a porter again prompted more interest in the style. By 1992 there were twenty-five beers being brewed in Britain under the name of porter.

The same year, Whitbread, another of the former London porter brewers that had grown to be a national beer maker, started brewing porter once more at its brewery in Castle Eden, Durham, as part of its 250th anniversary festivities. The new beer lasted only four years, but the baton of national brewer turned porter revivalist was picked up by Guinness, which introduced a beer in 1996 called Harwood's Porter. It was brewed at its 1930s Park Royal brewery in west London and named after the supposed father of the style. Unlike most of the other revival porters, this was a dark brown eighteenth-century-style beer, rather than a black nineteenth-century version and to add to the authenticity it had a proportion of aged beer mixed in.

However, the revived Harwood's, like the other national brewers' attempts at porters, also lasted only a few years. But by this time the revival was secure; more than sixty different porters were being brewed in Britain and Ireland in 1999, including examples from Fuller, Smith and Turner and Young & Co. in London, while around one in five of Britain's 'new' breweries were making a beer under that name. At least one, Flag Porter, was made to a recipe from 1850 from Whitbread's brewery in London and bottle-conditioned using yeast cultivated from bottles of porter found in a shipwreck from 1825.

The style had also been revived by the new wave of microbrewers around the world. In South Africa the Nottingham Road microbrewery in

Natal kept up the tradition with Pickled Pig porter. American microbrewers, however, with their penchant for radical reinterpretation of old styles, have some fascinating examples of 'new' porters. Alaskan Smoked Porter is, as its name suggests, made from smoked malt, which may well be (not everybody agrees) what a 'new' porter tasted like in the eighteenth century. At least one, Geary's London Porter, from Portland, Maine, is based on a recipe from a book published in 1802 called *Every Man His Own Brewer*. Others are more eclectic interpretations, including Coffeehouse Porter from the Berkshire brewery in Massachusetts, which has organic coffee beans added to the brew.

While American porters have generally been at or above 5 per cent abv, most of the revived porters in Britain are at strengths and with recipes that reflected the post-First World War idea of the beer. Fuller's London Porter, however, is a more late nineteenth-century-style 5.4 per cent abv available in bottle and, seasonally, on draught. The Meantime brewery in Greenwich, London, went even further in 2005 with a London porter that eighteenth-century drinkers might have recognised, containing seven different kinds of malt and a blend of different beers including one deliberately made with a *Brettanomyces* culture of the sort London's first porter brewers introduced accidentally while storing their beer in wooden vats. The beer even comes in corked bottles, as eighteenth-century versions would have, although these are 75cl glass rather than the one pint stoneware bottles Victorian brewers used.

5

STOUT

There enter in, for Drink well brew'd and clear.
For Ales well-colour'd, and stout humming Beer

*A Vade Mecum for Malt-Worms, c.*1718

Today only a daring brewer would produce a stout that was any colour other than black as squid ink. But to Georgian brewers stout simply meant strong beer, in any shade. In 1741, for example, Truman's brewery in East London had both brown and pale stout in stock. Whitbread, another big London porter brewery, was selling pale stout in 1767, for a price a third more per barrel than regular porter. Barclay Perkins, for a long time the biggest London porter brewery, was still brewing pale stout in 1805, made from 100 per cent pale malt, at an original gravity of 1079, the strongest beer the brewery made and even in the 1840s one Irish brewer was advertising a pale stout.

Stout as an adjective originally meant 'proud' or 'brave'. Later (around the fourteenth century) it gained the meaning 'strong'. The first recorded mention of its application to beer comes in the 1630s, when the English poet Robert Herrick wrote a poem about the harvest home supper, which included the lines

If smirking wine be wanted here
There's that which drowns all care, stout beer.

Over the next few decades 'stout beer' was shortened to 'stout'. A letter from 1677 (now in the British Library) declares to the addressee: 'We will drink your healths both in stoutt [sic] and best wine.' The *Vade Mecum for Malt Worms*, a rhyming guide to London pubs written (probably) by the tavern keeper and poet Edward Ward around 1718, mentions stout several times (along with two dozen other types of beer), including the 'famous stout' at the Cooper's Arms on the corner of 'Peter's Street'. Stout was still seen as a rather common expression when used on its own as the name of a drink, however. When Samuel Johnson recorded its meaning in his *Dictionary of the English Language*, published in 1755, he wrote that it was 'a cant [that is, slang] name for strong beer'.

The word continued to be used as an adjective as well as a noun for many years. A poem from Scotland called 'The ale-wife's supplication', which urged George III to cut the taxes on malt and ale, included the lines

> Here's to thee neighbour, ere we part
> But your Ale is not worth the mou'ing
> You must make it more stout and smart
> Or else give over your brewing …
> … Cries Maggy then, you speak as you ken
> Consider our Taxations
> And brew it stout, you'll soon run out
> Of both your Purse and Patience.

The opposite word to stout was 'slender'. In 1796, when restrictions brought in because of the war with France were forcing brewers to make their beers weaker, Thomas Greenall of St Helens told a customer that he would no longer send out larger casks, because the 'slender ale' that was all he could brew would turn sour before an innkeeper could empty the cask.

The porter brewers called the strongest versions of their beer 'brown stout', sometimes 'stout porter', to distinguish it from pale stout. *The Times* was carrying an advertisement for 'stout bottled porter' in August 1797. There was an advertisement for 'Brown Stout Porter' in the edition of 16 August 1800, and one for Stout Porter at £3 a (thirty-six gallon) barrel from the Imperial brewery, Battersea from the Friday 23 October 1807 issue (the brewery's ale, which was clearly stronger, was £4 a barrel). The Southwark brewer Barclay Perkins brewed a 'strong double-brown stout' in 1802, made using the same methods and grain bill as porter, but to a higher gravity. In 1810, Guinness in Dublin decided 'to try whether the publicans will encourage a stouter kind of porter'. This was Superior Porter, the forerunner of Extra Superior Porter, which eventually became Extra Stout.

For the public, 'strong porter' and 'brown stout' were completely interchangeable terms. In a court case reported in *The Times* in July 1803, which revolves around the marvellously named crime of 'sucking the monkey', the two phrases are clearly synonyms. An attorney called Johnson was suing a carrier called Ottadfield (sic) for the price of a thirty-six gallon cask 'of porter, of superior quality, called Brown Stout', which he had bought as a present for his mother and had paid to have delivered to her in Barnsley by wagon.

The cask arrived safely but on the way north 'an accident happened to it, which now and then took place, namely the *sucking the monkey*'. Someone had inserted a straw or tube into the cask through a hole bored into it with a gimlet and sucked out all the rich and doubtless deliciously alcoholic contents. All that arrived in Barnsley was what *The Times* called the '*caput mortuum*', the empty cask. The beer was described in court as 'remarkably fine old porter and very strong' and 'excellent brown stout'. Mr Johnson was awarded £5 2s 2d damages for the loss of the porter and the cost of the cask, the carriage and the booking.

Three decades later, in 1831, 'stout' still meant 'top quality porter': when the partners at Truman's brewery in Brick Lane, on the eastern edge of London, one of the three or four biggest porter brewers in Britain (and thus the world), renewed their lease on the premises for sixty-one years the payment was £1,500 per annum and four kilderkins of 'the Best Beer or Porter called Stout'.

For a long time it was felt necessary to continue to say 'brown stout', *The Times* of 6 January 1876 carried an advertisement for 'Bass & Co.'s European Extra Brown Stout', which the Burton upon Trent brewer had apparently just introduced. Even in 1923 the Leeds brewer Tetley & Co. was making 'brown stout', though this was probably an indicator that the beer was made with a proportion of brown malt, rather than just pale malt and black malt.

Gradually, however, stout stopped being a general term covering any strong beer. Barclay Perkins had evidently stopped brewing pale stout by 1812. A brewer's manual published around 1840 referred to 'stout ales', meaning strong ale in general. In June 1843 a series of small advertisements appeared in *The Times* for Bavarian Pale Stout, brewed, not in Munich, but by Beamish and Crawford of the Cork Porter brewery in Ireland:

> under principles personally explained by Professor Liebig to the manufacturers ... remarkable for its purity and agreeable flavour, and produces a grateful and cheering effect, without exciting any irregular

actions in the stomachs of persons even of the most delicate constitutions, or inducing the least drowsiness in those of sedentary or
studious habits.

This seems to have been a last fling for the term; to most of Queen
Victoria's earliest subjects 'pale stout' would probably have seemed an
oxymoron. The porter brewers had appropriated the word stout for
themselves, so that it became associated for the drinking public solely
with strong, dark beer and it was no longer necessary to add that the
beer was brown. Though stout lingered on as an adjective – in May
1854 Flower and Sons' brewery in Stratford-upon-Avon still listed 'stout
porter' at a price equal to other people's double stout – its general use in
Victorian breweries was solely as the name of a stronger version of porter.

By the 1840s the two great centres of stout brewing were London and
Dublin and stouts from both were available across the country. Dublin
was mostly represented by Guinness and Guinness was widely advertised
in newspapers such as *The Times* in London and the *Manchester Guardian*.
Not everybody liked the Dublin version, however. Charles Knight wrote
in 1851:

> Guinness is a respectable enough drink, but we must say that the
> ascendancy it has gained in many coffeehouses and taverns of London
> is anything but creditable to the taste of their frequenters. Its sub-
> acidity and soda-water briskness, when compared with the balmy
> character of London bottled stout from a crack brewery, are like the
> strained and shallow efforts of a professed joker compared with the
> unctuous, full-bodied wit of Shakspere [sic].

The big difference between the two cities' stouts was that the Irish
brewers, or at least Guinness, used just pale malt and patent roasted
malt, while the London brewers used brown malt as well. In 1838 John
Grattan Guinness Junior had been sacked from the brewery business
in Dublin started by his grandfather for drunkenness and 'mixing with
degraded society'. His uncle, Arthur Guinness II, bought him a brewery
in Bristol to try to give him another chance. Unfortunately John Grattan
Guinness does not seem to have been a businessman and the Bristol
brewery went under in 1845. (Much later, after he fell into poverty, John
Grattan Guinness tried ungratefully and unsuccessfully to sue his cousin,
Benjamin Guinness, for wrongful dismissal from the Dublin brewery.) While John G. Guinness was still running the brewery in Bristol,

however, he was evidently visited by the brewer and writer George Stewart Amsinck, who was shown several different brews, all apparently based on St James's Gate originals. Amsinck eventually printed the recipes for the beers as part of *Practical Brewings*, a manual of fifty different beer recipes published in 1868.

Their interest comes from their being the closest we have to genuine Dublin Guinness recipes of the late 1830s, showing us brewing methods and, in particular, ingredients and proportions of different grain types. Guinness had been among the first porter brewers to seize upon Daniel Wheeler's 'patent' malt for colouring porters and stouts after it appeared in 1817. This was the first properly legal beer colouring (because tax had been paid on the malt before it was roasted into stygianity) to let brewers make really dark beers (which is what the public then expected in their porters and stouts) while using almost entirely pale malt, which gave a much better extract of fermentable sugars than the high-dried and 'blown' malts the original porter brewers had used. An advertisement for Plunkett Brothers, the Dublin makers of patent malt, dated 1873, quotes a letter from Guinness saying the St James's Gate brewery had used its products for 'over fifty years' – in other words, since at least the very early 1820s.

The recipes Amsinck recorded at John G. Guinness's Bristol brewery included a Dublin stout of 1096 OG, using 96.8 per cent new pale Suffolk malt and 3.2 per cent 'black' (roast) malt; a Country Porter (the name that Guinness at St James's Gate gave to the beer delivered outside Dublin) of 1067 OG, brewed with the same ratio of black and pale malts; and a Town Porter (the name Guinness gave to the beer brewed for sale in Dublin) of 1061 OG, ditto for the grain bill again but with half the hops of the Country Porter. This last, town beer was kept for only a day after fermentation was finished, before being mixed with 10 per cent fresh wort, a technique called gyling, and put out into the trade for consumption within a fortnight, making it truly a mild porter, in the proper sense of mild as fresh beer made for quick consumption.

Just like Guinness, the London brewers made their porters and stouts with exactly, or almost exactly, the same grain bill for each grade, only varying the amount of water used to give a higher or lower OG as required. Research by Ron Pattinson into the brewing books of Whitbread's Chiswell Street brewery show that in 1805 the firm used 160 quarters of pale malt and 56 quarters of brown malt to make both its porter and single stout and 136 quarters of pale together with 40 each of amber and brown malt to make its double stout. From these 216 quarters of malt it would make 798 barrels of porter (3.7 barrels to the quarter, around 1060 OG) or 720 barrels of single stout (1070 OG or so) or 580 barrels of double stout (2.7 barrels to the quarter, around 1080 OG).

Four decades later, in 1844, the Whitbread brewing books show it was making five different black beers, porter, KP (keeping porter), single stout, double stout and triple stout, all from pale malt and brown malt only, in a ratio of approximately three quarters pale to one of brown. The stouts were generally parti-gyled with one or other of the porters. The only difference between stout and porter, therefore, was in strength.

In the second half of the nineteenth century, recipes for stout and porter start to diverge. Ron Pattinson's research into the big London brewers' records show that in the latter decades of the Victorian era, as the strength of the black beer grew, generally speaking, London brewers dropped the proportion of black (or roast) malt and increased the proportion of brown malt, while final gravities in the stronger beers climbed. The stronger stouts would thus have tended to be less roasted in flavour and rather sweeter than the porters, particularly if they were sold 'mild', that is, unaged.

This was the start of a long move towards English brewers producing sweeter stouts, which was definitely in progress by the 1880s and culminated in the arrival of 'milk' stout, containing some unfermentable lactose sugars, in the 1900s. In 1883 the *Brewer's Journal* made several references to sweet-tasting stouts brewed with a considerable quantity of non-malt saccharine, 'one-fifth or even larger proportions of Egyptian sugar ... This stout ... tastes extremely sweet.' The move to sweet stouts, the *Journal* said, was 'rendered necessary, perhaps, by a desire for rapid turn-over and a changeable public taste'.

How different in taste were those rival stouts, London and Dublin? In a lengthy article in *The Brewers' Journal* in June 1890, Frank Faulkner, author of *The Theory and Practice of Modern Brewing*, declared: 'The black product of the Emerald Isle is totally different on palate to any that is met with in England, softness being a predominating characteristic, while sweetness is almost entirely absent.'

The reasons for the difference, Faulkner said, were the very soft water used by Irish brewers; their using pale malt plus 6–8 per cent black or patent malt only, not the 'some half dozen varieties of malt, pale and coloured', plus sugar, used by English stout brewers; 'pressure boiling' the wort, which, Faulkner said, guaranteed a good head on the beer; extended primary attenuation to get as low a final gravity as possible; and 'worting' the beer, otherwise known as kräusening or gyling (adding a small amount of fresh still-fermenting wort to the product just before it left the brewery to give it condition).

London stout brewers, on the other hand, Faulkner said, employed pale, brown and black 'and in many cases crystal or amber' malts in making their stouts, generally in a ratio of 8–10 per cent black and 12–25 per cent brown, with the rest 'full-bodied pale'. In recent years, he said, the 'monopolists' had also started using 'black invert sugar of high–class quality' as a malt substitute. This meant the 'London black beer producer' could carry out a speedier fermentation and also 'cask his product at a much higher range of gravity', while 'the main portion of it is consumed perfectly young and green' – and presumably comparatively unacidic and quite sweet.

Despite Faulkner's comments, however, most writers on beer made no particular difference between Irish and London stouts. Herbert Lloyd Hind's *Brewing: Science and Practice*, after the invention of milk stout, said:

> There are a number of distinct types of stout and porter, for which different blends of materials are used. On the one hand, are the stouts brewed from malt only, or from malt and roasted barley. On the other are the sweeter stouts, for which a fairly high percentage of sugar is employed.

The almost universal names for black beers by the middle of the nineteenth century were, in ascending order of strength common porter; best porter; stout or single stout; double stout or extra stout; and imperial stout. The name imperial came from the idea that this was the sort of beer exported to the Russian court in St Petersburg. The best known version was brewed by the Anchor brewery in Southwark, owned by the Thrale family and then by Barclay Perkins. The artist Joseph Farington wrote in his diary for 20 August 1796: 'I drank some Porter Mr Lindoe had from Thrale's Brewhouse. He said it was specially brewed for the Empress of Russia and would keep seven years.' Mr Lindoe was underestimating; a London-brewed imperial stout has proved perfectly drinkable after thirty years in the bottle.

A recipe for Imperial Brown Stout from the Barclay Perkins brewing books of 1851, again uncovered by Ron Pattinson, show it was made from 63.6 per cent pale malt, 10.8 per cent amber malt, 23 per cent brown malt and 2.6 per cent roast barley (surprising, since roast barley was an illegal ingredient at that time – perhaps it did not matter if it was an export brew) at an OG of 1085, with a hop rate of a thumping

9lb to the barrel, though by 1856 it was being brewed at 1107 OG and 10lb 2oz of hops to the barrel. The recipe continued to change. In 1885 Imperial Brown Stout was brewed with 31 per cent brown malt in the grist (against 11.1 per cent brown malt for common porter) and 9lb 14oz of hops to the barrel (against 2lb 8oz for the porter).

Russian Stout, bottle-fermented and stored at the brewery for twelve months with an OG of 1101.8 and an abv of around 10.5 per cent, was still being made by Barclay Perkins at the Anchor brewery until 1958. After Barclay Perkins merged with Courage, production was transferred to Courage's own Anchor brewery downriver by Tower Bridge.

At the Courage brewery, Russian Stout was made as a parti-gyle beer with the weaker 1041 OG Velvet Stout (itself originally brewed by Reading's Simonds brewery), the first run-off from the mash being used for the stronger stout. After Courage's brewery closed in 1982, John Smith's brewery in Tadcaster, by then part of the Courage group, made the beer, turning out batches every couple of years until 1993, the last brewing. Five years later Scottish Courage, by now the owner of John Smith's, announced officially that it would be brewing no more imperial stout.

Another 'Imperial Russian' stout that made it through to the second half of the twentieth century was Simonds of Reading's Archangel Stout, described by the writer Andrew Campbell in 1956 as 'very powerful ... dry and strong to the taste'. Advertisements from the 1930s gave the beer the alternative name of 'XXXXXXX'. Baltic brewers themselves picked up on the style and Tuborg in Denmark was still making a 'Double Imperial Stout' in the 1950s. It was also made in Estonia by the A. Le Coq brewery, under licence from the Barclay Perkins brewery.

The *American Handy Book of the Brewing, Malting, and Auxiliary Trades*, 1908 edition, gives a good overview of the different strengths of stout at that time. Single stouts were made at an original gravity of 1065 to 1073, the authors, Wahl and Henius, said, double stouts at 1073 to 1080, imperial stout at 1080 to 1100, and Russian export stouts were 1100 upwards. Frequently the final beers were a mixture of a strong, aged, vatted brew, which would have all the *Brettanomyces* character of a beer stored for a long time in wooden vats, and a younger, sweeter beer. Thus, a proportion of well-aged stout with an OG of 1080 would be blended into a young 'running' stout or porter of 1049 to 1053 to give a beer with the alcoholic strength equivalent to an OG of 1065 or so. This, it was thought, gave better results than could be obtained with a single unblended stout brewed at 1065 to 1069 OG. Hop rates were 2lb 8oz to the barrel.

Few brewers made the complete range of stouts, however. In the 1880s, Fuller, Smith and Turner of Chiswick, to give one instance, brewed just single stout at 22s a kilderkin and double stout at 27s a kilderkin, with OGs of roughly 1055 and 1070 each. Around the same time M.A. Sedgwick of Watford in Hertfordshire brewed stout at 24s a kilderkin and imperial stout at 36s a kilderkin, at strengths of around 1060 OG and 1090 OG respectively, while Morgan and Co. of Yarmouth in 1884 sold imperial stout and double stout, one at 28s, the other 24s a kilderkin. Frederic Robinson's brewery in Stockport sold stout at 24s and extra stout at 30s.

At the best-known Dublin stout brewer, Guinness, the two main brews were referred to internally, until 1929, as single stout (SS or X) and double stout (DS or XX), though their official, public designations were porter and extra stout. It took a board resolution that year to force the brewery staff and workers to refer to the beers by their 'correct' titles. (Until the First World War Guinness's porter was brewed to the same strength as most English brewers' stout.) But a reflection of the time when stouts were not always completely black could still be seen on Guinness's original trademark label, issued only to those selected bottlers and brewers 'who sell no other brown stout in bottle'.

Guinness actually brewed two other stouts, Export Stout, also known as Invalid Stout, last brewed in 1916 and Foreign Stout or Foreign Extra Stout. FES is still around today and is the basis for most of the versions of Guinness brewed around the world. At an abv of 7.5 per cent, a hop rate even today of 3lb 8oz to the barrel (against more than 5lb in the nineteenth century) and with a proportion of aged, extremely dark old beer in the blend, this is a rare survivor to show the world what stout was like more than one and a half centuries ago.

The popularity of porter in Ireland meant its other brewers generally brewed a dark stout as well, intended for drinkers wanting something stronger. Among the better known were 'Wrastler' or 'Wrassler' stout from Deasy's brewery in Clonakilty, West Cork, supposedly a favourite with the IRA leader Michael Collins (he is said to mention drinking it in his diaries); 'Crown' nourishing stout from Findlater's Mountjoy brewery in Dublin; and the stout made by D'Arcy's Anchor brewery, also in Dublin, and Guinness's main competitor in Ireland until it closed in 1926.

London's best-known stout brewers were Barclay Perkins, Meux and Co. of Tottenham Court Road and Reid & Co. of the Griffin brewery, near Clerkenwell Road. While Guinness today has almost a monopoly as the beer to drink with oysters, this was not always the case. The journalist Alfred Barnard wrote in 1889: 'Who has not heard of Reid's stout? And what better accompaniment to a dozen of oysters could be found?' Reid's produced nothing but stout, in four grades, XX Imperial at 1080 OG, BS (brown stout), DBS (double brown stout) and CB (common brown), and porter until 1877, when it began making the increasingly popular pale ales. But when Barnard visited the brewery in 1889 it still had one racking store devoted entirely to the XX Imperial Stout and another store filled from end to end with stout for Russia, at 1100 OG, 'for which this house is justly celebrated'. When Reid's merged with its fellow London brewers Watney and Combe, in 1898, the Reid's name continued to be used for bottled Special Stout, Family Stout and Oatmeal Stout, and Reid's Extra Stout continued as the combined operation's draught strong dark beer. By the 1950s it had become 'container stout', an early keg beer that was a rival to the growing Guinness keg stout. It finally vanished in 1961, when Guinness paid Watney's £28,000 to stop brewing Reid's and take Guinness stout instead.

By the end of the nineteenth century, stout had won a reputation for its supposed restorative qualities, with doctors recommending it as a pick-me-up and for patients, particularly females, who had lost their appetites. Even in 1861, Mrs Beeton was recommending it for nursing mothers: 'As the best tonic, and the most efficacious indirect stimulant that a mother can take at such times, there is no potation equal to porter and stout, or, what is better still, an equal part of porter and stout.' (Porter and stout mixed was known as Cooper, supposedly because it was the drink most popular with coopers and Whitbread, for one, offered bottled London Cooper.)

The health-giving nature of stout was an image Victorian and Edwardian brewers played to. In 1887 the Richmond brewery in Surrey was advertising 'Ladies' Stout' and 'Double Stout (Invalids)', while its near neighbour across the Thames, William Gomm of the Beehive brewery, Brentford, sold 'Double Stout (for nursing)'. The same year Waltham Brothers' brewery in Stockwell, South West London, was calling its SN stout an 'alimental tonic', 'particularly suited for invalids, ladies nursing or anyone requiring a good sound strengthening beverage', while warning that its Double Stout was 'Highly nutritious, but too strong for some invalids'.

Barrett's, the brewery in Vauxhall, South London, that pioneered the screw-top beer bottle, issued story-telling posters in 1896 depicting in the first frame a sick woman being shown a bottle of stout by a gentleman

The Whistling Oyster, Vinegar Yard, Drury Lane, London, which sold Reid's XX stout to accompany its oysters

clearly meant to be from the medical profession. In frame two she was restored to full bloom, waving bottle and glass and declaring that Barrett's stout 'saved my life'. Vaux, the Sunderland brewer, carried an encomium from the *Lancet*, the medical journal, on posters for its stout in 1900. The posters quoted the magazine saying: 'As is well known, Stout appears to be easier of digestion than beer, and doubtless in the present case this is especially so.' Nurses appear in several advertisements for stout from the

1890s and 1900s, with Ind Coope of Romford actually listing the more than twenty hospitals where its beer was used.

Oatmeal stout, a variant that appeared around the end of the nineteenth century using oats, raw or malted, was pushed as even better than ordinary stout for the enfeebled. The Rochdale and Manor brewery in Lancashire in 1909, for example, advertised its Oatmeal Nourishing Stout as 'Refreshing and strengthening'. Walker and Homfray's of Salford in 1904 declared its own Oatmeal Stout was 'particularly suitable for invalids'. The allegedly health-enhancing properties of stout is why, when Guinness hired an advertising agency in the late 1920s to ask people why they drank its beer, so many declared: 'Because it's good for me', a response that prompted one of the most famous advertising slogans in the world.

Consumer protection legislation has killed 'Guinness is Good for You' in Britain and Ireland, as it has the rival Mackeson stout's line, 'Does You Good', though 'Good for You' still appears on bottles of Nigerian-brewed Guinness. It is doubtful if any brewer today would be able to name a beer, as Ansell's brewery of Birmingham did, Tonic Stout, and similarly Peter Walker, the Warrington and Burton upon Trent brewer, would not now be allowed to make the pre-First World War brew it called Dietetic Stout.

'Mild' stout, young and sweeter than aged stout, as we have seen, was popular at the end of the nineteenth century, but inevitably the beer aged and lost its sweetness. What was needed was something sweet to put in the beer that would not ferment. In the 1890s one sugar supplier in London was selling something called 'Viscosoline', which it said 'may be described as unfermentable sugar', for brewing light but full-tasting beers. However, Viscosoline is not heard of again after the end of the decade. The idea of a 'milk beer', made with an addition of unfermentable lactose sugar, derived from milk, to give a sweeter brew had first been suggested in 1875. It took a long time for the first successful product to appear, however. In 1907 the Kentish brewer Mackeson of Hythe, having acquired the patents to the idea, made its first brewings of a new stout brewed with lactose, which was put into the wort at a rate of nine pounds to the barrel, half an ounce per pint; the original label bore the claim that 'Each pint contains the energising carbohydrates of ten ounces of pure dairy milk'. The new beer was called 'milk stout'; 'stout' was now on its way to having the meaning 'black beer' rather than strong beer.

The original Mackeson milk stout was apparently 1054 OG and a version called Mackeson XXX is brewed in the United States at

5 per cent abv, but Mackeson stout as brewed today in the UK is only 3 per cent alcohol. This is less than most surviving mild beers, despite an OG of 1042, thanks to all that unfermentable lactose. Mackeson soon licensed the production of milk stout to other brewers. Massey's Burnley brewery was advertising its 'new Milk Stout' by January 1911, for example, and thirteen other brewers were also making milk stout by 1912. Others followed and in the 1930s Watney's even had an 'Extra Milk Stout'.

However, the beer's great boom came after Mackeson's was acquired by Whitbread in 1929. Sidney Nevile, the M.D. of Whitbread, says in his autobiography that at that time:

> the output [of milk stout] was small and at first there was doubt whether the product would be worth continuing … I found on investigation that the quality was impaired by certain restrictions imposed by the customs authorities on the use of lactose, restrictions which seemed to me capable of revision. I was able to arrange with the heads of Customs for these to be modified. This improved the product and … before long we had secured a large and growing market throughout the country.

Stout began to lose the image of a strong beer even faster after the great lowering of gravities in the First World War and the gradual disappearance of porter from British brewers' portfolios. It became, in effect, another name for a dark beer, a little stronger, rather darker, perhaps a little more bitter than a brown ale in the way that a best bitter was a little stronger and hoppier than an ordinary bitter. The Scottish brewer Maclays' oatmeal stout, for example, in 1909 had a gravity of only 1046. In 1920 Steward and Patteson, the Norwich brewer, had stopped brewing porter and was making a 'stout' that, at 1047, had an OG 13 per cent lower than its pre-war porter, which had been 1054 OG. By 1929 Steward & Patteson's stout had fallen to 1039 OG, only one degree above its Norfolk brown ale.

Since the passing of the Free Mash Tun Act of 1880, which finally permitted brewers to use ingredients other than malt to brew with, some had been substituting the roast malt used to give colour to stout with roast barley. Henry Stopes, writing in his 600-page bible *Malt and Malting*, insisted that roasted barley did not give as permanent a colour as roasted malt and 'the flavour is also very inferior; and the aroma can bear no comparison'.

But Alfred Henry Allen wrote in *Allen's Commercial Organic Analysis* in 1912 that: 'Roasted barley is now largely taking the place of roasted malt, the latter being used mostly in the brewing of export stouts.' Guinness seems to have continued using only roasted malt until the end of the 1920s; its guidebook for visitors to the St James's Gate brewery in Dublin, published in 1928 said: 'The chief difference between Ales and Stout are … in the use of roasted malt, which imparts both colour and flavour to the stout.' In the 1931 edition, however, the copy had changed to read '… the use of roasted malt, *or barley*' (my emphasis). It looks significant that this happened just after the death of Edward Guinness, first Earl of Iveagh, in 1928, who had effectively controlled the company for the previous sixty years. Had he stood out against using roasted barley and, after his death, did the 'progressives' at St James's Gate finally get its use approved? (Some time in the early 1950s Guinness began using flaked barley as well in its stout.)

At the time, stout was probably at the height of its popularity. Guinness opened a new brewery in Park Royal, north-west London, in 1936 to supply drinkers in the southern half of Britain with its bottled Extra Stout (although, like Steward & Patteson's stout, Guinness ES had fallen from its pre-First World War gravity to just 1044 OG). Sales of sweet, lactose-containing milk stout boomed, surviving the blow of a ruling by the British government in 1946 that beers could not carry the word 'milk' on the label. Brewers got round that restriction by giving their lactose-containing beers names such as 'Farm Stout' (Rayment's of Hertfordshire), 'Barley Cream' (Darley's of Thorne) or 'Dairymaid Stout' (Watney's), while Simonds of Reading had Velvet Stout (later produced by Courage after it took over Simonds) and Marston's of Burton upon Trent managed to get away with 'Mylki Stout'.

A little booklet on beer produced in 1956 by the now-vanished men's magazine *Lilliput* lists almost fifty different stouts from British and Irish brewers, of which not quite half are marked as 'sweet', including Mackeson (and one from Beasley's brewery in Plumstead, London, called 'Arsenal' – named for the nearby Royal Woolwich Arsenal, not the north London football team).

London-brewed stouts that were, like Guinness, not marked as 'sweet' included three from Watney's: Hammerton's, Reid's Special (described elsewhere as 'rather bitter') and Export; one from Whitbread; one from Taylor Walker; one from Mann's in the East End, Cream Label; and one from Barclay Perkins, Velvet Stout (not to be confused with the 'sweet' Velvet Stout brewed by Simonds of Reading). In the early 1950s the

London brewer Watney Combe Reid made one draught stout and seven different bottled stouts: the medium-strong Hammerton's Oatmeal Stout (brewed at the Stockwell brewery acquired by Watneys in 1951), the strong Reid's Special Stout, Country Extra Stout, Export Stout; Family Stout, 'specially brewed for the country trade', Isleworth Stout, from the Isleworth brewery in Middlesex, which Watney's had bought in 1924 and Dairymaid Sweet Stout.

One London brewer in the mid-1950s, Lovibond's of Greenwich, was producing two draught stouts called Oatmeal (containing oatmeal, naturally) and Yeoman (a nice play on the expression 'stout yeoman'). However, the writer Andrew Campbell, in *The Book of Beer*, said of the contemporary beer scene that 'Ordinary stouts are not often to be found on draught'.

At Whitbread, nearly half the trade in 1959 was in bottled Mackeson stout. Mackeson was one of the heavily advertised beers of the period, with the veteran actor Bernard Miles appearing on television to tell viewers in a strong Hertfordshire accent: 'Looks good, tastes good – and by golly, it does you good!' Sales of Mackeson were high enough for Guinness to feel threatened, even though its much dryer-tasting product appealed to a different sort of drinker, and in 1956 the Dublin Guinness brewery was asked to brew a sweet stout for testing in Britain to counter the Mackeson threat. However, whatever the test results were, Guinness sweet stout never appeared on the market.

Milk stout and the even sweeter versions of the style, such as Sweetheart Stout from Younger's of Alloa, at 2 per cent abv, about as far from the original idea of stout as it is possible to be, were frequently marketed at women. The regular sight of the television battleaxe Ena Sharples and her two equally elderly female pals ordering milk stout in the Rovers Return in the ITV soap opera *Coronation Street* in the early 1960s must have been undoing everything the brewers' marketing departments were then trying to achieve. From 1959 Guinness was making increasing progress with its 'draught' dispense system, using a mixture of nitrogen and carbon dioxide to serve its stout in metal kegs. This replaced the old 'high and low cask' system of serving the beer from two separate casks, one filled with young, highly conditioned beer to give a good head and the other older and flatter beer. Whitbread tried selling a pressurised draught version of Mackeson stout from 1958 to the mid-1960s, and again in 1969 as 'Mackeson D', but the project was a failure for two reasons: the association of milk stout with elderly working class women and the technical problems of serving keg stout, which tends to produce a very big head very easily under pressure. Too often bar staff were pulling a pint of froth and nothing else.

Meanwhile, the efforts of one milk stout producer to sell his beer abroad were providing a back door for the arrival of what would become the UK's biggest-selling lager. Hope and Anchor, a specialist bottled beer brewer in Sheffield, had been very successful with a milk stout called Jubilee, first produced in 1935, the year of George V's silver jubilee. The managing director of the Hope and Anchor brewery, Thomas Carter, was sure there was a market for Jubilee Stout in Canada. In 1951 Carter went to see E. P. Taylor, head of Canadian Breweries, who agreed to brew and bottle Jubilee Stout in Canada if, in return, Hope and Anchor would brew and bottle his Carling Black Label lager in Britain. Jubilee Stout was a flop in Canada, to the chagrin of Hope and Anchor, but Taylor's team found it was pushing at an open door in its efforts to sell lager to the British. Eventually, Taylor welded together an empire in the UK to sell Black Label lager, which became Bass Charrington, the largest brewer in the country.

Stout had been successfully exported as a style: the strong imperial version had taken root in the Baltic countries and there were stout brewers in former British bastions such as Jamaica, Nigeria, Malaysia and Ceylon (now Sri Lanka), all places where stout is still brewed and popular today (it goes remarkably well with spiced food). Brewers in Australia, South Africa and New Zealand made stouts alongside their ales. American and Canadian brewers also brewed 'Brown Stout' in the nineteenth century. In Malta the Simonds Farsons Cisk brewery still makes Lacto Milk Stout, first brewed in 1946, and 3.8 per cent abv.

A survey in the early 1970s by Frank Baillie of the UK's ninety or so surviving regional breweries found only forty-eight stouts being brewed, of which forty-one were sweet stouts, including the distinctly un-PC Blackamoor Stout from Hardys and Hansons in Nottinghamshire, first brewed in 1950. Only two brewers were making oatmeal stout, Wadworth of Devizes and the soon-to-close G.E. Cook in Essex.

Only Belhaven brewery made three different stouts, two sweet and one, Trinidad, brewed to a drier recipe. This last beer was exported to the West Indies to satisfy the local desire for strong dark brews, and also to Tahiti. All these stouts were bottle-only; the draught stout market had been surrendered to Guinness, after unsuccessful attempts in the late 1960s by Watney's to import draught Murphy's stout from Cork under the name 'Colonel Murphy' and Bass to market Cork's other stout, from Beamish & Crawford.

The Nottinghamshire brewer Hardy & Hansons made Blackamoor stout in the 1950s

A dozen years after Frank Baillie, another survey by *What's Brewing*, the Campaign for Real Ale newspaper, revealed just twenty-nine brewers in the UK and Channel Islands making a total of thirty-two stouts, all bottled. It might have been expected that stout would die out as a style, with old ladies sitting on their own in snugs apparently the only people ordering the beer; stout now had such a poor image, draught Guinness deliberately refused to use the 'S' word about itself, despite its ancestry.

Unlike the draught version, bottled Guinness had continued to be a 'live' beer, containing yeast that helped it condition, a tradition Guinness brewers had been extremely proud of, when almost all other bottled beers were filtered and pasteurised. However, the rise of central heating meant that British pubs, like British homes, were now much warmer places than they used to be, which meant the beer was conditioning too fast. With sales of bottled stout falling in the UK and turnover of bottles on the shelves lower, this meant too many customers were getting 'off' Guinness. In the mid-1970s Guinness stopped leaving live yeast in its bottled stout and filtered and pasteurised it just like almost everyone else.

But the small brewery boom in the United States saw brewers there start producing stouts as part of a general revival in old beer styles. The first microbrewery in the country, New Albion in Sonoma, California, had a stout in its repertoire when it began around 1978 and most American micros since then have included a stout in their line-up. An American beer importer read in Michael Jackson's *World Guide to Beer* in 1977 about oatmeal stout and persuaded Samuel Smith, the Tadcaster brewer, to start making it again for export in bottle to the United States. This encouraged American microbrewers to start making their own oatmeal stouts, while Sam Smith's also decided to introduce a bottled imperial stout, albeit at only around 7 per cent abv.

Gradually other brewers in the UK began making stouts as well, though they arrived at least ten years after the first revived porters appeared. The Oakhill brewery, near Bath, was making a bottled stout in 1986. One of the first 'new wave' draught stouts was from the Big Lamp brewery in Newcastle upon Tyne, which appeared in 1987 with an OG of 1044. The chosen gravity was probably, under the influence of bottled Guinness, seen as the 'traditional' stout strength. At the same time the Reepham brewery in Norfolk was making a draught stout with an OG of 1048.

By 1992 the *Good Beer Guide* was listing a dozen draught stouts, though the strongest were only 1050 OG and one was as low as 1036, well below many of the newly revived porters. The new stouts included three cheekily named offerings, Goodness Stout from the Jolly Roger brewery in Worcester, Guiltless from West Coast in Manchester and Guineas from Linfit in Huddersfield. (After the closure of the Park Royal brewery in 2005, the only British stout with a true Guinness heritage is Elvedon Stout, 5.2 per cent abv, brewed on the Suffolk estate of the head of the Guinness family, the current Lord Iveagh, and sold in stoneware bottles.)

Today there are some fifty draught stouts available in British pubs, including Comrade Bill Bartram's Egalitarian Anti-Imperialist Imperial Soviet Stout from the Bartram brewery in Bury St Edmunds, which, at 6.4 per cent abv, may not be the strongest stout ever brewed, but has to be the one with the longest name. Bartram also does several other bottle-conditioned stouts, including a damson stout and a cherry stout, both at 4.8 per cent abv. Few are up there for strength with Liquid Lobotomy Stout from the Garton brewery in East Yorkshire, at a Victorian-style double stout OG of 1080, or Russian Stout from Wessex of Warminster, also 1080. They also include mixtures old brewers never dreamed of: Port Stout (O'Hanlon, among others), Espresso Stout (Meantime) and Blackberry Stout (Burton Bridge), to list three. Some have picked up on the chocolate flavours found in roasted grain, such as Young's Double Chocolate Stout, made with real chocolate. Harvey's brewery in Lewes has done the world a huge favour by reviving the Imperial Extra Double Stout once brewed in Estonia by the Le Coq brewery, a marvellous bottle-conditioned beer at 9 per cent abv, best drunk at least three years old.

In Japan, Asahi has made a traditional stout at around 1064–1068 OG that is pitched with *Brettanomyces* yeast as well as conventional brewer's yeast, to give a flavour like Guinness Foreign Extra Stout. American microbrewers have happily seized on stout as a beer it is possible to make extreme drinks with, such as Brooklyn Black Chocolate Stout (which contains no chocolate) and Expedition Stout, 12.55 per cent abv, from the former Kalamazoo brewery in Michigan, which has offered up to ten different stouts at the same time. Today's king of stouts, however, has to be the now infamous Dogfish Head brewery of Lewes, Delaware's World Wide Stout, at a knock-out 18 per cent abv. One version released in the UK went as far as 21 per cent. With beers like that around, nobody will be wanting 'smirking wine'.

However, since the revival of porter brewing, or to be more accurate, 'the revival of beers being called porter', with several brewers making 'stouts' that are weaker than their 'porters', it is no longer possible to say, as it used to be, that the difference between porter and stout is one of strength. Indeed, it looks impossible now to draw a line and state categorically about dark beers being brewed today: 'Everything over here is a stout and everything over there is a porter'. In terms of strength, ingredients, flavour and appearance, modern-day stouts and porters, except for 'milk stouts', occupy effectively identical spaces, as shown by this survey of thirty more or less randomly chosen porters and stouts from the 2009 Campaign for Real Ale *Good Beer Guide*, fifteen of each, with their abvs and the adjectives used in the *Guide* to describe them:

Porters		
Brewer	*ABV*	*Adjectives*
Elland	6.5%	creamy liquorice chocolate roast malt
Larkins	5.2%	roast bitter-sweet fruity
Oulton	5.2%	fruity bitter-sweet
Cox & Holbrook	5.0%	caramel roast malt very sweet
White Horse	5.0%	dark red chocolate fruity berry
Wicked Hathern	4.8%	ruby lightly smoked chocolately nutty
Beowolf	4.7%	mint-chocolate liquorice roast fruit toffee
Berrow	4.6%	ruby hops
Bartrams	4.5%	ruby hops
Burton Bridge	4.5%	malty roast fruit liquorice bitter
Enville	4.5%	sulphurous sweet fruity
Moor	4.5%	fruity roast malt slightly sweet
RCH	4.5%	chocolate coffee roast dark fruits
Vale	4.3%	roast rich fruitiness sweet to dry hoppy
Pilgrim	4.0%	roast bitter-sweet berry fruit
Average	4.8%	

Stouts		
Brewer	*ABV*	*Adjectives*
Outstanding	5.5%	bitter liquorice
Burton Bridge	5.0%	roast malty fruity
Famous Railway Tavern	5.0%	full bodied intense roast grain sweet to dry
Eynsham	5.0%	roast liquorice smoky
Wapping	5.0%	bitter fruit dry
Bartrams	4.8%	biscuity smoked lightly roast coffee
Beowulf	4.7%	charcoal liquorice raisins
Wye Valley	4.6%	smooth roast bitter
B&T	4.5%	bitter coffee roast
Goachers	4.5%	Irish-style
Hop Back	4.5%	roast sweet malty
Titanic	4.5%	tobacco smoke liquorice chocolate dry
Town House	4.5%	roast chocolate toffee sweet to bitter
Big Lamp	4.4%	roast malty
Woodlands	4.4%	creamy roast dry
Average	**4.7%**	

The porters are on average slightly stronger than the stouts, though if you take the Elland 1872 Porter out, the averages are exactly the same. Most common adjectives used for porters: roast (60%) fruity (53%) chocolate (33%) sweet (27%) liquorice (20%) ruby (20%). Most common adjectives used for stouts: roast (67%) liquorice (27%) bitter (27%) dry (27%) fruity (20%) smoked (20%). This suggests that porters (in the UK at least) have a tendency to fall on the fruity-chocolate-sweet side, stouts on the liquorice-bitter-dry side, but the differences are not that marked. When a brewer brews something today that he or she calls 'stout' this is simply meant to indicate that it will be a dark beer, while if it is named 'porter', the beer is very probably meant to be making a nod at an idea of authenticity, a suggestion that it is true to an earlier model.

6

INDIA PALE ALE

'Take away this clammy nectar!' said the king of gods and men;
'Never at Olympus' table let that trash be served again.
Ho, Lyaeus*, thou the beery! Quick – invent some other drink;
Or, in a brace of shakes, thou standest on Cocytus'† sulphury brink!'
Terror shook the limbs of Bacchus, paly grew his pimpled nose,
And already in his rearward felt he Jove's tremendous toes;
When a bright idea struck him – 'Dash my thyrsus!‡ I'll be bail
For you never were in India that you know not HODGSON'S ALE!'
'Bring it!' quoth the Cloud-compeller; and the wine-god brought
      the beer.
'Port and claret are like water to the noble stuff that's here!'
And Saturnius drank and nodded, winking with his lightning eyes,
And amidst the constellations did the star of HODGSON rise!

'Jupiter and the Indian Ale', from *The Bon Gaultier Ballads*, William
Edmonstoune Aytoun and Theodore Martin, 1845

*An epithet of Dionysus †One of the five rivers of Hades ‡A staff
with a pine come on the end, one of the symbols of Bacchus

Horace Walpole, the writer and son of the former prime minister Sir
Robert Walpole, invented the word serendipity in 1754 in a letter to
a friend written at his home, Strawberry Hill, near Twickenham,
Middlesex. He took the word from an old oriental tale, *The Three Princes
of Serendip* (an Arab name for Sri Lanka), basing its meaning on the idea
that the princes were always making happy discoveries while actually
looking for something else entirely.

Two years earlier, in 1752, a small brewing operation had begun over
the other side of Middlesex, at Bow on the River Lea, that would have

its own serendipitous discovery involving the Indian subcontinent. The Bow brewery, founded by George Hodgson, was comparatively small, making an average of just 11,200 barrels a year in the 1750s and 1760s and a little under 20,000 barrels in 1786 when, for example, Samuel Whitbread's porter brewery in Chiswell Street, on the edge of the City, was brewing 130,000 barrels a year.

But Hodgson's lucky break was that his brewery was just up the Lea from Blackwall on the Thames, where the ships of the East India Company docked. The East India Company, founded in 1600, had become the most powerful force, economic and political, in the subcontinent. It had a monopoly on trade between Britain and India, which was carried on some seventy or so sailing ships known as East Indiamen. The ships' commanders and crews were allowed to conduct private trade on their own accounts, shipping English goods to India, generally for sale to the East India Company's 'civil servants' (traders, tax collectors and the like) and 'military servants' (the soldiers in its three private armies).

The goods the commanders and officers of the East Indiamen bought out from London in the holds of their ships included clothes, perfume, china and glass, hams, cheese, cider, wine – and beer. An East Indiaman ship's commander might well make up to £12,000 a year from private business, an enormous sum for the time, and by 1784 it had become the usual, albeit illegal, practice for an East Indiaman captain to sell his command to his successor for between 4,000 and 7,000 guineas.

For their beer supplies, the ships' commanders did not bother going to any of the better-known London brewers, although several of the largest, such as Thrale, Calvert and Parsons, were handily placed by the banks of the Thames. Instead they went to the rather nearer Hodgson at Bow. One important reason for buying from the Bow brewery was that Hodgson gave the commanders and captains lengthy credit of up to eighteen months. They bought a mixture of different beers from the Bow brewery, including porter (Hodgson was listed among London's porter brewers, albeit not one of the big twelve, and was still sending porter to India in 1823), small beer and October beer. This last was the pale, well-hopped autumn-brewed stock bitter beer, popular with the eighteenth-century landed classes, who brewed it themselves on their country estates and kept it as 'stock' beer was meant to be kept, for a year to two years to mature.

However, something serendipitous happened to Hodgson's October beer on the long, three to four-month voyage by sea from Blackwall to Bombay, Madras or Calcutta. The journey was a rough one, as the ships sailed down to Madeira, on to Rio de Janeiro in Brazil to pick up more food and water, then across the South Atlantic via St Helena to Cape Town, up the Mozambique Channel and finally to India, crossing the equator twice on the way down through the Atlantic and then the Indian Ocean. The ships themselves received a serious battering; an East Indiaman would normally make only four or five round-trips before being broken up or sold off. But for the October beer in the ships' holds, the slow, regular temperature changes on the journey and the rocking it received in the oak casks that it sat in had a transforming effect. The beer arrived in India with the maturity and depth of flavour previously only found after years in a cellar and the Indian expatriates loved it.

Despite many claims otherwise, there is no evidence George Hodgson had to design a special beer for shipping to India. Brewers already knew how to make beers that would keep a long time in cask; the anonymous *Every Man His Own Brewer* of 1768 gives a recipe for two hogsheads of October 'malt wine' made from the first two mashes off 22 bushels of malt, with 6½lb of hops per 8 bushels of malt to ensure 'a year's keeping'. Nor was he the first to export pale ale to hot climes. This was taking place fifty years before Hodgson got going, according to a book called *Social Life in the reign of Queen Anne: taken from original sources*, since it quotes an advertisement apparently from the early eighteenth century that said: 'Any Merchant that has occasion for Pale Ale and Stout, to send to the West Indies, may at any time be supplied at the Fountain Brewhouse, by the Hermitage, with Beer for Shipping at reasonable rates.' The Hermitage is likely to be the one by the river at Wapping, just to the east of the Tower of London; the district was a centre of export brewing and when the Sun brewery, Wapping, which looks to have been in existence since at least 1735, was put up for auction in June 1819, it was described as having 'a highly respectable and lucrative shipping trade', which had been established 'for many years'.

When the Bow brewery's ales started to be exported to the east is not known, but in 1844 the brewery was claiming that its beer had been 'held in high repute in India for nearly a century'. Certainly Hodgson's beer eventually won a tremendous reputation among the expatriate drinkers of India. Harry Abbott, grandson of a later partner in the brewery, Edwin Abbott, and an officer in the Indian Army, recalled in his autobiography:

Hodgson's was the favourite tipple then … The following was a song which used to be sung at many a pigstick party and race meeting in the thirties, forties and fifties:

Who has not tasted of Hodgson's pale beer
With its flavour the finest that hops ever gave?
It drives away sadness, it banishes fear,
And imparts a glad feeling of joy to the grave.

Oh! to drink it at morning, when just from our bed
We rise unrefreshed, and to breakfast sit down,
The froth-crested brimmer we raise to our head,
And in swigging off Hodgson, our sorrows we drown.

Or to drink it at tiffin, when thirsty and warm,
We say to the khidmutgar, 'bring me some beer,'
Soon, soon do we feel its most magical charm,
And quickly the eatables all disappear.

Or at ev'ning, when home from our ride we return,
And jaded and weary we sit down to dine;
We ask but for Hodgson, and willingly spurn
The choicest the dearest the rarest of wine.

Then hail to thee Hodgson! of Brewers the head,
Thy loss we in India would sadly bewail;
May you live long and happy, and when you are dead,
I will think of you daily whilst drinking your ale.

Beer for breakfast, it will be noted, was apparently still a habit of the English upper classes, at least in India, as it had been in Tudor times and before.

However, Hodgson's reputation seems to have taken some time to build. An advertisement in the *Calcutta Gazette* from 8 April 1784 mentions 'cyder, 20 rupees per doz.', and 'London porter and pale ale, light and excellent, 150 rupees per hogshead, 12 rupees per doz. bottles'. Among the points to be noticed here are (1) the brewer's name is not mentioned; (2) porter, as well as pale ale (and indeed cider) were being exported to India in 1784; and (3) pale ale was not seen as anything out of the ordinary. It received no special underlining and it was selling for the same price as the porter.

Another advertisement from the *Calcutta Gazette* a couple of years later, 8 June 1786, deserves quoting more fully:

> Per ship Phoenix: The whole of Captain Rattray's Investment, purchased by messers Sanders & Lacey ... exposed for sale at their warehouse on Wednesday next. From the very quick passage of the Phoenix (she having been little more than four months from England) they have every reason to expect that the eatables and drinkables will be in the highest perfection ... wines, Herefordshire cyder, Porter in casks, ditto in bottles, small ale and strong ale ... cheese, hams ... china, glass ... perfume ... clothes ... and everything else to fit out a home.

So, not only porter, but 'small ale' was being shipped to India. Small ale was made at a strength of four or five barrels from a quarter of malt, was lightly hopped and probably was not much higher than about 4.5 per cent or 5 per cent abv; so much for the idea that malt liquor had to be strong and well hopped to survive the journey east. We can guess that the 'strong ale' was probably pale ale, but it was not specifically being described as such and nor, again, was the brewer's name given.

The first named advertisement for Hodgson's beers appears in the *Calcutta Gazette* in September 1793, brought out on the East Indiaman *Britannia*. Two months later the *Hillsborough* arrived bearing both 'Pale ale and porter in hogsheads from Hodgson'. The market was clearly not just for pale ale. Indeed, in January 1801 the *Gazette* printed an advertisement for the 'Investment of Captain Lambe' of the *Melville Castle*, 'just landed and now exposed for sale for ready money only ... Beer from Hodgson', no more specific than that, at Sicca Rupees 140, alongside 'claret 43 per doz, port 25 ditto, gin in pipes 3½r per gall ... hams, cheese, pickles, tongues ...' The price suggests beer was selling for about 6s 6d a gallon, more than four times the cost in England.

The business was small, with only 9,000 barrels being exported in total from the whole of Britain to India in 1800, not even half a per cent of the amount of beer brewed in London that year. Hodgson was not short of rivals; Barclay Perkins brewed 'India Ale' from 1799, for example. In 1817 *The Times* was carrying advertisements from W.A. Brown of the Imperial brewery, Bromley-by-Bow (further down the Lea and thus even closer to Blackwall and the East India Company's docks, than Hodgson's brewery), which said: 'Captains and Merchants supplied with Pale Ale, prepared for the East and West India Climate, on liberal terms'. Another London brewer, Drury, Thompson and Neale of Southwark, 'near the New Bridge', was telling readers of *The Times* in February 1819 that it had 'Ale, Pale Ale, Stout and Porter always ready for export orders'.

Hodgson's name was becoming a guarantee of quality, however; n 1809 it was being described in the *Calcutta Gazette* as 'Hodgson's select Pale Ale, warranted of superior excellence'. The *Gazette* from 20 January 1822 contained an advertisement for the 'select investment of prime London goods just landed from the HC [Honourable Company] ship Sir David Scott', including 'Hodgson's warranted prime picked pale ale of the genuine October brewing, warranted fully equal, if not superior, to any ever before received in the settlement'.

George Hodgson's son, Mark, was running the Bow brewery by 1802. Eleven years later he was shipping some 4,000 barrels of beer a year to the east, four times the amount shipped in 1801. Four years on, in 1817, the brewery had moved 230 yards east, to Bow Bridge, where a pub called the Bombay Grab had been running since at least 1805. (There has been much inaccurate speculation about the name of this now-closed pub, which almost certainly comes from the name of an East India Company warship, the *Bombay Grab*, a three-masted armed cruiser of the Bombay Marine active in the 1780s, of which an oil painting exists in the British Museum. A 'grab' was a two-masted Eastern coasting-vessel or galley, from the Arabic *gurab*.)

Another four years passed and in 1821, when the brewery was being run by Frederick Hodgson and Thomas Drane, it was rebuilt. Hodgson and Drane now decided they were able to cut out the East Indiamen's officers and ship their beer to India themselves. If they retailed it themselves once it arrived, they could gather all the profit of the Indian beer trade, instead of just the producer's share. The two opened an office in Cornhill in the City of London and set up as shippers. Because most trade was from India to Britain, shipping costs in the other direction were very low. The charge for shipping a barrel of beer to the east, even for an outside trader, was no more than the charge for shipping one to Edinburgh.

Hodgson and Drane ended the twelve or eighteen months' credit previously given on the beer they sold to the East India Company's employees, refused to sell on any terms but cash and raised the price to buyers by 20 per cent. In India, if the local merchants tried to import someone else's beer, Hodgson and Drane dropped their prices so low that they frightened their competitors away. In any case, Hodgson and Drane reasoned, if the East Indiamen commanders did get supplies of beer elsewhere, the Bow brewery's product had such a reputation in India, no one else's brew would find buyers.

However, the men who ran the East India Company had not ended up in control of much of India just to roll over against a couple of comparatively small-time brewers. Early in 1822 one of the East India Company's most powerful members, Campbell Marjoribanks, who represented the shipping interest on the company's court of directors, invited Samuel Allsopp, the Burton upon Trent brewer, to dinner at his house in Upper Wimpole Street, London. The Burton brewers had just been hurt badly by the loss of trade to Russia, their main export market, after the Russian government imposed a huge tariff on English ale imports. Marjoribanks told Allsopp that the Indian market, with 10,000 barrels of English beer exported to India every year, could easily replace the Russian one. There was an opening for a new supplier, he said, for 'we are all now dependent upon Hodgson, who has given offence to most of our merchants in India'.

Allsopp returned to Burton to see if he could reproduce 'Hodgson's India beer', which was paler and bitterer than the ales the Burton brewers made. Serendipity once again played a role; Marjoriebanks was looking simply for a replacement for Hodgson and turned to Allsopp because he knew the Burton brewer was experienced in exporting beer to distant countries. But the well waters of Burton, rich in calcium sulphate, produce a much better pale, bitter ale than London's water, which is high in calcium carbonate and more suited to dark beers such as porter. A Burton brewer was going to make a superior pale beer to a London brewer, because his type of hard water made for better conversion of starch into sugar when pale malt was used in the mash tun. The beer could also be made paler, because the sulphate-rich water extracted less colour from the malt that London water did.

Once Allsopp's maltster, Job Goodhead, had succeeded in making a suitably pale 'East India' malt and after experiments, Goodhead revealed thirty years later, with a brew made in a teapot, the first consignments of Allsopp's new pale ale went out to India in 1823. Within a year the Burton brewer was receiving letters from the subcontinent telling him his beer 'is almost universally preferred by all old Indians [that is, Europeans in India] to Hodgson's'. The beer was bottled in India after arriving and took three months to come into condition; by eight months it was 'excellent indeed, of a bright amber colour, clear as crystal and a very peculiar fine flavour', one merchant wrote to Allsopp from Calcutta, the only complaint being that it needed to be a little more bitter and a little less strong.

Another correspondent in 1828 told Allsopp that in the hot season his beer was 'always cooled with saltpetre [potassium nitrate] before it is drank: we can make it by this article as cold as ice'. The letter is one of the earliest references in English to drinking chilled beer. The technique of cooling containers by placing them in a solution of water and potassium nitrate was an ancient one, though in India it was normally used to make ice-cream and sorbets rather than chilled pale ale. It must have been a similarly chilled beer that Charles Knight was remembering fondly when he wrote in 1851 of 'Hodgson's pale India ale, so grateful at tiffin when the thermometer is upwards of 100 and the monotonousness-creating punkah pours only a stream of heated air on the guests'.

Allsopp's new market could not be kept a secret from Burton's other brewers, then numbering five, and both Bass & Ratcliff (founded 1777) and Thomas Salt (a brewer from 1800) began to brew pale ale for the India trade in 1823. However, neither claimed to be the first; Salt's merely said that they were 'among the first to bring the experiment' to produce a pale ale to compete with Hodgson's India Ale 'to a practical issue', while Bass told Alfred Barnard in 1889 that it was merely 'the first brewers who sent out large consignments to India'.

Certainly by 1832–33 Bass had 43 per cent of a yearly trade of 12,000 barrels, Hodgson and Drane just 28 per cent and Allsopp 12 per cent. Hodgson's trade declined until by 1841–42 it was down to only 6.5 per cent of 18,300 barrels a year, against 29 per cent to Bass and 36.5 per cent to Allsopp. The other 20–30 per cent was going to brewers such as Ind & Smith (later Ind Coope) of Romford and Charrington of East London, which had started exporting pale ale to India in 1828. William Tizard, writing in 1846, said these last four were among the successful exporters of beer to India from the mid-1820s. Others included the Burton brewer William Worthington, who is said to have entered the Indian trade in 1829 (though Worthington's name does not appear in a list of exporters from 1833).

The first tasting of India Pale Ale at home in England, according to William Molyneaux, writing in 1869, came after a shipwreck in the Irish Channel 'about the year 1827' of a ship carrying 300 hogsheads of beer. Several casks of 'Burton bitter beer' salvaged from the wreck, the writer said, were sold off in Liverpool by the underwriters. The beer was highly enjoyed by those who tried it and according to this story the 'fame of the new India ale' beer then spread 'in a remarkably rapid manner' throughout the country.

No record of any such incident is known, however, and in addition there is no evidence for IPA taking off in Britain until the early 1840s. In any case, the beer was already available at home; 139 hogsheads of 'Pale Ale brewed expressly for the India market' and 'suitable for warm climates or home consumption' were advertised for sale by auction 'at the

Glasgow and Leith wharf, near the Tower [of London]' were advertised in *The Times* on 11 January 1822.

The use of the expression 'Pale Ale brewed expressly for the India market' leads on to a curious fact: the term 'India Pale Ale' was not coined until decades after brewers such as Hodgson began supplying pale ales for sale in India. Before 1837 the beer we now call India Pale Ale, or IPA, was labelled simply 'pale ale' or 'beer' when it was being sold in India, or 'Indian beer' back home in England, or, in the early to mid-1830s, 'Pale Ale as prepared for India'. Even Hodgson's product, when it was being advertised directly at 'Families from India', as it was in an advertisement in *The Times* in July 1833 (clearly the brewer was hoping for custom from people now back in England who had enjoyed its beers out East), was still only referred to as 'Hodgson and Co.'s Bottled Pale Ale' – no mention of India in the name of the beer, no indication that this was special or different from other sorts of pale ale, except for the brief hint in the note that 'The Nobility, Gentry and others (especially Families from India)' could be supplied with the product.

In October 1834 a London wine and spirit merchant, W.G. Field and Co., of Henrietta Street, Covent Garden, was advertising in *The Times* 'Burton, Edinburgh and Prestonpans Ales, Pale Ale as prepared for India, Dorchester Beer and London and Dublin Brown Stout'. Earlier in the century Thomas Field of London had been a big customer of Bass in Burton upon Trent and it seems quite likely this was the same firm, probably selling Bass 'Pale Ale as prepared for India' carried down from Burton by canal or wagon. In the 1840s Field was certainly selling Bass pale ale.

Field, and its successor firm, Field Wardell, continued to use this expression 'Pale Ale as prepared for India' until at least 1846, probably in part because that was the expression used by one of the early nineteenth century's best-known medical men, Dr William Prout, in a book on the treatment of diabetes and dyspepsia *On the nature and treatment of stomach and urinary diseases*, which recommended Burton bitter beer for dyspepsia sufferers. People with stomach disorders cannot, he said, 'assimilate the sweeter ales. Some of the finer kinds of Burton ale, however, are unobjectionable; particularly those prepared for the Indian market, which are not only carefully fermented, so as to be quite dry, or free from saccharine matter; but they also contain double the usual proportion of hops.'

However, in 1835, Hodgson's beer was advertised in the *Liverpool Mercury* using the apparently newly coined term 'India Pale Ale', the first time the expression seems to have been used in print. It took some time for it to spread; the first use of the phrase in *The Times* does not occur for another couple of years. But on Thursday 15 June 1837, George Shove, a wine and beer merchant of Threadneedle Street, close to the Bank of England in the City of London, advertised for sale, alongside 'Guinness's extra Double Stout', 6s 6d a dozen bottles, Barclay's brown stout, 6s 6d, and best porter, 4s 3d, and Edinburgh ale, 7s 6d, 'Hodgson's India pale ale, 6s 6d'.

A year later Mr Shove had evidently lost the agency for Hodgson's beers to Edwin Abbott, who had been the owner of the Sun brewery in Wapping and who was shortly to be a partner in, and then owner of, the Bow brewery. Abbott was advertising himself in *The Times* as the only London depot for the 'long-celebrated beers', 'Hodgson's East India Pale Ale and Stout', the latter beer shortly afterwards renamed 'Export Stout', underlining the fact that Hodgson was not just sending pale ale out East. (While some later brewers sold both an India Pale Ale and an East India Pale Ale, incidentally, the latter beer being in these cases more expensive and thus stronger, in general the two terms, IPA and EIPA, were used as synonyms.)

Hodgson's grip on the London market was about to be lost, however, just as it had been lost in the East, to rivals from Staffordshire. In August 1839 the Derby to Birmingham railway arrived in Burton upon Trent, with another line opening to Leicester soon after, slashing the cost to the town's brewers of getting their goods to market elsewhere in England. Freight charges between Burton and London fell from £3 a ton to 15s and the time it took a cask of ale to travel from Staffordshire to the capital dropped from a week to twelve hours. Over the next eighteen months London's wine merchants began advertising anonymous India pale ales, without names of brewers. Then, on 15 April 1841, the following advertisement appeared on page seven of *The Times*:

EAST INDIA PALE ALE – BASS & Co respectfully acquaint the public that a printed list of the bottlers of their INDIA ALE may be procured on application at the London Store, 49 Great Tower-street, where it may be had in casks of all sizes. This particular kind of ale differs greatly from the common malt liquors. It is more perfectly fermented, and approaches nearly the character of a dry wine; it has the light body of a wine combined with the fragrance and subdued bitter of the most delicate hop. That it is wholesome in an eminent degree is proved by it being drunk as the common beverage in India, where, from the nature of the climate, nothing which is not friendly to health can be used as an article of diet by Europeans, Many of the faculty also prescribe this ale to invalids. Dr Prout, who has examined that brewed by Bass & Co, in his work on diet &c, especially recommends it to weakly persons on account of its dryness, its mild tonic properties, and because it is not liable to turn ascecent in the stomach as other malt liquors are. The high esteem in which the pale ale of Bass & Co is held in India will be seen by a statement given below of the comparative quantity shipped by them and by Hodgson & Co to Calcutta in the season 1839 and 1840: Shipped by Bass & Co 4,936 hogsheads, by Hodgson 1,463 ditto.

It is important to note that East India pale ale, India ale and pale ale are all used as synonyms of the same article and that Bass reckoned its EIPA had a 'subdued' bitterness of 'delicate hop' – not a teeth-puckering, hop-filled wallop. But Bass was not calling this 'Pale Ale as prepared for India' – it clearly liked the sound of 'India Pale Ale'.

Another cheeky point is that Bass failed to mention its biggest rival and fellow Burton brewer, Allsopp, in the statistic for beer shipped to India. Allsopp responded with its own advertisement in *The Times* the very next day:

> EAST INDIA PALE ALE – In consequence of the increased consumption of this malt liquor, and at the request of several eminent medical men, who are strongly recommending its use to their patients, Messers ALLSOPP and SONS beg to inform the public, and the trade generally, that they can be supplied with their ALES in casks of various sizes, by application to Mr John Edwards at their stores, Old Swan-lane, Upper Thames-street. The reputation which this ale has acquired in all parts of India can be ascertained by a reference to the mercantile prices current, by which it can be seen that it commands a preference over all other ales which are now offered to the public … Parties in the country can be supplied with casks direct from the establishment, by addressing their letters to Burton-on-Trent, or to Old Swan-lane.

April 1841 appears to be the moment 'Pale Ale as prepared for India' took off, at least in London, with up to five or six small advertisements from wine merchants in *The Times* every day for 'India Ale', 'pale India ale', 'pale export India ale' and other variations. Bass and Allsopp were not the only Burton brewers selling to the London market. Others included Mason and Gilbertson, whose brewery in Horninglow Street was later owned by the Thompson family, eventual partners in Marston's, and who were advertising their India Pale Ale, 'now so much recommended by the medical profession', in *The Times* on 29 October 1841.

Another was Saunders & Co. William Saunders began brewing on the north side of Horninglow Street around 1835 and was 'probably' (according to Colin Owens' *The Development of Industry in Burton upon Trent*) absorbed by Allsopp's in 1865. On 8 December 1842 *The Times* carried an advertisement for Saunders's 'East India Pale and Golden Ales' with the claim that 'The fermentation being conducted upon a principle which renders them entirely free from acidity has brought them under the notice of several of the most eminent physicians in London … Invalids generally will find these ales an agreeable and refreshing beverage.'

No brewer, incidentally, ever took credit for discovering stronger, hoppier beers worked best for export to the East, not even Hodgson, and no brewer was given credit for it until William Molyneaux in 1869 claimed that:

> The origin of India ale is by common consent accredited to a London
> brewer named Hodgson, who … discovered the process of brewing a
> beverage peculiarly suited to the climate of the East Indies and which,
> under the name of 'India Pale Ale', monopolised the Indian trade in
> English ale … The brewery where pale ale was first brewed, according
> to popular opinion, was the Old Bow brewery.

But as we have seen, there is no evidence that Hodgson made any such discovery; he did not have a monopoly of exporting beer to India, even before the Burton brewers moved in on the trade. The Old Bow brewery was not the first place to brew pale ale, which was a known style of beer before Hodgson, and Hodgson's beer wasn't called India Pale Ale until 1835, when it had already lost its pre-eminence in the east. However, Molyneaux's narrative has had the same effect as John Field's claim sixty-five or so years earlier, that Ralph Harwood invented porter, so that the story of Hodgson's alleged creation of IPA has been repeated constantly almost every time the history of the beer is discussed.

What exactly was 'Pale Ale as prepared for India'? William Loftus explained, under the heading 'India Pale Bitter Ale', in his book *The Brewer: A Familiar Treatise on the Art of Brewing*, published in 1856. He said that 'Bitter Ale', 'prepared for the home market is less bitter and spirituous than that which is prepared for exportation to India'.

A book written in 1843 by Jonathan Pereira with the lengthy title *A treatise on food and diet: with observations on the dietetical regimen suited for disordered states of the digestive organs* said 'the Pale Ale prepared for the India market, and, therefore, commonly known as the Indian Pale Ale, is … carefully fermented, so as to be devoid of all sweetness, or, in other words, to be dry; and it contains double the usual quantity of hops; it forms, therefore, a most valuable restorative beverage for invalids and convalescents.'

It looks as though while pale ales for export were, as Pereira indicates, massively hopped at six pounds per barrel or more, 'domestic' IPAs were hopped at getting on for half that rate. This would speed up the time it took them to become drinkable. The brewer Michael Combrune, writing in the 1760s, suggested that hops should be used at the rate of one pound to the quarter of malt for every month that a beer was to keep. If early IPA brewers were looking for their beers to mature as long as eighteen months or two years and followed Combrune's advice, they probably were hopping at around six pounds to the barrels, which would have made for a very bitter beer, one that would take eighteen months or so to round down. The anonymous *Art of Brewing* said India Pale Ale, 'now becoming an article of such general demand as to deserve the attention of every brewer', should be made from best palest malt at three barrels per quarter, around 1065 to 1080 OG, and 16lb of hops to the quarter of malt, 5⅓lb a barrel, plus dry-hopping in the cask.

However, the Victorian brewer George Amsinck, who included several recipes for 'East India Pale Ale' in his book *Practical Brewing*, seemed to think that even a well-hopped 6lb to the barrel IPA was 'fit to deliver to the trade' after just two months. Amsinck also included recipes for IPA with hop rates of 3½lb to the barrel, still high by modern rates, which was probably the norm for IPAs meant for 'home' consumption. The strengths, at least, of early Burton IPAs seem to be much the same as later nineteenth-century versions, at around 1065 to 1075 OG.

India Pale Ale continued to be regarded as an autumn speciality for decades; in the *Leeds Intelligencer* of 18 October 1856, Tetley's brewery announced to its customers: 'East India Pale Ale – This Season's Brewings are now being delivered.' The development of decent refrigeration meant by the end of the nineteenth century brewers could brew all year round. The original justification for strong March and October stock beers, that it was too hot to brew successfully from April to September meaning well-hopped beers needed to be brewed before and after to cover the gap, was lost. But even in the 1890s J. Harris Browne of the Hadley brewery near Barnet was calling its IPA 'Stock Ale' and in 1898 Waltham Brothers' brewery in Stockwell, South London said of its India Pale Ale: 'This Ale is heavily hopped with the very best Kent hops, and nearly resembles the fine *Farmhouse Stock-Beer* of olden times.' Overseas imitators also emphasised that this was a beer which needed to be matured; an advertisement from the end of the nineteenth century for C.H. Evans's brewery in Hudson, New York for its IPA said the beer was 'Allowed two years to ripen in the Wood before bottling'.

Hodgson's, at least, used East Kent-grown hops in its IPA, bought from specific growers rather than, as other brewers did, from the hop factors across the Thames in Southwark. A report on the hop harvest from *The Times* on 12 September 1840 said that Ospringe, a village in East Kent almost due south of Faversham,

> is highly favoured; for although the bulk will be deficient, the quality is generally good. Mr John Abbott's (so much esteemed for their preservation quality in the celebrated 'Hodgson's Pale India Ale',) falling short, may this year be assisted by his neighbours, Mr Alfred Cobb and Mr Wilks, who seem to vie with Mr Abbott and each other in superior culture and attention to their plantations.

Very likely the hops grown by Mr Abbott (who must have been a relative of Edwin Abbott) were East Kent Goldings, the best known and most highly prized variety from the most highly regarded hop-growing area in the country. Nineteenth-century brewers regarded the variety as particularly 'adapted to the brewing of store beers', beers that, like IPA, needed ageing. In 1857 a parliamentary select committee on the hop industry was told that Goldings made up a third of all the hops grown in East Kent. The Burton brewers look to have had the same views on hops as Hodgson's. Around 1820 at Bass 'East Kent hops were generally regarded as being the best and were used in varying proportions with other Kentish and North Clay (Nottinghamshire) hops', according to Colin Owen's history of Bass, Ratcliff and Gretton, *The Greatest Brewery in the World*.

Burton-brewed India Pale Ale sold in Britain for 8*d* a quart retail, twice as much as either porter or lesser pale beers. Other brewers began brewing a cheaper 'East India Pale Ale' or 'India Pale Ale' to compete with the Burton brewers' product by the middle of the 1840s. One of the first was Kirkley, Swinburne & Co. of the Low brewery, Fairless Quay, South Shields, which was advertising 'Pale East India Ale equal to the

best Burton qualities, especially suited for ships bound for warm lati-
tudes'. J.W. Baker of the Castle brewery, Leamington, Warwickshire, was
advertising East India Pale Ale at 1s 4d a gallon in 1846, the equivalent
of 6d a quart pot retail. Most brewers outside Burton sold their IPA or
EIPA at 1s 6d a gallon wholesale, or 7d a pot retail.

However, it looks as if what many brewers were doing was simply
renaming their 'stock' strong bitter as IPA, to give it the cachet the
Burton IPAs had. Almost all Victorian brewers brewed four, five or six
different strengths of pale bitter beer; around two thirds seem to have
called the 1s 6d or 1s 8d a gallon product in their bitter beer range, which
would have had a strength of 6.5–8 per cent abv, 'IPA', while the rest
called it 'Strong Bitter', 'Rich Bitter' and the like. This lack of consistency
raises doubts over whether IPA was ever a properly distinguishable style
or just a fancy piece of marketing for well-hopped bitter.

Some brewers seem to have responded to the popularity of IPA by
cheating with their existing beers. *The Encyclopædia of Domestic Economy*
of 1855 said that IPA:

> was first prepared for the India market but has come into general use
> here. To make it keep in a warm climate, it has more than the usual
> quantity of hops, and is, of course, much more bitter than the ordinary
> ales. It has been recommended by some physicians as being proper for
> certain invalids, with whom the usual ale does not agree. It is said that
> some brewers, in preparing it, merely add an infusion of hops to some
> of their already brewed ales.

A few brewers brewed two versions; the Northampton brewery
Company in 1873 sold India Pale Ale at 1s 6d a gallon and East India Pale
Ale at 1s 8d a gallon. Not everybody rushed to produce an IPA; Steward
& Patteson of Norwich, for example, only introduced a beer under the
IPA name in 1893.

Some brewers made West India Pale Ale. This appears to have been an
Irish speciality, with William Lane & Co. of the South Gate Lane brewery, Cork, advertising West India Pale Ale alongside 'Mild, Bitter and XX
Ale, Export and Bottling Stout and all Kinds of Porter' in the latter half
of the nineteenth century. Charles Day, author of *Five Years' Residence in
the West Indies*, wrote in 1852 that 'London stout or porter is too heavy
for the climate', but 'West India pale ale is in high favour'. Ashby's brewery in Staines, Middlesex, was advertising Australian Pale Ale in *The
Times* in 1842, exported to 'the Australian colonies' since 1829, which

'resembles the East India pale ale in flavour and colour, with rather more body'. Ashby's advertisement appeared in competition with those for 'Bass's Pale Ale, as prepared for India', 'Hodgson and Abbott's pale ale' and 'Allsopp's East India pale ale, as prepared for India'.

Brewers who tried to imitate Burton pale ale were handicapped by the need to make it with sulphate-impregnated water, which could be found in only a few places. The true chemical nature of the well-waters of Burton upon Trent, in particular, which drew up brewing waters from the Keuper marls below the town, does not seem to have been properly understood until the Burton brewers brought a libel action in 1830 against the Society for Diffusing Useful Knowledge for claiming, in a treatise on the 'Art of Brewing', that they adulterated their beers with a mixture of various 'noxious' ingredients including 'salt of steel' (iron chloride) and 'sulphate of lime' (calcium sulphate).

The Court of King's Bench in London heard that the author of the treatise, David Booth, claimed he could only make beer that matched the Burton brewers' products by adding gypsum, a hydrated form of calcium sulphate. The Burton brewers, however, produced affidavits from chemists who had analysed their brewing waters and found that they naturally contained calcium sulphate derived from the gypsum found in the Keuper marls.

Brewers soon realised that it was the geology of the area that made Burton beers so successful. William Tizard, in *The Theory and Practice of Brewing Illustrated*, wrote: 'The Burton ales principally owe their superior qualities and uniform permanency to the nature of the water there used, and which, according to the best evidence, is strongly impregnated with this hardener of water, gypsum or sulphate of lime.'

In the 1850s, as pale ales grew in popularity, Burton's output more than tripled to 971,000 barrels a year. While the workers still drank porter and mild ale, the secretary of the maltsters' association, William Ford, wrote in 1862 that the class of ale 'termed "India Pale"' was 'an article in great and increasing estimation with middle and higher classes of society.' At the end of the 1860s Burton's output had risen to 1.75 million barrels a year, from twenty-six active breweries. Two decades later, in 1888, thirty-one breweries produced 3 million barrels of beer a year.

The Hodgsons, their grip on the Indian trade long smashed, had faded away – they were gone from the Bow brewery by 1849. (According to Harry Abbott, 'Hodgson was a very handsome man and ran away with the lovely Mrs Trower, wife of an Indian Army officer, she was one of the reigning beauties of Paris for many years afterwards.') Meanwhile, several London brewers set up branch breweries in Burton to try to brew the pale ales they could not make properly with London water, including Ind Coope of Romford in 1856 and the East London brewers Charrington & Co. in 1872, Truman Hanbury & Buxton in 1873 and Mann Crossman & Paulin in 1874.

Regional brewers also came to Burton. Andrew Walker of Warrington and his brother Peter Walker, who had a brewery in Wrexham, both opened branch breweries in the Staffordshire town in 1877 and 1880 respectively, while the Leicester brewery Everard & Co. took over the Trent Bridge brewery in 1885.

One way for brewers who did not have a natural supply of calcium sulphate-impregnated water was to add the mineral to the water they did have, a system first named 'Burtonising' by Egbert Hooper in *The Manual of Brewing*. By the early 1890s brewing journals were carrying a host of advertisements for 'gypsum specially prepared for brewers' use', 'saline blend for water treatment – used in hundreds of breweries', 'Burton ale salts' and the like.

The discovery of the 'Burtonising' technique is frequently credited to the chemist Charles Vincent, who is said to have analysed Burton water in 1878 and discovered what salts helped the local brewers make such good pale ales. However, Whitbread was adding gypsum to its brewing water to make pale ales as early as 1866. Brewing manuals in the 1880s were showing how to construct a 'gypsum tank' for treating water and in 1891 Alfred Barnard saw one in action at Fox's brewery in Farnborough, Kent, filled with 'gypsum quarried from the Trent side'. In 1904 it was reckoned that more than 150 tons of gypsum a year were being quarried and used in breweries to Burtonise their brewing liquor for making pale ales.

Some lucky brewers lived in towns that had similar water to Burton; Stratford upon Avon, for example, where the well water also contained quantities of gypsum. In 1854 Flower's brewery in the town was selling a 'Pale India Ale' at 1s 8d a gallon, 8d a pot retail, the same price as Burton pale ale. Another town with a reputation for Burton-like brewing water was Alton in Hampshire, where in 1903 Courage took over a brewer called G.& E. Hall to supply its London pubs with pale ale. Brewing in Alton has lasted through to the twenty-first century, though Director's, the pale ale that was originally supposed to be brewed for the Alton brewery boardroom, is no longer made there, but in Bedford.

In Yorkshire, Tadcaster, which had five breweries in 1890, also had a reputation for sulphate springs and fine pale ales. Edinburgh brewers, who took their brewing liquor from an underground ring of water-bearing sandstone known as the 'charmed circle', which, like Burton water, was rich in gypsum, were the only big rivals to Burton for IPAs. William Younger & Co. brewed IPA at its Abbey brewery from at least 1854, later transferring production to the newer Holyrood brewery alongside it.

Younger's also copied one of Burton's great discoveries in the brewing of pale ales – the union cask system of fermentation. The union method, which became known because of its use in the great Staffordshire brewing town as the Burton union system, was the climax of a series of developments designed to solve the problem of removing excess yeast from the fermenting beer without wasting beer and without having to constantly top the fermenting vessel up manually. The union system was patented in 1838 by a Liverpool brewer called Peter Walker, originally from Ayr in Scotland. It was, effectively, an automated version of the cask fermentation method used by brewers for centuries, where the fermenting beer was removed from one big vessel after a day or so and allowed to continue fermenting in smaller casks, with the excess yeast flowing out of the cask through the bunghole at the top. Walker's system had

The union room at Allsopp's Brewery in Burton upon Trent in 1889, where one of the country's best-selling IPAs was brewed

banks of casks arranged in double rows. Each had a swan-neck pipe in the top of the cask through which the excess yeast foamed, dropping into a trough above the twin rows of casks. The yeast and beer separated out in the troughs and the beer flowed back down into the casks.

When the journalist Alfred Barnard visited Burton around 1890 he found all the brewers he saw using the union system to finish off their pale ales. Each brewer had hundreds, sometimes thousands, of union casks, each cask holding between 144 and 160 gallons, joined in sets of up to thirty. The yeast they used thrived best in Burton's high-sulphate water under the union system, though whether the union system bred a yeast that fitted in perfectly with that method of brewing or Burton brewers already used a yeast that was waiting for the union system to arrive, is not clear. Whatever the case, the yeast used in Burton unions gave excellent flavour and good stability, just what pale ale brewers wanted. Its disadvantage in a conventional fermenting vessel was that it formed a poor head and did not flocculate or form into clumps at the end of fermentation for easy removal from the finished beer. This did not matter under the union system, which automatically removed the yeast from the beer.

At the end of the twentieth century the union system had disappeared from every British brewery except one, Marston, Thompson & Evershed of Burton, killed by economics – even an ex-head brewer at Marston's was compelled to describe it as 'surely the most expensive fermentation system in the world'. It requires ten times the manpower to clean out a union set than to clean a conventional fermenting vessel, supervision costs are also high to ensure proper control of fermentation and the whole set has to be dismantled every two years for refurbishment. Only the desire to keep the yeast strain going, which would not happen outside a union, has persuaded Marston's to continue with the system.

The great gravity drop of the First World War and its aftermath, where greatly increased taxes meant brewers pushed down the strengths of their beers to try to keep them affordable, meant that IPA fell from around 1070 OG to 1050 or so. It was now much closer in strength to a best bitter and the cachet associated with the name began to vanish. Indeed, in the mid-1930s Ind Coope at Burton was brewing an IPA that had a lower OG, at 1041, than its best bitter, at 1046. Often, as at Benskin's brewery in Watford in the 1950s, or Watney's of Pimlico, IPA was simply a synonym for best bitter; Benskin's IPA also had an OG of 1041, while its draught bitter, PA, was 1037 (though the PA was a tad darker, with a Lovibond number of 11.5, mid-amber, against the 11 of the IPA).

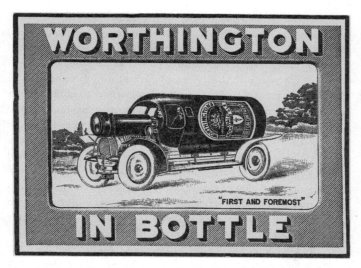

An advertisement from just before the First World War for Worthington IPA, now known as Worthington White Shield and one of the few original IPAs still being made

Certain brands that had begun as India Pale Ales were still highly thought of, particularly draught Bass Red Triangle Pale Ale (which was still 40 per cent of the company's output even in 1952), Ind Coope Double Diamond and Worthington IPA, one of the last bottle-conditioned pale ales. But by 1948 a book published by Whitbread on *The Brewer's Art* could say that the term India Pale Ale was 'now nearly obsolete'. It became obscure enough for the 1051 OG Worthington IPA, one of the oldest India Pale Ale brands, which was always unofficially known as White Shield (from the colour of the Worthington trademark on the label, which distinguished it from the filtered and pasteurised 'Green Shield' version), to be officially renamed Worthington White Shield by the 1970s. Perhaps the Burton brewers felt that beers such as Greene King IPA, which had an OG of just 1036, or Wadworth's, at 1035 OG debased the idea of IPA as a strong export ale so much it was no longer worth proclaiming.

IPA was never as widely reproduced around the world as porter, but other countries still made their own versions of it. In Australia, Coopers of Adelaide was brewing India Pale Ale for bottling in the 1870s, while the Castlemaine brewery in Fremantle, Western Australia, brewed 'Best

India Pale Ale' around 1900. However, it was North America that picked up on the style. John Labatt, for example, whose father bought a share in a brewery in London, Ontario in 1847, was apprenticed in 1859 to an English brewer, George Weatherall Smith, in Wheeling, West Virginia, where he undoubtedly learned to brew India Pale Ale. Labatt returned to the family brewery in Ontario in 1864 and developed his own IPA in the 1870s so that it became the firm's best-known brand. Molson's brewery in Montreal was brewing India Pale Ale by 1859 at the latest and was still doing so in the 1930s, while Alexander Keith's brewery in Halifax, Nova Scotia, claimed to have been brewing an IPA since 1820.

In the United States, particularly in the more British-influenced north-east, brewers such as P. Ballantine & Sons of Newark, New Jersey, Bartels's in Syracuse, New York and Granger & Gregg and C.H. Evans, both of Hudson, also New York, produced India Pale Ales. The highly admired Ballantine IPA, when brewed at Newark, was a deep amber colour with a whopping 60 IBUs (international bitterness units) and 7.5 per cent abv, aged in oak storage tanks, where hop oils distilled from Bullion hops at the brewery were added to the maturing beer. After the Newark brewery closed in 1971 the IPA was brewed in Narragansett, Rhode Island, where the ageing was reduced to six months, the bitterness fell to 45 IBUs (and the hops changed to Brewer's Gold and Yakima) and the strength was reduced to 6.7 per cent abv. Several other changes of home followed, until the beer disappeared in the 1990s.

But it was the microbrewery revival from the 1980s onwards that saw a big interest in the idea of IPA develop in the United States, as brewers looked to the style to provide inspiration for big-hopped, bitter, aromatic beers. Bert Grant, the Scot who began brewing in Yakima, Washington State in 1981, was one of the pioneers of the new American IPA style, with other leading examples being Sierra Nevada Celebration Ale, first brewed in 1983. There are even extra-strong versions for hop lovers called Double IPA or Imperial IPA from brewers such as Dogfish Head of Delaware. The official American style guidelines for Imperial IPA include 'high to *absurdly* high hop bitterness ...' (my emphasis).

Few brewers in Britain have echoed this American revival, one of the exceptions being the Burton brewer Marston, Thompson & Evershed, with its 1057 OG Old Empire, introduced early in the twenty-first century as a deliberate revival of the recipe of nineteenth-century IPAs, albeit with a slightly lower gravity. In December 2005 the St Austell brewery made what it called 'Proper Job IPA', again inspired by nineteenth-century versions, at 5.5 per cent abv, with what brewer

Roger Ryman called 'assertive hop bitterness and aroma'. The beer was well enough received to be launched in bottle in March 2006. The same summer, Greene King, perhaps stung by the criticism of its IPA as being too weak for a proper India Pale Ale, has brought out the tautologically-named 'Export Strength IPA' in bottle at 5 per cent abv, with a considerable amount of hop flavour.

The most successful new IPA in Britain comes from an old Victorian brewery, Caledonian, in Edinburgh. Deuchars IPA, is a modern 3.8 per cent abv in cask, 4.4 per cent in bottle, with an American lemony hop flavour. It appeared in the 1990s, but became extremely successful after winning the 2002 Champion Beer of Britain contest. A couple of British brewers have produced even stronger nineteenth-century IPAs, notably Meantime of Greenwich, just across the Thames from where the East Indiamen once docked, with a 7.5 per cent abv bottle-conditioned beer authentically hopped with East Kent Goldings.

7

GOLDEN ALE

... her muscles felt sore from the unaccustomed strain of riding astride. Nothing had ever tasted so good as the cool golden ale she swallowed from a pewter tankard. She slept deeply that night and longer than she had intended ...

Forever Amber, Kathleen Winsor, 1944

History is seldom straightforward, even when it's only twenty-odd years old. In 1986 the Golden Hill brewery in Wiveliscombe, Somerset made a one-off beer to celebrate the 1,000th brewing of its Exmoor Ale. The beer, made only from pale Pipkin lager malt, with no crystal malt to bring it up to the amber/cornelian colour of most British bitters, but enough hops to give it the bitterness of an IPA, was given the name Exmoor Gold. It became a popular choice for drinkers and the brewery carried on making further brews of the beer.

Since then an army of similarly golden-coloured beers has appeared. There are currently more than 125 beers brewed in Britain with 'gold' or 'golden' in the name plus a dozen or so others in the same style called 'summer ale' or 'blonde ale' and others whose name does not immediately give them away, such as Big Lamp of Northumbria's Prince Bishop Ale.

Based on the fact that Exmoor Gold was first brewed before any of its competitors, the Golden Hill brewery, now known as Exmoor brewery, markets its version of the style as 'the original golden ale'. But was it? The tradition of golden beer went back at least to 1842, when William Saunders's brewery in Burton upon Trent was advertising its 'East India Pale and Golden Ales' and Josef Groll was producing the first pale lager in Pilsen, Bohemia. The Germans now have Helles – 'light' – and the pale top-fermented Kölsch from Cologne and the

French have bière blonde. Belgium has its own strong golden ale style pioneered by Duvel in 1970.

While most British beers continued to be ruddy-to-dark, there were very pale-coloured bitters in England before 1986, notably Boddington's Bitter from Manchester and the 'straw-coloured' Taddy Bitter from Samuel Smith of Tadcaster, the forerunner to Old Brewery Bitter. Strong's brewery in Romsey had Golden IPA; Holden's brewery in Dudley was making Holden's Golden Pale Ale before 1974, Offiler's of Derby sold Golden Bitter and Burt's brewery on the Isle of Wight brewed Golden Ale in the 1960s, while J.W. Green, the Luton brewer, called its Masterbrew pale ale a 'golden brew' in the 1950s. Earlier still, Duncan Gilmour of Sheffield sold a bottled Golden Pale Ale and Barclay Perkins of Southwark, London, brewed Golden Hop Ale. Back in 1887, exactly ninety-nine years before Exmoor Gold appeared, Charles Watkins & Son of the Hereford brewery was advertising Golden Sunlight Pale Ale.

Hall & Woodhouse in Dorset introduced the pale, strong Tanglefoot bitter in 1981, but it was always described as 'lightish' or 'straw-coloured', not golden. After 1986 more very pale beers began to appear, such as Miners Light from the Miners Arms brewery in Somerset, first made in the summer of 1989, but this was described as 'a light straw-coloured brew with a clean bitter flavour' rather than a golden beer. None of these started a trend for very pale ales in what could be described as a new category or style, however – and neither, to be honest, did Exmoor Gold.

By 1990 there were still only six brews in Britain called 'gold' or 'golden'. The beer that was to kick the 'golden ale' or 'summer ale' category into life first appeared the previous year, in 1989, when John Gilbert of the Hop Back brewery, then behind the Wyndham Arms pub in Salisbury, Wiltshire, produced a one-off brew for a local beer festival. Again, it used only pale malt, with Challenger and East Kent Goldings hops and a late addition of hops in the boil to give a refreshing citrus note and enough hops all contributed to make it, again, high in bitterness.

When Gilbert opened the Hop Back brewery in 1986 he announced plans to brew a lager, a style he had made while he was a brewer at the Brixton brewery in Stockwell, London. The lager never happened, but the idea of it may have inspired him to make an ale that could appeal to lager drinkers with its very pale colour, refreshing taste and surprising drinkability for a beer with an OG of 1050 and without the sweetness and maltiness of most ales of that strength. The brew, which Gilbert called Summer Lightning, after the title of one of the novels in the 'Blandings' series by P.G. Wodehouse published sixty years earlier, was tremendously successful from the beginning. It instantly picked up the 'new brewery champion beer' title at the Great British Beer Festival in Leeds. This was the first in a long string of awards for Summer Lightning, including Best Strong Beer in Britain at the 1992 Great British Beer Festival.

Imitators quickly followed, with forty different draught summer ales and golden ales on the market in Britain by the summer of 1994. Tweaks on the theme of 'summer refreshment' quickly began to appear, with Bateman's of Wainfleet, for example, in 1995 producing 'Lincolnshire Yellow Belly Bitter', a 4 per cent abv 'late summer bitter' named after a fenland frog and flavoured with vanilla pods as well as hops. Not all golden ales were summer ales: Elgood's Barleymead, for one, was described as a 'golden autumnal ale', available from the end of September and made with new-season hops and malt at 4.8 per cent abv.

Although Summer Lightning was brewed with solely English hop varieties (and in its bottled version with just one, Goldings), an increasing number of golden beers were being produced with American hops, which give a more pronounced citrus flavour and aroma. One of the most successful and influential of this strain was Oakham Ales' Jeffrey Hudson Bitter, at an OG of 1038, quite light in alcohol compared to most beers in the style, but not much less bitter, with English Challenger and American Mount Hood hops and Maris Otter malt. It was named after the diminutive Rutland hero who was 'court dwarf' to Henrietta Maria, wife of Charles I, and a Civil War army captain (and who appeared on a couple of now-vanished London pub signs with his fellow royal servant, the seven feet six inches tall doorman and messenger William Evans as the 'Gentleman and Porter'). After the Oakham brewery moved from Rutland to Peterborough, J.H.B. began to pick up national awards, culminating in the Champion Beer of Britain title in 2001.

Another user of American hops is Helvellyn Gold from the Hesket Newmarket brewery in Cumbria, which contains American Cascade hops alongside the much more traditional Goldings and Fuggles. Helvellyn Gold also adds 3 per cent malted oats and 'aromatic pale' malt, a 'stewed' variety (like crystal malt but without the dark colour) alongside Maris Otter. Most golden beers have used traditional English malts, especially Maris Otter, for malt flavour, but some brewers have chosen specifically lager malts, such as Harvest Gold from the Museum brewery (now the White Shield brewery) in Burton upon Trent, made in 1997. This used Pipkin malt as Exmoor Gold did, but Bramling Cross hops (a cross between a Goldings variety and a Canadian wild hop) and an ale

Not all golden ales are designed for summer drinking: the Cambridgeshire brewer Elgood's made Barleymead as an autumn speciality

yeast to produce a very pale ale. St Peter's Golden Ale, 4.7 per cent abv, is one that mixes ale malt with lager malt.

The tendency was also developing for golden ales to be served cooler than traditional amber bitters. This was partly to encourage more uptake among lager drinkers already attracted to the style by its familiar colour (to them), partly to emphasise their refreshing character as summer drinks. The trend reached its acme in Discovery, a 'blonde beer' developed at great expense (using brewhouse-scale brews as trials) by Fuller, Smith & Turner, the London brewer. Discovery uses some malted wheat and includes Liberty hops, an American variety not as assertively citrusy as many transatlantic strains. The beer, the brewery's first new permanent draught ale for two decades, was deliberately designed to be served cool during the summer and at more normal cellar temperature during the winter, with a flavour profile that worked well at both temperatures. Eventually, however, the 'cool' version found such popularity it became an all-year-round offering.

By 2001, American brewers had noticed the new British ale style and were producing a few examples themselves, though with influences that did include Bavarian Helles, Kölsch and Belgian golden ales. Unlike most British golden ales, however, American blonde beers, such as Goose Island Blonde and Bridgeport Pintail Ale, were low in bitterness and hop aroma and were perceived as closer to American lagers.

Victory for another golden ale, Pale Rider (from Kelham Island of Sheffield, made with American Willamette hops) as Champion Beer of Britain at the 2004 Great British Beer Festival, after it won the Best Bitter category helped push forward a move to recognise golden ales as a separate category entirely from bitter in the 2005 competition. It marked what might be called the coming-of-age of golden ales after just about eighteen years since their 'birth'. The official CAMRA definition of the style was given as pale amber, gold, yellow or straw-coloured with a low to strong bitterness, light to medium body and a strong hop presence, creating a refreshing character. Light to medium malt flavours may be present 'but should be minimal' and 'fruitiness may be present'.

The first winner of the golden ale category was Crouch Vale Brewers Gold, one of the versions of the style made using lager malt, which went on to show what a strong presence golden ales now have by winning the champion beer title as well. With more than one in four British brewers making a golden ale, it is now as much a part of the nation's brewing history as porter or stout.

8

DINNER ALES AND LOW-GRAVITY BEERS

Only a pint at breakfast-time, and a pint and a half at eleven o'clock, and a quart or so at dinner. And then no more till the afternoon; and half a gallon at supper-time. No one can object to that.

Jan Ridd in *Lorna Doone*, R.F. Blackmore (1825–1900)

Beer, as the national drink of England and Wales (though not of Scotland and Ireland), was always the beverage of choice for drinking with meals. When the young Victoria succeeded her uncle William IV in 1837, 'Beer was universally taken with dinner', Sir Walter Besant wrote fifty years later and 'even at great dinner parties some of the guests would call for beer. In the restaurants every man would call for bitter ale, or stout, or half-and-half [ale and porter mixed] with his dinner, as a matter of course.'

The custom of beer with dinner persisted throughout the Queen's long reign. It survived even though in the early 1860s William Gladstone, as Chancellor of the Exchequer, had cut duties on French wines, especially table wines, in part to encourage wine drinking with meals. Thirty years later, in 1894, Baedeker's guide to London still told visitors from abroad that if they wished to dine out, 'beer, on draught or in bottle, is supplied at almost all the restaurants' and 'is the beverage most frequently drunk'.

Beer and ale with meals was a centuries-old (millennia-old) habit, from the time when unboiled water and milk were not safe, fruit juices unavailable, and tea and coffee had not yet arrived. Indeed, water remained a dangerous drink to rely on until the 1870s, when public health measures started to become effective. In the earliest written household accounts in the medieval period, the allowances of ale per head look stupendous to twenty-first-century eyes.

Although the government now tries to tell us we are binge drinkers if we have two pints at lunchtime and two more in the evening, six to eight pints of ale a day, every day, for every adult member of the household was the norm right through to the seventeenth century. Henry VIII, who had two personal brewers, one making ale and one the new hopped drink, beer, ran a household at Hampton Court in the 1530s and 1540s which consumed 600,000 gallons of ale and beer a year, more than 13,000 pints a day. Ordinary servants were allocated six pints of ale a day with their meals on meat days and four pints a day on fish days; higher ranks received more, so that dukes were to get three gallons a day (shared, presumably, with others), disbursed at breakfast, lunch and supper.

While the royal household's consumption of ale and beer was on an industrial scale, others brewed domestically in considerable quantities as well. Pamela Sambrook's *Country House Brewing in England from 1500 to 1900* shows the aristocracy and gentry supplying their servants with hundreds, sometimes thousands of gallons of home-brewed small ale and beer a month, all drunk with meals, at an average of around five or six pints per head a day. Lady Griselle Baillie, a Scottish aristocrat, was instructing her butler in 1743 to ensure he had enough ale and small beer on the sideboard so that he would not need to leave the room while the family was dining to fetch more.

Small beer was the common drink of the people. One of the glories of the British brewing tradition is the ability of the nation's brewers down the years to produce delicious, refreshing, attractive beers that are also low in alcohol. Sometimes this was down to necessity; during the First World War, for example, the British government forced brewers to produce as much as half the nation's beer at a gravity of 1030 or below, with some apparently being produced as weak as 1019 OG. But since the introduction of hops to brewing in this country around the start of the fifteenth century, which first allowed brewers to make a drink that would keep without having large amounts of alcohol in it, the delights of 'small beer' have been appreciated.

The brewer William Brande, for example, writing around 1830, said small beer

> is best calculated for common use, being less heating and stimulating than other malt liquors. Drank soft and mild [young], after being well-fermented and fined, it forms an excellent diluent [sic] with food, more especially at dinner … it is unquestionably the best fermented liquor that can be used at meals, by persons of middle and higher

ranks, who are in the habit of drinking wine after dinner; and as it abounds with fixed air [that is, carbon dioxide], it is the most useful beverage for labourers, as it cools the body, quenches thirst and at the same time moderately stimulates the animal powers.

Brande's words echo Gervase Markham, writing two centuries earlier in the reign of James I, who said small beer was 'that wherewith either Nobleman, Gentleman, Yeoman or Husbandman shall maintain his family the whole yeere'. Not everybody agreed: William Shakespeare had Prince Hal in *Henry IV* condemn 'the poor creature, small beer'. But this was still an era when beer allowances for the whole family would be four or more pints per head a day and small beer was what everybody, especially servants and farm workers, drank as a matter of common necessity. Most householders of yeoman class or above brewed their own small beer and others bought it off the professional brewers. In 1701 the common brewers of England and Wales brewed 1.1 million barrels of small beer, against 1.5 million barrels of strong beer and strong ale.

Small beer was generally the product of a second mashing of the 'goods', or ground malt, after a first mash had been collected to make strong beer. (Sometimes it was made from a third, almost cold, mash left standing for three quarters of an hour, though Thomas Tryon, writing in 1690, condemned this as 'a very ill sort of drink') When 'intire' small beer was made, using all the wort collected from the mash tun, the recommended rate, according to William Ellis's *London and Country Brewer*, published around 1736, was five or six barrels of beer from each quarter of malt, suggesting an OG of between 1030 and 1035, against just one barrel from a quarter of malt for strong stout and one and a half barrels for 'common' brown beer.

Small beer's close relative was table beer, reflecting the idea that, as Brande said, low-gravity beer was the best drink with meals. Excise regulations from 1782 specifically recognised a class of beer called 'table', midway between strong beer and small beer. Small beer was normally comparatively lightly hopped, at around a pound per barrel, against three pounds of hops or more for a barrel of strong beer. However, small beer, because of its low alcohol content, did not keep as long as strong ales and the brewer and beer writer Michael Combrune, writing in 1762, recommended almost doubling the quantity of hops used when brewing in the hottest weather. Combrune also recognised that brewing good small beer was more difficult than brewing strong beer:

Common small beer is supposed to be ready for use, in winter, from two to six weeks, and in the heat of summer from one to three ... its chief intent is to quench thirst ... the incidents attending its composition, and the methods for carrying out the process must be more various and complicated than those of any other liquor made from malt.

Small beer was not always 'common'. At Wrest Park, Silsoe, Bedfordshire, home of the de Grey family in the 1770s, there were two 'small beer' cellars, one containing 'common small beer' for the servants' hall and the other 'best small beer' for the family. The need to calculate the amount of beer servants should be allowed exercised the upper classes through the centuries. In 1800, the engineer Matthew Boulton worked out that his female servants required half a pint of ale (that is, a stronger brew) and a pint of beer for their midday dinner and the same again at suppertime, while the men would need twice as much – six pints a day at mealtimes, two of ale and four of beer. In 1879, servants at Trentham Hall, Staffordshire, home of the dukes of Sutherland, were still allowed four pints a day for men and two for women.

What the servants were getting in drink was only what they would have expected had they been living in their own homes. The pot boy was a familiar street sight, delivering beer in pewter pots from the local inn or pub to the houses of nearby families for mealtimes. A pot boy can be seen handing in a pint at the door of the pawnbroker's in Hogarth's great 1753 engraving Beer Street and a poem by the eighteenth-century writer Mary Darby Robinson called 'London's Summer Morning' says that amid 'The din of hackney-coaches, waggons, carts', 'the pot-boy yells discordant'. He carried the pots in an open wooden container with a handle, rather like a carpenter's tool box; he wore an apron, and he shouted 'Beer-ho!' as he walked through the streets to attract purchasers. George Dodd, in *The Food of London*, published in 1856, described the pot boy and his 'tray filled with quarts and pints of dinner-beer, carried out to the houses of the customers', though Dodd complained that the pot boy's tray 'seems to have undergone some change, for it is less frequently seen than "in days of yore".'

The potboy was in competition with those brewers who specialised in brewing beer for domestic customers. *The Encyclopædia of Domestic Economy* of 1855 said that:

in London, professional brewers who brew ale and table beer are distinct from those who brew porter, and some brewers confine

Beer Ho.

An early Victorian
cartoon of a potboy,
carrying his quarts of ale,
and calling: 'Beer Ho!'

themselves to the manufacture of table beer only. They make this malt
liquor from the best pale malt, or amber and pale malt. They usually
draw six barrels of beer from one quarter of malt [implying an OG
of 1035 to 1045]. The quantity of hops is from four to five pounds per
quarter of malt [eleven to thirteen ounces to the barrel]. Being sent
out in small casks, by proper management it may be drunk fresh and
in good condition; it is not calculated for long keeping.

Even in the second half of the nineteenth century the cask of ale at
home, delivered by the brewery roundsman, was still common and many
small concerns advertised themselves specifically as 'family brewers'.
Young's of Hertford, for example, ran advertisements in the local paper
in the 1870s promoting its 'superior pale bitter ales, brewed expressly for
the supply of Private Families and delivered in 9 or 18 gallon casks …

AK for family use, 10d per gallon.' Richard Reeve's West Ham brewery in what was, in 1900, still Essex, on the edge of London, had a huge sign across the front of its Romford Road premises declaring its beers, including Nursing Stout and Pale Dinner Ale, to be 'brewed expressly for private families from English malt and hops only'.

The normal prices for beers sold as 'family ale', 'table ale' or 'dinner ale' were 10d or 1s a gallon, implying OGs of around 1035 to 1045. They were the weakest Victorian beers, apart from the harvest ales sold to ease the thirsts of farm workers in hot August fields. Charles Ashby and Co. of Staines, 'Brewers of Pale and Mild Ales for Family Use', sold mild table ale at 10d a gallon, pale Family Table Ale at the same price and a better Family Pale Ale at just over 11d a gallon. Sich and Company of the Lamb brewery, Chiswick, west London (next door to Fuller's), which would 'supply private families direct from the brewery', also sold table ale at 10d a gallon. Locke and Smith of Berkhamsted in Hertfordshire wanted customers to know that 'Our DINNER ALE, BX, is specially Brewed for family use' and sold at 1s a gallon, 4s 6d a pin (4½ gallons).

But by the 1880s, while a pint of beer with dinner or supper was still popular, there was less demand for a whole 4½ gallon cask of dinner ale to be delivered to the family home. Overall beer consumption was falling and the chances of the beer turning sour before it was used were too great. Some brewers had started selling their beers in one or two-gallon screw-top stoneware jars, with brass taps. Healey's of Watford, just north of London, would let you have a gallon jar of its 'family bitter ale' for 1s 2d, 'jars and stoppers charged and allowed for when returned'.

Even a gallon was too much for many families, however. Fortunately the hour had brought forward its hero, Henry Barrett. Bottled beers had been available for centuries and Whitbread had started a considerable bottling operation in 1870. But these were corked bottles, which meant brewers needed an army of workers to knock home the corks (Whitbread employed more than a hundred corkers, each man working a twelve-hour day in 1886). They were also inconvenient for the drinker – a corkscrew was always required and bottles could not be easily resealed. In 1879 Barrett invented the screwtop beer bottle, a cheap, convenient, reusable container that meant little or no waste for the man desiring his lunchtime or suppertime pint. Four years later Barrett started his own brewery in Wandsworth, south London, Barrett's Brewing and Bottling Co. His early advertisements contrasted the ease with which a screw-top bottle could be opened against the potentially gory disaster of trying to open a corked bottle, with broken glass, blood and beer everywhere.

The screw top caught on rapidly (Whitbread started using them in 1886) and a thirty-year period began where almost every brewery had to have a bottled dinner ale or its equivalent. Even a tiny concern such as the Richmond brewery in Friars Lane, just off Richmond Green, Surrey, which brewed an AK Dinner Ale, offered its customers screw-topped imperial pint bottles at 2s 6d a dozen in 1887. This sum, half a crown for a dozen pints, was the standard price (Barrett's actually used the brand name 'Half-Crown Ale'), though in 1893 you could get Fuller, Smith and Turner's Pale Dinner Ale for 2s 4d, and in 1896 the Victoria Wine Company would sell you a single pint bottle of Devenish's 'celebrated Weymouth Dinner Ale' for 'tuppence ha'penny' – 2½d. The other favourite way to buy bottled beer was in wooden crates containing four screw-topped quart bottles, retailing at 1s 4d.

Most dinner ales were light ales, though Ash and Co. of Canterbury sold a 'Dinner Stout' and their rivals at the Canterbury brewery Company had a 'Luncheon Stout', as did the Ebbw Vale brewery in Wales, Ind Coope of Romford and several others; Ward's of Foxearth, Essex had 'Special Dark Family Ale'; the Friary Brewery Company in Guildford bottled something called 'Anglo Lager Dinner Ale'; Young's of Wandsworth brewed 'family stout'; while in Scotland, Calder's of Alloa bottled 'household stout', 'household' ale or beer being the Scots equivalent of the expression 'family ale'.

But all these early bottled beers were naturally conditioned, which meant a yeast deposit and the chance of cloudy beer if the customer did not take care. In 1897 the brewing scientist Horace Brown was reporting to the Institute of Brewing that in the United States they had solved the problems involved in chilling and filtering beers so that they would remain 'bright' in the bottle. It did not take long for the technology to cross the Atlantic. By 1899 the Notting Hill Brewery Company in west London was advertising its 'Sparkling Dinner Ale' as 'a revolution in English bottled beers, produced entirely on a new system … no deposit, no sediment, brilliant to the last drop, no waste whatever'.

The new, bright beers were popular with the public and other brewers had to buy in the necessary equipment themselves to keep up. Many, like the Notting Hill brewery, gave their beers names that reflected the perceived advantages of filtered beers. The Chester Northgate brewery, for example, sold 'All Clear' light dinner ale; Thomson and Wotton of Ramsgate sold 'All Bright' light dinner ale, 'guaranteed free from sediment'; Phillips and Marriott of the Midland brewery, Coventry, also sold 'Sparkling Dinner Ale'; while in Scotland, Maclays of Alloa sold

'Sparkling Table Beer' (table beer was the standard Scots name for dinner ales). The labels on Brickwoods of Portsmouth's Dinner Ale declared it 'Bright to the Last Drop'. Others relied on advertising; Huggins & Co. of the Lion brewery, Golden Square, Soho, printed posters declaring their Light Dinner ale was 'The Beer that's Clear from Here [arrow points to top of bottle] to Here [arrow points to bottom of bottle]'.

Off-licence sales of bottled beers, particularly lower-gravity beers, boomed with the arrival of the new technology. When Julian Baker wrote his book *The Brewing Industry* in 1905, he observed that of the three 'weights' of beer, strong, medium and light, 'increasing quantities' of light beers were being brewed every year. These beers, Baker said, were 'more or less the outcome of the demand of the middle classes for a palatable and easily consumed beverage. A good example of this type of beer is the so-called "family-ale".'

However, the First World War brought restrictions and tax increases in the name of victory that saw beer consumption and average gravities tumble while prices doubled. At certain times even pubs went short of beer. A pint with your dinner was often an unobtainable luxury. High taxes meant that even after the war, alcohol levels never recovered to pre-war levels. Steward & Patteson of Norwich, for example, brewed its two most popular beers, Light Bitter and XX mild, each at a gravity of 1047 in 1914. By 1920 they had fallen to 1029, lifting only slightly to 1030 in the 1930s. Meanwhile, changing social habits meant there was no big rush back to drinking beer with meals at home; by now the main evening meal in working class homes was called 'tea', which reflected the drink that was expected to go with it.

Some brewers did continue producing dinner ales. In 1929 the little brewery of Christie and Lucas in Ware, Hertfordshire, was selling 'John Gilpin' brand light dinner ale (a curious name, since William Cowper's 'Ballad of John Gilpin' is all about the poor man's problems in trying to get to his dinner and how he ended up in Ware in error), and family stout, at 6s and 5s 8d respectively for a dozen pints. Burge and Co. of the Victoria brewery, Windsor, was bottling three different 'beers for meals', Windsor Dinner Ale, Mild Dinner Ale and Luncheon Stout, when it was taken over by Meux's of London in 1931. Fremlin's of Maidstone, which was still calling itself a 'family pale ale and stout brewer' in the 1920s (when it first started to acquire tied houses), sold its Number 5 Family Ale at 6s 6d for a dozen bottles in the mid-1930s. But of the forty-six bottled beers in the Victoria Wine price list in 1936, its own Victoria Dinner Ale at 3s 8d for a case of four quart flagons was the only dinner ale there.

The Second World War brought much the same problems for beer drinkers as had the first: prices rose, strengths fell, pubs were often out of beer and (if anybody could get hold of any bottled beer to drink at home) shortage of paper meant sometimes the only way of telling one type of beer from another was the colour of the bottle top. Gravities dropped to save raw materials, so that Greene King in Bury St Edmunds, for example, was producing just one beer in 1943 at an OG of 1027 – though it did come in both light and dark versions. However, the average gravity stayed around the 1035 mark, higher than the 1030 of the First World War. The *Brewers' Journal* wrote in May 1945: 'Although the gravity of beer has progressively declined during the war, the quality and drinkability of the extremely light beers which have constituted the bulk of the beverage of the country have been higher than one could have dared to hope.' In part, however, this was down to high demand; while weak beers with low hopping rates would rapidly turn sour, 'the beer has scarcely had time to go off' before it was drunk, the *Journal* said.

Dinner ale and its companions did make a small comeback after 1945. The Victoria Brewery, Plymouth, was brewing family stout in the early 1950s. Around the same time, Bushell, Watkins & Smith's brewery in Westerham, Kent, was making dinner ale for Taylor Walker of the Barley Mow Brewery, Limehouse, East London, which had acquired Bushell's in 1948.

But while bottled beers were increasing enormously in popularity, to reach more than 50 per cent by value, these were mostly the big nationally-advertised brands, Double Diamond and the like, generally strong pale ales. As the 1960s arrived, dinner ale had sunk away. One of the very last was Melbourn's of Stamford, Lincolnshire, which still bottled a dinner ale (actually a bottled version of its draught bitter) when it closed in 1974. A brave attempt to revive the style was made by the little Paine's brewery of St Neot's, Cambridgeshire, in the summer of 1978 with the launch of Lunch Light, a draught light mild with an OG of just 1031. The beer lasted until 1982, when it was withdrawn because of lack of sales (Paine's itself lasted only a few years longer, selling out to Tolly Cobbold of Ipswich in 1987 and closing the following year).

Perhaps the last bottled dinner ale was the Luncheon Ale brewed and bottled by the Home brewery in Nottingham, which was still on sale in the early 1990s when the company was owned by Scottish and Newcastle. In 1998, however, the year after the Nottingham brewery was closed, the Sussex brewer Harvey's of Lewes introduced 'Harvey's Family Ale', which it described as a 'Light Bitter Dinner Ale' at just

The bottle label for the Luncheon Ale produced by Fordham's brewery in Ashwell, Hertfordshire, showing the brewery itself

2.2 per cent abv. This was available on draught 'for a limited season', the weakest draught beer since the Second World War.

However, the struggle to revive dinner ales was running in the face of a general decline in low-gravity beers. Even in 1976 there were more than a hundred different draught ales available at OGs of 1034 or less, with around twenty of those brewed at less than 1031 OG. Gradually, however, they disappeared, or had their strength quietly increased; McMullen's AK, for example, rose in OG from 1033 to 1034 in 1999, then 1036 in 2002 and 1037 in 2003.

In 2001 Brakspear & Sons, then still brewing at Henley-on-Thames in Oxfordshire, introduced a 2.5 per cent abv beer, Brakspear 2.5, hoping it would be part of a new category of low-gravity beers that the Chancellor of the Exchequer could be persuaded to tax less heavily than regular-strength brews. Sadly, he could not. But low-gravity beers continue to appear; in 2008 the Dorset brewer Hall & Woodhouse brought out bottled Harvester's Ale, a tasty, well-hopped brew with an abv of just 2.8 per cent.

9

BROWN ALE

When the chill Sirocco blows
And winter tells a heavy tale;
When pies, and daws. and rooks, and crows
Do sit and curse the frost and snows
Then give me ale,
Old ale,
Stout brown,
Nut brown
O, give me stout brown ale

Anonymous, 1656

Brown ale is one of the oldest styles of beer in Britain and it finds equivalents in some of the more ancient beers of other brewing lands, such as the *Oud Bruin* (old brown) of Belgium and the *dunkel* (dark) lagers of Bavaria. Oddly, however, current British brown ales all have twentieth-century origins. At the same time, despite a couple of well-known brands, brown ale is largely ignored in Britain today, though British brown ales have inspired a brown ale boom across the Atlantic.

In the Venn diagram of beer styles, brown ale overlaps with dark mild on one side, porter on another, amber ale on a third and Burton and old ale on a fourth. While it is not true to say, as some have claimed, that once all beer was brown (sun-dried malts, straw-dried malts and wheat malts would have made for pale beers and 'red ales' have been around for at least 1300 years), it seems to be true that for centuries the browner the beer, the more highly regarded it was. The medieval poet, William Langland, in 'Piers Plowman', written *c.*1380, had peasants whose work was in demand because of the labour shortages caused by the Black Death rejecting weak 'halfpeny [sic] ale' and drinking instead 'of the beste and of the brunneste that in Burgh is to selle' (or 'that brewsteres do sell', depending on which manuscript you have).

Another poet, John Milton, in 1645, in his poem 'L'Allegro' tied brown ale firmly into rural life, using an adjective regularly applied to describe the colour of the drink: 'Young and old come forth to play On a Sunshine Holyday, Till the live-long day-light fail: Then to the Spicy Nut-brown Ale'.

Brown ale, or to be exact, brown beer, since it contained more hops, was actually particularly associated with urban drinkers rather than rural ones, however, and London 'common' brown beer, with an alcoholic content of 6 per cent abv or so, was the capital's chief beer style at the end of the seventeenth century. But it did not have a good reputation. Michael Combrune described old-style London brown beer in 1762 as 'heavy, thick, foggy, and therefore justly grown to disuse'. It was replaced in the alehouse by a daughter style, porter, the even hoppier, drier, more aged beer that London's brown beer brewers developed from the 1720s onwards. The stronger version of old-style 'common' brown ale, called Stitch, which had an OG of around 1075 and sold for 21s 4d a barrel, similarly gave way to 'stout' porter, which was also known, in a nod to its descent from the older style, as 'brown stout'.

Brown ale did survive long enough to be taken to Britain's colonies, though. An advertisement in the *Sydney Gazette* of 23 December 1804 reads: 'LARKEN'S BREWERY. Ales – Pale, Brown and Amber; Twopenny and London Porter, etc., prepared after the system of the British breweries.' However, with the rise of porter and stout, and later of pale, bitter beers, brown ale as a recognised style went into sharp decline across the British Isles. Dublin, like London, had its own version of brown ale, which was also ousted by porter in the second half of the eighteenth century.

Brown ale, as a named style, dropped off the list of beers offered by British brewers until the first 'modern' version of brown ale was developed at the turn of the twentieth century. The new beer came from the East End firm regarded even by some of its rivals as London's leading mild ale brewer, Mann, Crossman & Paulin of the Albion Brewery. Mann's premises in the Whitechapel Road, next door to the Blind Beggar pub, was selling 500,000 barrels of XX mild a year at the beginning of the twentieth century.

The inventor of this modern style of brown ale was Thomas Wells Thorpe, son of a Lincolnshire farmer, who had started at Mann's in 1875 as junior brewer at its then new brewery in Burton upon Trent, brewing

T. W. THORPE, Esq.

Thomas Wells Thorpe, the creator of Mann's Brown Ale, which introduced a new style of brown ale to Britain

pale and Burton ales. His talents as a brewer were soon clear and in a short while he was moved south to be head brewer at the Whitechapel Road brewery. In 1883 Thorpe became general manager of the firm and in 1901, when Mann, Crossman & Paulin was turned into a limited company, he was appointed as its first managing director. The next year, 1902 (though one source claims 1899), Thorpe introduced a new bottled beer, Mann's Brown Ale, promoted as 'the sweetest beer in London'. It was part of a trend towards sweeter beers that included the development of milk stout in the same decade. Its recipe included wheat malt for head retention and roasted barley for colour and flavour. Its sweetness came from its low attenuation; despite an OG of 1033 its abv was just 2.7 per cent.

However, the new beer did not properly take off until after the First World War. In 1924 bottled beers in total, including stouts and bitter ale, made up just 14 per cent or so of Mann's production. But the 'great gravity drop' during and after the war meant the strengths of British beers ended up 25 per cent lower in 1919 than in 1914, because of government legislation designed to reduce drunkenness and save raw materials by promoting lower-strength beers. The result was a crisis in the pub as landlords struggled to keep their now weaker, more easily spoilt draught beers in good condition. Drinkers went for disguising the poor quality of much draught beer by mixing it with the highly carbonated, stable bottled variety. Dark mild had become the country's biggest selling beer style and the natural mixer with it was bottled brown ale, as brown-and-mild.

Mann's found sales of brown ale rushing ahead and rival brewers were forced to introduce their own versions under such names as Nut Brown. A fellow East End brewer, Truman's, brought out a bottled brown ale in 1924. It was being sold under the name Trubrown by 1929, when the Truman's house magazine revealed that over the previous five years 'the trade has increased by leaps and bounds and brown ale now outstrips all other brands [of the company's bottled beers]'. Also in 1924, Whitbread acquired the Forest Hill Brewery Co. in South East London, a firm with a reputation for 'bright' (filtered) bottled beers, which brought with it the Forest Brown brand, destined to become one of Whitbread's best-selling bottled ale brands.

Across the country, other brewers followed. Young & Co. of Wandsworth, London, had brought out bottled Amber Ale in 1924, but in 1927 the company was forced to announce that 'owing to many enquiries for Bottled Ale with more colour than we now supply we have decided to brew our Amber Ale to conform with more general demand', the result being labelled Brown Amber Ale. After experimental brews, the Norwich brewer Steward & Patteson introduced Norfolk Brown Ale in the summer of 1928 with a gravity of 1037.5 and soon declared that demand had 'greatly exceeded expectations'.

At Benskin's Watford brewery, in the 1950s, the Nut Brown Ale was fractionally weaker than the XX dark mild, at 1032 OG against 1033, and marginally lighter, with a Lovibond colour of 37, a dark brown, against 38 for the mild (the brown ale was the same colour, incidentally, as Benskin's stonking 1093 OG XXXX Colne Spring Ale). But rather than produce a new beer, some simply bottled their mild ales to sell as brown ale. When the two neighbouring brewers in Kimberley, Nottinghamshire, Hardy's and Hansons amalgamated, albeit with a continuation of their separate estates, and the Hansons brewery closed in 1932, Hansons took Hardy's Nut Brown Ale and relabelled it for its own pubs as Hansons Special Mild. Tollemache, the Ipswich brewer, which also brewed in Walthamstow, East London, made two different brown ales for its different markets, London Brown, which was smooth and sweet and a drier version, County Brown.

Some brewers, such as Arkell's of Swindon and Warwicks of Newark, bottled their mild under the name Home-Brewed, a reflection of the large number of home-brew pubs once found in areas such as the West Country and the West Midlands whose main beers were generally dark milds. Arkell's version, at 1032 OG, was first bottled in 1937 and lasted until the 1960s. Many beers sold as 'Home-Brew' were strong, however, such as Gray's of Chelmsford's version, which was its bottled dark stock ale. Just after the Second World War, George's of Bristol sold draught Home Brewed at a price almost two thirds more than its mild; the beer lasted in bottle until the early 1990s.

After the Second World War, with declining beer sales placing even greater strain on draught beer quality, bottled beers continued to increase sales, hitting 35 per cent of total beer volume by the mid-1950s and more than 50 per cent by value, up from 25 per cent by value in the 1930s. At some breweries the proportion was even higher; Mann's, in 1958, bottled nearly 70 per cent of its beer production, much of it Mann's Brown. Mild was still the most popular draught beer and the amount of brown-and-mild being drunk meant that brown ale was also a big seller.

Many brewers had two brown ales, one at around 1032 OG, the other at 1038 or so; Everards of Leicester had five, including Bradgate Brown, Burton Brown, Nut Brown and Belvoir Strong Brown. This last was one of a number of 'double brown ales', including Bateman's Double Brown, Mitchell & Butler's Sam Brown Ale, Ruddles' Strong Brown at 1048, first brewed around 1970 and Whitbread Double Brown, launched in 1927, and sold as 'a fine strong ale' that blurred the line between brown ale and stout.

From 1960, however, mild sales began to fall like a shot duck, with mild drinkers growing older and dying out. As the output of mild fell, brown ale sales declined in proportion. A survey in 1973 found some 112 brown ales still being brewed, with 90 per cent of Britain's regional brewers producing at least one, and eighteen brewers who were each making two different brown ales. Over the next couple of decades, however, the number of brown ales shrank dramatically as many regional breweries closed and others simply stopped making the style. Mann's Brown, which was acquired by Watney Combe Reid of Pimlico when it took over the Mann Crossman brewery in 1958, was one of the few survivors, replacing dozens of former rivals in other brewers' pubs as they stopped brewing their own brown ales.

Starkey Knight and Ford of Tiverton in Devon was one of a number of brewers to make a brown ale under the description 'Home Brewed', recalling the beer made by home-brew pubs

When the Mann's brewery closed in 1979, production of the brown ale was moved around, ending up at the Watney-owned Usher's brewery in Trowbridge, Wiltshire. Usher's became independent in a management buy-out in 1991 after the Courage group acquired Watney's brewing interests and the Wiltshire brewer also gained the rights to the Mann's Brown brand, which had been selling 30 million bottles a year in 1989, around 25,000 barrels. When Usher's closed in 2000 the brand passed to a new company, Refresh UK (today owned by Marston's) and Mann's, which now has at least 90 per cent of the UK's surviving market for sweet brown ales, was being brewed in 2008 at the Thomas Hardy Burtonwood brewery in Cheshire.

One other English brown ale type introduced in the twentieth century, however, has prospered and even inspired a flood of successful overseas imitators. The 'North East Strong' style of brown ale is generally said to date from 1927, when Newcastle Breweries launched a deep amber-coloured, fruity beer, drier and stronger than beers such as Mann's, under the name Newcastle Brown Ale. The beer had been developed after Barras Ramsey, chairman of Newcastle Breweries, asked the company's young head brewer, Colonel James H. Porter, to work with the brewery's chief chemist, Archie Jones, to develop a new product that would suit the then-growing bottled-beer market.

It took three years, but the new beer, when it appeared, was rewarded almost instantly with the Challenge Cup for bottled beers at the 1928 Brewers' Exhibition in London. When Newcastle Breweries merged with Scottish Brewers to form Scottish & Newcastle in 1960, the beer gained a national presence. It also began to find a growing market overseas, with today, more than half of the 4.7 per cent abv beers' sales made abroad.

In Sunderland, however, they tell a different story. The town's big brewery, Vaux, brewed a special beer called Maxim in 1901 to celebrate the safe return from the Boer War of Major Ernest Vaux, who had commanded a Maxim gun detachment in the Northumberland Hussars. Maxim was originally a strong amber-brown ale, but Sunderland legend says the strength was quickly reduced because local landlords complained that their customers kept falling asleep. However, in 1938 the strength was increased again to 4.7 per cent abv and the name of the beer changed to Double Maxim, evidently in response to the challenge from Newcastle Brown. The Vaux brewery closed in 1999, but the Double Maxim brand name was bought by two former Vaux directors, Doug Trotman and Mark Anderson, who formed the Double Maxim Brewing Company and had the beer made in Robinson's brewery, Manchester. In August 2006 it was announced that Double Maxim Brewing had commissioned a new brewing plant at Rainton Bridge, bringing the beer back to Wearside.

Two other brewers also made beers in the North East brown ale style. One was Samuel Smith of Tadcaster in Yorkshire, with Nut Brown Ale, at 5 per cent abv. The other was the Northern Clubs Federation brewery, originally of Newcastle, later of Dunston, Gateshead, with Strong Brown Ale. The Federation brewery's beer was later renamed High Level brown ale after one of the bridges over the Tyne. However, in 2005, Scottish & Newcastle announced the closure of its Newcastle brewery and the acquisition of the Federation brewery in Gateshead to take its place. High Level brown ale was dropped, and Newcastle Brown Ale replaced it. In late 2009 it was revealed that Newcastle Brown Ale production was moving to Tadcaster, Yorkshire.

Meanwhile in the United States in the 1980s, a new style of brown ale was being born. Brown ales had gone to America with its founding fathers – the style is mentioned in 1810 along with porter, pale ale, small beer and strong beer as one of the types made by US brewers. Like brown ale in Britain, the style died out until a former electrical engineer, Pete Slosberg, went into the growing microbrewery business in California in 1986. His first beer was based on Samuel Smith's Nut Brown Ale and was a brownish-red, 5.5 per cent abv beer, with maltiness balanced by plenty of hop flavour, which he called Pete's Wicked Ale. The beer won a silver medal in the 'ale' category at the Great American Beer Festival the following year. In 1988 the festival created a new category, brown ale, and in 1992 it introduced an American Brown Ale category, specifically to encompass Wicked Ale and its imitators.

Today, American microbrewers brew a wide variety of beers in the American Brown Ale style, including Indian Brown Ale from Dogfish Head in Delaware at 7.2 per cent abv; Imperial Brown Ale from the Legend brewery Company, Virginia, at 7.5 per cent abv; Hazelnut Brown Nectar from Rogue of Oregon, which 'puts the nuts in nut-brown' by containing real hazelnut extract; Old Brown Dog Ale, at 1060 OG, from Smuttynose of New Hampshire, and Kick-Ass Brown, at 5.3 percent abv from the C.H. Evans brewery in Albany, New York.

However, brown ale is not a completely forgotten style for Britain's small brewers. Partly thanks to the mini-revival of dark milds over the past few years, there are now a number of draught and bottle-conditioned brown ales in the UK. They include Maiden's Magic from the Alcazar brewery in Nottingham, smooth and lightly hopped in what might be called, in honour of Mann's, the 'Southern' brown ale style, but at 5 per cent abv rather stronger than the 'urtype'; Bodger Brown from Wissey Valley in Norfolk, at 4 per cent abv; Marld, from Bartrams of Bury St Edmunds, a bottled version of the company's mild ale and a more typical Southern brown ale strength of 3.4 per cent abv; and Black Bear from Beartown in Congleton, Cheshire, another bottled dark mild. In 2006 the Highgate brewery in the West Midlands, for many years a dark beer specialist, introduced Old Ember, at 6.5 per cent abv a welcome revival of the strong brown ale style, brewed with honey for a delicious twist. There is even a draught 'Northern brown ale', Tyne Brown, 4.6 per cent abv, from the Reepham brewery in Norfolk.

10

WHEAT BEER

Tell Davy this Cornwall is such a vile county, that nothing but its merit, as his birth-place, redeems it from utter execration. I have found in it nothing but rogues, restive horses, and wet weather; and neither Pilchards, White-ale, or Squab-pie, were to be obtained!

Letter to Joseph Cottle, Robert Sothey, 1800

If James II had not alienated everyone except his most loyal supporters before fleeing the country in 1688 after the landing of the Dutch ruler William of Orange, and if the Dutchman, who was subsequently crowned in Westminster as William III, had not needed money to pay for the eight-year 'War of the British Succession' with Louis XIV of France that followed, then Britain might still have a tradition of wheat beers to rival Belgium or Germany.

Unfortunately, as part of the money-raising to pay for the enlarged army and navy required to keep a French invasion on behalf of the deposed James away from British shores, the first tax on malt in England was introduced in 1697 (Scotland, which had many supporters of James II, and which William did not wish to alienate further, escaped the malt tax for another couple of decades). The regulations that came with the Act, in an attempt to maximise revenue, prohibited commercial brewing with anything other than (taxed) malted barley. After many centuries, English brewers could no longer use wheat, malted or otherwise, in their beers and ales. It was a painful blow; an anonymous book published in 1768 called *Every Man His Own Brewer* declared: 'Wheat has the most spirit and body, and was formerly the only grain esteemed worth malting, and may probably be so still, if other reasons [the tax laws] did not interfere.'

In fact, a couple of obscure styles of wheat beer did survive in Britain. One was known in the nineteenth century as 'Devon white beer', although it was certainly brewed in Cornwall as well and, as a largely hopless brew, is probably better referred to as West Country white ale. A recipe from 1850 for 'White Ale', a 'very nutritious Wheat Beer and wholesome drink ... probably one of our old English ales, slightly improved or altered', has a grain bill of one 'sack' of pale or pale and amber malt, almost certainly meaning 1½ bushels, around 60lb, and 24lb of 'fine wheaten flour', or just over 70:30 barley to wheat.

As the 1850 writer guessed, white ale certainly looks to be among the oldest types of ale brewed in Britain, dating back to at least the medieval period and hopfree or (after the sixteenth century) only very lightly hopped. Its first mention is in a book by the Tudor traveller and physician Andrew Boorde, who wrote around 1540 that Cornish ale 'is stark nought, lokinge whyte and thycke, as pygges had wrasteled in it'.

The whiteness would have come from the wheat, which gives a characteristic protein haze to the beer. The thickness was probably because it was then an unboiled or lightly boiled hopless ale, with the proteins that coagulate out of boiled wort still in the drink and also because recipes for white ale generally used a considerable quantity of eggs, actually in the brewing rather than, as in ale flip, added afterwards.

Boorde was not impressed by this West Country drink, declaring that 'it wyll make one to kacke, also to spew'. But it was extremely popular locally; William Ellis, author of the *London and Country Brewer*, published almost two centuries later, said that 'the Plymouth People ... are so attach'd to their white thick Ale, that many have undone themselves by drinking it'.

The tradition of brewing with wheat comes from the earliest millennia of brewing. The favourite brewing grain of Celtic brewers at the time of the Romans, as with the Sumerians in the Middle East around 2000 BC, appears to have been emmer, a 'primitive' hulled wheat (which makes it easier to malt than modern unhulled wheat). Wheat and honey were the ingredients in Welsh *bragawd* or bragot, a honey ale that was made by private brewers right through until the seventeenth century in England as well as Wales and which probably takes its name from the Celtic for malt, *bracis*. The pre-Norman Conquest English used *hwaetene mealt*, wheat malt, in some of their ales and in 1286 the brewery at St Paul's Cathedral in London was making ale for the monks using malted wheat, malted barley and oats in a ratio of 1:1:4 by volume.

Wheat continued to be used by English brewers after the arrival of hops. The first description of how to make hopped beer in England, in 1443, said 'pure barley and wheat' should be used and in 1576, in an

Andrew Boorde, the Tudor physician, was the first man to describe Cornish White Ale. He didn't think much of it

attempt to keep the price of grain down, the brewers of London and surrounding counties were banned from brewing 'any extraordinary beare with wheate or wheate meale commonlye called March beere'. A recipe for home-brewed beer from the following year used eight bushels of barley malt to half a bushel of wheat meal and half a bushel of fine-ground oats. In 1615 Gervase Markham was still recommending half a 'peck' (a quarter of a bushel) of wheat and half a peck of oats to two quarters of malt and a peck of 'pease' to make 'the best March bere'.

In 1671 the household brewery at Wrest Park in Bedfordshire was making six hogsheads of best quality beer, three hogsheads of next best and one of small beer from a recipe involving sixty bushels of new malt, three bushels of wheat and three of beans, plus three bushels of old malt. The likely strength of the best beer looks to have been somewhere above the 1100 OG mark.

Private households continued to use wheat as an ingredient in beer after the introduction of the ban on commercial brewers using wheat in 1697, though often they used cracked wheat rather than the malted variety. At least two surviving recipes suggest throwing a couple of handfuls of rosemary flowers into the wort along with the hops. A recipe from the Dyott family of Freeford Manor near Lichfield for 'Lord Granby's Ale' includes five bushels of malt and half a bushel each of white oats and unground wheat to make five 'London barrels' of beer. Although this suggests an OG of only around 1035, the recipe stated the beer would 'keep four years'.

All of these were fairly conventional beers. Descriptions of the ingredients of West Country white ale, however, generally involve the brewers purchasing something called 'grout' or 'ripening' to make it ferment, suggesting it may have been similar to the gruit ales of the Continent, with the brewers buying a grain-and-herb mix from specialist retailers to add to their own grist, just as Dutch and German brewers did before hopped beers took over. On the Continent the precise make-up of the 'gruit', which would include bittering herbs such as bog myrtle or yarrow, was normally kept secret by the sellers and the same seems to have been true of the mystery ingredient in white ale. Bishop White Kennett, writing around 1700, called white beer a 'grout ale'. He may have meant the English equivalent of gruit, that is a herb-and-grain mix, or groats, that is crushed wheat or oats. But the *Publican, Innkeeper and Brewer's Guide* of 1850 says that 'Gray, in his Practical Chemist' (which may be a reference to Samuel Gray's *Operative Chemist* of 1828) gives a recipe for 'Grouts for White', made from 6–8lb of ground malt in 1½ gallons of water, kept warm by a fireside until it began naturally fermenting and then boiled down to a thin paste. This would make the 'grout' a source of wild yeast rather than flavouring. William Ellis, who gave the first known recipe for white ale in *The London and Country Brewer*, said the drink was 'a clear Wort made from pale Malt, and fermented with what they call ripening, which is a Composition, they say, of the Flower [flour] of Malt, Yeast and Whites of Eggs, a Nostrum made and sold only by two or three in those Parts'.

However, the sellers of the 'ripening' did not make the ale, Ellis said, instead 'the Wort is brewed and the Ale vended by many of the Publicans; which is drank while it is fermenting in Earthen Steens, in such a thick manner as resembles butter'd Ale, and sold for Twopence Halfpenny the full Quart.' Ellis added that 'It is often prescribed by Physicians to be drank by wet Nurses for the encrease of their Milk, and also as a prevalent Medicine for the Colick and Gravel.'

A recipe for 'Western White Ale' from *Every Man his Own Brewer* said the beer was made from 'pale, slack dried malt of the lowest quality, and without the use of any hop, or other alkaline preservative, as being for spending immediately after fermentation'. The fermentation was brought about 'without yeast' by adding wheat flour, bean flour or malt flour, 'it matters not which', made into a paste with egg white, which 'being thrown into the wort sets it a fermenting'. The wort is 'most usually let down from the mash into glazed jars, called steens, and worked in [allowed to ferment], and drawn from them for use'. The similarity of this 'spontaneous' method of fermentation to what we know today as Belgian lambic beers, which are also made with a quantity of wheat in the recipe, evidently occurred to the writer of *Every Man his Own Brewer*, who said: 'All over Flanders an ale of the like kind, in taste and colour, is drank very freely by the ladies, and seems the cause of their plump and healthy appearances.'

The *Town and Country Brewery Book*, written by William Brande *c.*1830, listed 'Devonshire White Ale' among the regional speciality brews of Britain. In a narrative that owns a lot to Ellis a century earlier, Brande said white ale was drunk in Plymouth 'by the first people of the town'. The local ale-wives, 'whose province this comes under to manage', fermented the ale 'in a row of earthen steens, holding about two or more gallons each', having brought on the fermentation:

> by the purchase of what they call ripening, or a composition, as some say, of the flour of malt mixed with the whites of eggs ... a nostrum not generally known, and for a great length of time was only in the possession of a few master brewers, who sold it out as yeast is now done, at so much for a certain quantity; and at every time a fresh brewing of this ale took place, a great ball or lump of it was generally sufficient to work four or five steens of wort, and convert it from a very clear body into a thick fermenting one, near the colour and consistence of buttered ale.

Brande warned that white ale had to be drunk quickly, 'for if it was let alone to fine or stale, it was rejected as not worthy of buying or drinking. Yet some, out of curiosity, have kept it in bottles, racked it off clear, and made of it flip and other very good compositions.' His recipe for the drink gave the ingredients as: pale ale wort, twenty-five gallons; hops, two handfuls; yeast, three pounds; groats, six or eight pounds. When the fermentation is at its height, bottle in strong stone half pints, well corked and wired. This ale effervesces when opened.

The *Publican, Innkeeper and Brewer's Guide* is more specific in identifying 'ripening' with 'groats' or 'grouts' and linking it to the sort of 'wild' fermentations found in wheat beer lambic. The author wrote that the preparation of 'ripening' had been 'held by one or two families for many years, no one else in the neighbourhoods where the ale is drank but these knowing how to prepare it'. However, it did not seem to be too secret, for the book went on: 'The Ripening, sold at Plymouth, for causing the fermentation, is a mixture of malt, hops and wort, which is quite sour, and without any appearance of fermentation, and is evidently a preparation in which a natural state of fermentation has occurred.' The same effect can be had, he wrote, by keeping some of the first wort in a jar in a warm place 'till the next brewing'. The lees from white ale 'are in great request by the bakers, at those places where they are made for raising the fermentation of their bread, and are retailed to them at threepence per quart'.

The *Publican, Innkeeper and Brewer's Guide*'s recipe for white ale suggested two mashes of thirty gallons each on sixty pounds of pale or pale and amber malt, which would give around forty-five gallons of wort, which should be boiled for just twenty minutes or half an hour with only eight ounces of hops – giving very little bitterness. To the boiled wort should be added a batter made from twenty-four pounds of wheat flour and twenty-four fresh eggs; a pound of salt; and a pound of 'ripening', giving an OG of perhaps 1045. Ferment in a tun for ten hours, 'cleanse' by passing through a fine wire sieve into casks with their heads out and ferment for another eight to ten hours, and the ale would be ready to drink, the guide suggested.

White ale seems to have disappeared from Cornwall in Georgian times. The poet Robert Southey made a trip to the county in 1800 and had evidently been told by his friend, the Cornish-born scientist Humphrey Davy, to look out for it as one of several local delicacies. However, Southey complained in a letter from Falmouth to another friend: 'neither Pilchards, White-ale, or Squab-pie, were to be obtained!'

The drink continued to be brewed in South Devon through into the Victorian era, however. In 1850 William White's *Directory of Devonshire* said Dartmouth and its neighbourhood were still 'long celebrated for white ale, said to have been first brewed here', while further west along the south Devon coast at Kingsbridge, the directory said, 'White Ale is extensively used in this neighbourhood, where it is said to have been introduced by a German regimental surgeon [confusion here, perhaps, with the drink mum], some centuries ago, at Dodbrooke [the town's eastern suburb], where it pays a small tithe to the rector.' The fact that the white ale brewers paid a tithe on the drink to the church seems good evidence of its antiquity.

In 1868 Salcombe, four miles south of Kingsbridge harbour, was still 'celebrated for the manufacture of white ale', according to the *National Gazetteer of Great Britain and Ireland*. By 1877, however, just a few years later, white ale was being described as 'said to have been a common drink until recently in the South Hams of Devon and in Cornwall'. The journalist John Bickerdyke, writing in 1889, said white ale was 'a milky-looking compound' and, 'judging from the flavour', milk, spices and gin were among the ingredients, something which, again, seems unlikely. Bickerdyke claimed that 'at the present time a considerable quantity of white ale is made in and about Tavistock', in Devon, though this was 'brewed in a simpler manner than before, and consists simply of common ale with eggs and flour added'.

However, others were having difficulty finding the drink. George Saintsbury, the critic and scholar, said in his *Notes from a Cellar Book* that 'The curious "white ale", or lober agol', 'within the memory of man, used to exist in Devonshire and Cornwall', though 'even half a century ago', that is, around 1870, 'I have vainly sought [for it] there'. While Saintsbury said the alternative name for white ale was 'lober agol', two words, Bickerdyke wrote in 1889 that 'an ale of a similar nature to white ale goes in Cornwall by the rather uneuphonious title of "Laboragol"'. The name may have something to do with the extremely obscure brewing term 'lob', meaning a thick mixture, found by the *Oxford English Dictionary* in a reference from 1839.

The other post-1697 wheat beer survivor in Britain was mum. It was the only wheat brew specifically permitted under the malt-tax legislation and it was taxed at 10s a barrel for both the British-brewed and the imported version. However, figures given by the economist Adam Smith for tax revenues for 1774 suggest fewer than 2,000 barrels a year of mum were being consumed in Britain.

Mum was defined by Samuel Johnson in his dictionary of 1755 as 'ale brewed with wheat'. In reality it was much more complicated than that, being flavoured with an apothecary's garden's worth of herbs. The drink looks to have originated in the north German city of Brunswick, where it is traditionally said to have been invented by a man called Christian Mumme in 1492. Unfortunately, there are no records from Brunswick showing anyone by that name in the late fifteenth century, while there appears to be a mention of '*Braunschweiger Dickbier*' (Brunswick Thickbeer) under the name 'Mumm' as early as 1390. It may not even be German originally; a beer called Dordrecht mom from Holland is referred to in 1285.

By the 1660s the drink was being sold in England in specialist 'mum houses'. Samuel Pepys's diary records on 28 May 1662 that he and his father and uncle went 'to the Mum House at Leadenhall, and there sat awhile'. Two years later he again went 'to the Fleece, a mum house in Leadenhall, and there drunk mum'. Licences to sell mum were issued in Cambridge and probably other places, and it was popular enough for a petition to be made in 1673 to the English Parliament for it to be prohibited, along with tea, coffee, brandy and 'chocolata', on the grounds that they all reduced the demand for beer and ale made with native ingredients. The Black Country ironmaster Andrew Yarranton in his book *England's improvement by Sea and Land to out-do the Dutch without fighting ... to set at work all the poor*, published in London in 1677, suggested making Stratford upon Avon a centre for English mum-brewing, saying that 'There may as much Mum be made there as at present is made at Brunswick', which could be exported to Ireland, the West Indies, France, Spain and the Mediterranean, thus 'getting away the Mum trade from Brunswick'.

A recipe for mum by John Houghton, a Fellow of the Royal Society, from 1683 gives the grain bill for forty-two gallons of mum as seven bushels of wheat malt, one bushel of oat malt and one bushel of beans. Once fermentation begins, Houghton wrote, the flavourings should be added, thirteen in all, including three pounds of the inner rind of a fir tree; one pound each of fir and birch tree tips; three handfuls of 'Carduus Benedictus', or blessed thistle (in modern botanical parlance *Cnicus benedictus*, an intensely bitter plant, though not actually a thistle, used by herbalists to stimulate appetite); two handfuls of 'flowers of Rosa Solis', or sundew, the insect-eating bogplant that has a bitter, caustic taste (according to the seventeenth-century medical writer William Salmon, *Rosa Solis* 'stirs up lust', and the plant was the main ingredient in a popular medieval cordial); elderflowers, betony, wild thyme, cardamom and pennyroyal. Houghton also said that his father made beer from malted wheat when wheat was cheap, 'and the Tradition is that it yields more liquor and stronger, the quantity used considered, than Malt made of any other grain'.

The bitterness of mum is underlined by an anonymous poem from around 1725 which talks about mum from 'Hamborough' (Hamburg) that was 'yellow. and likewise/As bitter as gall/And as strong as six horses/Coach and all'. A recipe for mum very similar to Houghton's appears in *Every Man His Own Brewer*, which added that 'our English brewers, instead of the inner rind of fir, use cardamom, ginger and sassafras; and also add elecampane [*Inula helenium*, a dandelion-like bitter plant with antiseptic properties, still used in herbal cough mixtures], madder and red saunders' [the heart-wood of *Pterocarpus santalinus*, a tree from Coromandel and Sri Lanka, which gives a red colour in the presence of alcohol, suggesting English mum was red, or at least pinkish].

Gradually, however, mum gave way to tea and coffee and more conventional beers, so that it seems to have vanished from Britain soon after Adam Smith mentioned it in passing in *The Wealth of Nations*. Sir Walter Scott referred to mum in his novel *The Antiquary*, published in 1816, describing it as 'a species of fat ale, brewed from wheat and bitter herbs, of which the present generation only know the name by its occurrence in revenue acts of parliament'.

Thus, with the demise of West Country white ale around 1870, Britain's wheat ale tradition was effectively dead. When William Gladstone passed the Free Mash Tun Act in 1880, which allowed commercial brewers in Britain to again use wheat after nearly 200 years and any other grain they wanted in making beer, there was no rush to use the newly legalised ingredient. British brewers did use wheat in small quantities after the Free Mash Tun Act, mainly because it gave 'outstandingly good' head retention to their beers. However, they rarely added more than 10 per cent or so of wheat to a beer, be it mild, bitter or sweet stout, to avoid problems caused by too much protein in the wort, which made the beer hazy and also because wheat flour could cause drainage problems in the mash tun. The lack of a British tradition in wheat beers and probably the lack of experience among British brewers at making them meant it was some time after the 'microbrewery revolution' took off before new wheat beers began to appear in Britain.

This was in high contrast to the United States, where a greater openness to brewing different styles of beer meant its new small brewers happily made south-German-style wheat beers alongside porters and IPAs and Belgian-style spiced wheat beers as well. Even Australia was

King and Barnes, the now-closed Sussex brewer, made a wheat beer in the 1990s

producing a wheat beer in 1984, the well-regarded Red Back from Freemantle.

The first new British wheat beers appear to have come from the regional family brewer Vaux in Sunderland, which in 1988 was making a south-German-style *Weizen* with a proper Bavarian-type yeast and another wheat beer with a more normal British ale yeast. The micro-brewer Bunce's brewery in Netheravon, near Salisbury, made in 1991 what it called 'Bunce's Vice', a play on *Weisse*, or white, a German word for wheat beer, as a summer occasional beer.

A couple of years later, in 1993, the nearby Hop Back brewery in Salisbury started brewing a 1052 OG wheat beer which later became Thunderstorm. The following year the Hoskins & Oldfield brewery in Leicester produced one of Britain's first Belgian-style wheat beers, White

Dolphin, flavoured with orange peel and coriander. Another wheat beer with a punning name, which appeared in 1997 from the Fenland brewery in Cambridgeshire, was the Belgian-style Sparkling Wit, a play on the Flemish word for white.

The Bavarian tradition of dark or *Dunkel* wheat beers also found its expression in Britain in 1997 with Silent Knight, a dark wheat beer from the Quay brewery in Weymouth. Perhaps the most intriguing new wheat beer, however, came in 1999 from an appropriate source, the Cornish brewery St Austell. Rather than revive Cornish White Ale, however, St Austell's head brewer, Roger Ryman, decided to recreate a south-German-style wheat beer, but with actual vanilla, clove and coriander, plus maple syrup, standing in for the special *Weissbier* yeast, which gives vanilla/clove/banana aromas to Bavarian *Weizen*. The beer was originally called Hagar the Horrible, after the cartoon character, but was launched in 2000 under the name Clouded Yellow, a type of butterfly (on the grounds that the beer was cloudy, yellow and, like the butterfly, a summer visitor). The bottle-conditioned beer makes a fine drink with food and a terrific base for fried fish batter.

Wheat beers are still comparatively rare from British brewers, however, despite the Belgian wheat beer Hoegaarden (pronounced hoo-garten), one of the few unfiltered keg beers in the world, becoming popular in the UK. Guinness launched a draught wheat beer in Ireland called Breo (pronounced 'bro'), the old Irish for 'glow', at a cost of million Irish pounds, but withdrew it in 2000 after a couple of years of poor sales.

Others include a Belgian-style unfiltered beer from the St Peter's brewery launched in 2005; George Gale's Summer Breeze, now brewed by Fuller Smith & Turner of Chiswick; a proper Bavarian-style wheat from the Meantime brewery in Greenwich; the curious Chimera Wheat Porter from the Downton brewery in Salisbury; Arran Blonde from the Isle of Arran, Scotland; O'Hanlon Double Champion Wheat; and a couple of Irish examples.

Porterhouse in Dublin, one of the few brewers confident enough to give out the recipes of its beers, admits to using torrefied wheat in several of its stouts and lagers, though not in its German-style wheat beer, while the Carlow brewery uses torrefied and whole wheat in its Cuirm (the old Irish word for beer) wheat beer. A modern-day Southey, however, would still search in vain for West Country white ale, which so far remains unrevived.

11

BARLEY WINE AND OLD ALE

There's a lusty liquor which
Good fellows use to take-a;
It is distilled with Nard* most rich,
And water of the lake-a.
Of hop a little quantity,
And Barm to it they bring too;
Being barrell'd up, they call't a cup
Of dainty good old stingo.

'A Cup of Old Stingo', from *Merry Drollery Complete*, 1650
*Spikenard

Drinkers in the Help Me Through the World pub in Codicote, Hertfordshire, in the 1890s had a resonant nickname for the strong beer supplied by their local brewer, Lattimore & Co. of Brewhouse Hill, in nearby Wheathampstead. Whatever its official name might have been, the locals called it Crackskull – and doubtless the morning after two or three pints that's what it felt like.

Crackskull would today probably be called a barley wine. Strictly, barley wine is not a style since the term is, today, applied to any strong beer of any type, that is from around 7 per cent abv upwards, except for black beers, where the hefty imperial stouts are kept (with no particularly logical reasoning) in a category of their own. 'Barley wine' thus covers the strongest beers in a range of different styles: strong sweetish Burton or 'winter warmer' old ales, strong stock bitter and strong pale, amber and brown ales. Some feel that barley wine should be restricted to beers over 8.5 per cent abv or to paler varieties of strong ale, with the darker types then called 'old ale'. But this is a definition far too fuzzy around the edges – London drinkers called the Burton style 'old', for example, but the best-known Burton-style strong ale, Bass No 1, is generally held up as an archetypal barley wine, despite its comparative darkness.

The term 'barley wine' is, in any case, a fairly new one, except when used as a literal translation of '*oinos krithios*', the phrase used by Xenophon in 300 BC for the beer that the Greeks had found the Armenians drinking in the lands near the Black Sea. Barley wine does not generally appear in brewers' advertisements until after the start of the twentieth century. Although the *Town and Country brewery Book* spoke of 'Barley wine and Dorchester beer' brewed at a huge ten bushels of malt to the barrel and a small brewer in Dartmouth, Devon around 1880, John Madocks & Co., advertised its beers as 'Barley Wine from the English Rhine', using a phrase for the valley of the River Dart coined by Queen Victoria. Bass only began using the words 'barley wine' to describe its strong No 1 Burton Ale in 1903.

But Lattimore's Crackskull is just one of dozens of legendary strong ales and barley wines, beers for lying down and enjoying as they mature that once delighted drinker, beers such as Benskin's Colne Spring Ale, also from Hertfordshire, Dutton's O Be Joyful from Lancashire, Trinity Audit Ale and Ind Coope's Arctic Ale.

There appears to be little or no evidence that very strong ales were in use before hops arrived in Britain in the early fifteenth century; unhopped strong ales would probably have still soured quite quickly, since they would have been quite sweet when new. But after beer brewing with hops began, brewers found they could make extra-strong beers which, if well hopped to act against infection, would stay drinkable, improving all the while for many months or years. In particular they began heavily hopping the beers made in March, the end of the brewing season, and October, the start of the new brewing season, these March and October beers being designed to last for at least a year and maintain supplies of drink through the summer when it was too hot to brew safely before the invention of ways to cool fermenting wort.

By the middle of the sixteenth century brewers were making, as well as the usual single and double brews ('double beer' was made using the first mash poured back over the grain in the mash tun to pull out more sugars from the grain and give a stronger wort), an even stronger version called 'doble-doble', which was regularly banned by the authorities for being too strong. A brewer called Peter Jool from Middlesex was indicted for selling 'doble-doble ale' in the reign of Edward VI (this does look to have been an unhopped or very lightly hopped strong ale) and in 1557–58, in the reign of Edward's sister Mary I, the Corporation of Norwich passed a prohibition against any 'Berebruer' making 'any Beyer called doble-doble bere'. Three years later, in 1560, Elizabeth I was complaining that the London brewers had stopped brewing single beer completely and instead made 'a kynde of very strong bere calling the same doble-doble bere which they do commonly utter and sell at a very greate and excessyve pryce'. Double-double was again prohibited and the brewers told to brew only single and ordinary double beer.

These attempts to outlaw extra-strong beers do not seem to have succeeded for very long, since by 1577 the Essex clergyman William Harrison was describing the popularity among the 'maltbugs' who frequented alehouses of 'heady ale and beer' sold under names such as huffcap (commemorated in the Mother Huffcap pub in Great Alne, Warwickshire), merry-go-down, mad dog and dragon's milk. It was not just the Tudor labouring classes who liked powerful beers. Harrison also described the strong March beer made at the end of the brewing season by the English nobility on their country estates. This, he said, was drunk when it was 'commonly of a year old' and sometimes 'of two years' tunning or more', though 'this is not general'.

The nobility competed to serve the oldest beer, Harrison said, 'each one coveting to have the same stale as he may, so that it be not sour', an odd-sounding sentence today, since Harrison was not using 'stale' in the modern sense, but with the meaning of something that had 'stood' and 'so' in the sense of 'except'. He meant that the titled classes tried to let their beer mature in cask for as long as possible without it actually going vinegary or sour.

By the beginning of Queen Anne's reign, in 1703, the anonymous *Guide to Gentlemen and Farmers for Brewing the Finest Malt Liquors* was saying there were 'many country gentlemen' who 'talk of, and magnify their stale Beer of 5, 10 or more years old'. The guide recommended using eleven bushels of malt to make a hogshead of strong March or October ale from the first mash, which would have given an enormous OG, somewhere up in the 1130s or 1140s, and which explains why it would keep so long.

These extremely strong, sweet beers were increasingly used by the gentry through the eighteenth century as substitutes for brandy, which had become prohibitively dear after huge rates of duty were imposed on French wine imports. The squires and knights of the shires who could not obtain smuggled brandy drank tiny glasses of their own brewed

powerful, aged, sticky beer at the end of dinner in glasses holding three
to four fluid ounces, less than a quarter of a pint. The glasses themselves
were decorated with wheelcut engravings of hops and barley or, in the
case of glasses for honeyed or buttered ales, bees and butterflies.

The best description of such a strong, long-lasting beer comes from a
book written in the 1860s, but set in the 1820s, *Wives and Daughters*, by
Elizabeth Gaskell. In one scene, Squire Hamley has broached a cask of
ale laid down at least twenty-one years earlier, at the birth of his first-
born son, Osborne, and invites the local physician, Mr Gibson, to try it
in honour of his second-born son, Roger, who has been chosen to lead a
prestigious scientific expedition to Africa:

> You must have a glass full. It's old ale, such as we don't brew now-a-
> days. It's as old as Osborne. We brewed it that autumn and we called
> it the young Squire's ale. I thought to have tapped it on his marriage
> but I don't know when that will come to pass, so we've tapped it now
> in Roger's honour.' The old Squire had evidently been enjoying the
> young Squire's ale to the verge of prudence. It was indeed, as he said,
> 'as strong as brandy', and Mr Gibson had to sip it very carefully as he
> ate his cold roast beef.

Strong beers were enjoyed, again, by Georgian workers as well as the
gentry. Among the drinks mentioned in the *Vade Mecum for Malt-
Worms*, the rhyming 'good pub guide' to London written about 1718,
are 'Humming Stingo' at the Peacock in Whitecross Street; October at
the Fountain in Cheapside; Bull's Milk Beer at the Bull in Wood Street;
and Burton Ale at the Guy of Warwick in Milk Street. This last beer
was probably the same as or similar to the nut-brown, sweet, extremely
strong ale that brewers in Burton upon Trent were exporting to Baltic
cities such as St Petersburg and Danzig, Riga and Königsberg from at
least the 1740s. This trade lasted, with hiccups during the Napoleonic
Wars, until the Russians imposed heavy tariffs on beer imports from
Britain in 1822 and the Burton brewers turned to brewing paler, more
bitter beers for the Indian market.

However, the Burton breweries continued making darker, sweeter
beers at a range of strengths, the strongest being around 1110 OG, and
10–11 per cent abv (the top-of-the-range Burton ales were generally
known as Number One, as they were at the Bass, Ind Coope and Truman
breweries in Burton, though Worthington, in typically perverse fashion,
called its best strong ale 'G'). These were beers with astonishing longevity;

the Ratcliff Ale, a version of Bass's No 1 strong ale brewed and bottled in 1869 to celebrate the birth of a son, Harry Ratcliff, to one of the company's partners, is still drinkable today, 140 years on. After surviving unopened for the whole of the twentieth century in bottles in the cellars at the brewery in Burton, the beer is now completely dry, with a flavour like a cross between sherry and smoky Christmas pudding.

The Burton brewers occasionally reproduced beers of the strength of the kind once exported to the Baltic, for Arctic explorers to take with them. Alfred Barnard, on his trip to Samuel Allsopp & Sons in Burton in 1889, wrote that 'the celebrated "Arctic ale" of which we have heard so much in days gone by' was specially brewed at the request of the government for the five-ship Arctic expedition in 1852–54 under Sir Edward Belcher (which was looking for Sir John Franklin's famous lost expedition of 1845). Belcher reported that the ale was 'a valuable antiscorbutic' (that is, scurvy-preventer) and 'a great blessing to us, particularly for our sick, as long as it lasted' and that it refused to freeze until the temperature dropped to twelve degrees Fahrenheit, or minus eleven degrees Celsius. Even when the temperature went down to minus fifty-five Fahrenheit (minus forty-eight Celsius) the beer was unharmed by being frozen, Belcher said.

It was brewed again for the 1875 Arctic expedition under Sir George Nares, which set out to reach the North Pole and managed to get to within 400 miles of the top of the world before scurvy forced the men, by now on sleds, to retreat, four of them dying. Nares wrote of the beer in February 1875: 'Excellent. Would recommend as large a quantity as can possibly be stowed away to be supplied to every future voyage.' The expedition's senior medical officer wrote to Allsopp's that it 'kept splendidly in the Arctic region, and the fact of its freezing did not appear to detract from its good qualities in any way. It was highly appreciated by the men'.

Barnard was disappointed to find there was none of the 1852 vintage left, but he tried the 1875 version, then fourteen years old, and 'found it of a nice brown colour, and of a vinous, and at the same time, nutty flavour, and as sound as on the day it was brewed'. He wrote that it 'did not show a very high alcoholic content', though the OG was all of 1130, about 47lb of extract per barrel, and an analysis in 1881, he said, 'proved that it contained not much more than about nine per cent alcohol by weight' (though since this is 11.25 per cent abv it sounds about right) and 'owing to the large amount of unfermented extract still remaining in it, it must be considered as an extremely valuable and nourishing food'. For comparison, William Molyneux writing in 1869 said the ale brewed for the old Russian trade varied from 42–48lb of extract to the barrel, while the brewery's 'normal' strong ale in the 1860s only went up to 42lb, an OG of 1116.7.

The Arctic Ale was, again, a long-lasting brew. William Henry Beable, writing in *Romance of Great Businesses*, said 'favoured visitors' to Allsopp's brewery in Burton upon Trent were 'sometimes invited to taste a bottle of ale similar to the celebrated "Arctic Ale" supplied to the Polar expedition of 1875' (i.e. fifty years earlier). Beable said of the beer: 'It is mellow as old Burgundy and as nourishing as a beefsteak.'

Some time in the 1930s, after the big merger with its Burton neighbour Allsopp of 1934, Ind Coope renamed its No 1 Burton Barley Wine Allsopp's Arctic Ale. The beer returned to the polar regions in 1952 when cases went off with that year's British North Greenland Expedition. However, while contemporary advertising in the 1950s called Arctic Ale a barley wine, *The Book of Beer* by Andrew Campbell, described it as 'less sweet than a barley wine', suggesting that fifty years ago not everybody put all strong ales in the barley wine category.

Arctic Ale appears in an Ind Coope price list of 1959 at a public bar price of 1s 5½d a 'nip' bottle, that is, one third of a pint. However, it looks as if Arctic Ale was no longer as strong as it used to be, because Colne Spring Ale, which had an OG of 1093, was a third dearer at 1s 11½d the nip (a pint of bitter, for comparison, was 1s 3d, three and a half times cheaper per fluid ounce). By 1961, the beer's name had changed to Arctic Barley Wine. It was still being brewed in 1965, but the brewery knocked it on the head a few years after that.

Arctic Ale and other super-strong English 'stock' ales were brewed to lie in wooden casks or vats for at least a year, often longer, where they would be worked on by *Brettanomyces*-type yeasts lurking in the wood, which took over from the standard brewing yeasts to consume the more complex sugars found in quantity in strong beer worts. Indeed, 'Brett' yeasts were first isolated by the Danish brewing scientist Niels Hjelte Claussen in or just before 1903 from an English 'stock beer', in the Carlsberg brewery's laboratory in Copenhagen and the name that Claussen gave them honours their origins: *Brettanomyces* literally means 'British fungus', as *Saccharomyces*, the name given to the standard brewing yeast, means 'sugar fungus'. Other types of *Brettanomyces* yeast were later found in Belgian lambic beers and aged Guinness stout.

While wine makers regard *Brettanomyces* as a defect to be avoided, loathing the 'farmyard' aromas that it delivers, British brewers, after Claussen's research, believed the yeast type was essential to give strong stock beer its correct flavour, which, they were told, could not be produced by the standard brewing yeast, *Saccharomyces cerevisiae*. To quote from Wahl and Henius' *American Handy Book of the Malting and Brewing Trades*, 1908 edition:

> The secondary fermentation of English stock beers – as shown by Claussen in 1904 [sic] – is entirely different from what is called secondary fermentation of American or European beers ... [it is] due, not to a genuine *Saccharomyces*, but to a certain torula, called *Brettanomyces* by its author ... forming large quantities of acidic and ethereal substances, thus producing the typical flavor of the English stock beers ... A pure cultivated yeast cannot produce the flavor that is characteristic to stock or ale or stout, and is due exclusively to the action of *Brettanomyces*. [To make the secondary fermentation more reliable and predictable] Claussen recommends the addition of cultures of *Brettanomyces* to bring about the secondary fermentation.

Colne Spring Ale, for one, was deliberately infected with 'Brett' yeast in its production. The Watford brew had a massive reputation; Alfred Barnard, who visited Benskin's brewery in 1890, said of it: 'Never was there a more delicious beverage than this ... full flavoured, soft, creamy yet vigorous.' The journalist Maurice Gorham, writing in 1949, called Colne Spring 'the joy of connoisseurs' and said the licensees of Benskin's pubs were not supposed to serve more than four bottles of Colne Spring to any one customer – 'and four bottles is quite enough'.

Andrew Campbell wrote in 1956 that Colne Spring Ale 'is probably the strongest of all the commercially bottled ales available in Britain today. Matured for seven years, it is dark [thirty-seven on the Lovibond scale, as dark as Benskin's Nut Brown Ale], mellow, and pours like wine, very slightly carbonated. It is rich and luscious in flavour, in no way edulcorated [sweetened] ... beer that should be treated with the very greatest respect'. Its restorative powers were legendary. A Colne Spring and an aspirin would cure any cold, it was said, while sick Benskin's drayhorses were given a pint a day. The beer survived the takeover of Benskin's by Ind Coope in 1957, albeit in pasteurised form rather than, as before, bottle-conditioned. But even so, a fifty-year-old Ind Coope bottling opened recently was still perfectly drinkable and extremely powerful, its flavour hinting at what a great beer it once had been. The last brewing of Colne Spring Ale was made in February 1970, two years before the Watford brewery itself closed.

Benskin's Colne Spring
Ale, matured for seven
years and 'the joy of
connoisseurs'

The lengthy ageing of strong ales was widespread among commercial brewers in Victorian Britain. Alfred Barnard in his tours of British breweries around 1889–90 tried two-year-old KK strong old ale at Hanley's City brewery, Oxford, and found it 'in splendid order ... very luscious'. When he visited Thomas Berry & Co. in Sheffield he found the brewery still selling its Jubilee stock ale, brewed two years earlier for Queen Victoria's golden jubilee, which 'on examination ... proved to be of a very high quality'.

At W.J. Rogers's Jacob Street brewery in Bristol, Barnard saw a huge cellar dug out of the red sandstone beneath the premises, containing thirty beer vats, each twenty or so feet high. They were filled with maturing 'Bristol Old Beer', some of it up to three years old and none allowed to leave until at least eighteen months after its brewing. The brewery manager, Mr Clifford, told Barnard that 'to a large extent' West of England drinkers 'will only drink old beer', hence the need for so many vats of ageing beer.

A rival Bristol brewer, George's, was still brewing old beer and maturing it for at least a year in huge oak vats ('some of the largest in the world') just before the Second World War. Brewing of these West

Country vatted strong ales always began in the autumn, using a mixture of old and new malts, often a 'high-dried' English malt with plenty of colour mixed with a mild ale malt. The *Brewers' Journal* in 1936 was advising that such strong stock ales 'of 30lb gravity and upwards' (that is, OGs of around 1085 or more) should go through two or three secondary fermentations in cask before being bottled after nine to twelve months not fully worked out, but still 'in slight "creamy" condition'.

The West Country old beers were one of several different traditions of strong ales. Another was the 'college' ale made in the breweries attached to colleges at the universities of Oxford and Cambridge, one of which, at Queen's College, Oxford, ran until the early 1950s. In the 1930s the Queen's College Brewery made two beers, College Ale, at 25lb gravity (around 1068 OG) and the thumping Chancellor's Ale, still brewed, at least in the 1920s, at an amazing 50lb gravity, or around 1135 OG. This was weaker, it appears, than in the past; Alfred Barnard in 1890 was told the Chancellor was brewed at sixteen bushels of malt to the barrel, which would have given an OG of as much as 1230. He drank the 1884 brewing, then six years old, declaring that 'two wine-glasses would intoxicate a man' and if thrown on a fire it would (allegedly) 'flare up like whisky'. Even in the 1920s it was made, in the old tradition, only in March and October, stored for a year in upright casks and passed around among fellows and scholars on special occasions in the Hall in a two-handled silver mug. Despite (or perhaps because of) its high OG, the 1920s beer only fermented down to around 1053 OG, with just under 8.5 per cent alcohol by weight or 10.6 per cent abv and it must have been very sweet.

Other famous college beers included the audit ales brewed at Trinity College and Jesus College, Cambridge. As its name suggests, this was originally to drink at the feast celebrating the end of the annual audit or examination of the college accounts by the fellows, but it was later made for consumption at other times. Another was the Archdeacon ale of Merton College. Oxford, brewed in the sacristy of the college chapel when George Saintsbury was a student there in the 1860s and served regularly at cheese time 'in proper beer-glasses, like the old "flute" champagnes'. The audit ale brewed at All Souls Oxford was 'served in small round silver cups with the cheese', where the brewery was still running in 1890. Audit ale was sometimes drunk warm, at least according to Sir George Otto Trevelyan, who wrote in 1869 of life at Trinity College, Cambridge that:

Filling a 'cleansing cask' from the fermenting vessel at the Queen's College brewery in Oxford in 1935; the strong beer would complete its fermentation in the cask

Connoisseurs treat audit ale like claret, and place it for a while in front of the fire: but the effect is seldom ascertained; for the corks, (such corks, at any rate, as fall to the portion of gentlemen *in statu pupillari*,) almost invariably leap from the bottles and are followed by the best part of the ale.

However, when Barnard visited Oxford in 1890, several college breweries, including the well-known Brasenose brewhouse, which had brewed a strong Shrovetide ale just before Lent every year, had recently closed down and colleges were having their strong beers brewed by commercial brewers. Mitchells & Butlers in Birmingham brewed College Ale and Audit Ale for several Oxford colleges until the 1950s and Dales of Cambridge made Audit Ale for Pembroke College, while Lacons of Great Yarmouth, which acquired a couple of breweries in Cambridge in the 1890s supplied Audit for Trinity in the late 1920s, at 8 per cent abv. Lacon's supplied other Cambridge colleges with audit ale as well, including, it appears, Corpus Christi, St Catharine's, Trinity Hall, Jesus and St John's. However, Greene King, which owned a brewery in Cambridge, brewed Trinity's Audit Ale in the 1950s, while around the same time Wells & Winch of Biggleswade gave St John's, Cambridge, its Audit Ale.

Other regional varieties of strong ale included Yorkshire Stingo, which Alfred Barnard in 1890 found being brewed by John Metcalfe & Son at the Nidderdale brewery in Pateley Bridge, and Joshua Tetley in Leeds, where he found it 'very luscious, full of body and well flavoured without being heady'. Yorkshire Stingo was registered by Samuel Smith's brewery of Tadcaster as a trademark in 1891 and is still a registered Smith's mark. The Yorkshire Stingo brewery, however, was in the Marylebone Road, London. It was taken over by Watney Combe Reid in 1907 and Watney's continued brewing a dark Stingo barley wine ('semi-sweet and malty, it is a powerful and respected drink,' Andrew Campbell said in 1956) until it vanished in the 1990s.

Other brewers of Stingo outside Yorkshire included Adey and White of St Albans until its closure in 1936 and the Northampton brewery Co., which was selling 'Imperial Stingo' in 1878 for 2s a gallon, a third more expensive than its XXXX Strong Ale and with an implied gravity of 1110 or more. NBC's Stingo survived through to the 1950s (albeit at a rather lower gravity), by which time it was being canned; in 1954 the brewery sent 100 cartons of cans of Stingo to British troops serving in Korea.

Another northern strong beer style was Old Tom, found in 1890 by Alfred Barnard at Smith's Don brewery in Sheffield (he called it 'a rich, full-bodied drink and a great favourite with the Sheffield grinders') and also brewed, among others, by the Tadcaster Tower brewery in the 1890s (when its price, 30s a kilderkin, suggested an OG around 1080) and the Oldham brewery. Old Tom may have taken its name from Old Tom gin, a sweeter style of spirit than London dry gin. However, 'Old something' was always a popular name for strong beers as an indication that they had been properly aged. Duttons of Blackburn brewed Old Ben on draught, which was bottled as OBJ, short for 'O Be Joyful'; Warwick & Richardsons of Newark had 'Ole Bill', named for the First World War cartoon character and sold in the 1930s at 9d a nip when mild was just 4½d a pint; Wadworth's of Devizes had Old Timer; Youngs Crawshay of Norwich brewed Old John; and Young & Co. of Wandsworth brewed Old Nick, to list just a few. Sometimes brewers wanted to show a beer was even stronger than Old Tom; Beverley Brothers' Eagle brewery in Wakefield registered the trademark Old Tom's Grandfather in 1890.

Analysis by Dr Keith Thomas of the University of Sunderland of brewing records from Hammonds' brewery in Bradford, Yorkshire, in 1903 shows that Old Tom, XXXX, was brewed by Hammonds at an original gravity of 1071 using just under 70 per cent pale malt, 15 per cent maize (probably to keep protein levels down and make for clearer bottling), slightly less than that invert sugar and a tiny amount, less than 1 per cent, of black malt for colour. The final gravity was relatively low, with an abv of around 7.5 per cent and the amount of hops used indicates a bitterness of a high 72 IBU. Dr Thomas suggests this was a pale, dry, bitter, astringent old ale with a strong ester character.

Hammonds also brewed a stronger XXXXX Stingo, using 82 per cent pale malt and 18 per cent glucose, with the wort boiled for three hours to concentrate it and give it more colour, an OG of 1100 and an abv of 9.5. The quite high final gravity of 1027, suggesting a sweet beer, would have been balanced by the massive amount of hops used, which may have given a bitterness level as high as 119. This, Dr Thomas suggests, was a classic barley wine, with an aftertaste that was likely to be richly hoppy and bitter, and an estery and alcoholic background from the high gravity fermentation. As he says: 'One can only speculate on its complexity.'

One mysterious, and now lost aged Yorkshire strong ale style is Australian ale, which seems to have been a speciality of Sheffield's brewers in Victorian times. Bradley & Co. of the Soho brewery, Sheffield, for example, sold No 3 Australian Strong Ale in 1870 at 1*s* 8*d* a gallon, implying an OG of 1080 or more, and H.J. Dearden's High House brewery, Hillfoot, Sheffield, sold Bushman in 1888 in bottle and cask. When Alfred Barnard visited Marrian's Burton Weir brewery in Sheffield in 1890 he was handed 'a sample of Australian beers four years old, which we found very delicious but far too strong for our Cockney taste'.

Barnard commented that the brewery's founder, Thomas Marrian, had built up 'an extensive trade in the Colonies, where his beer gained a great reputation, and commanded the highest price in the market'. Thomas Berry, of the Moorhead brewery, Sheffield, also 'at one time did a large export trade to the Cape, Australia and New Zealand', Barnard wrote, and it looks as if Sheffield brewers may have devised a strong, well-aged beer designed to appeal to the Antipodean market. However, its specific characteristics do not appear to have been recorded.

Scotland had its own strong ale style known as 'wee heavy', a more powerful version of the country's pale bitter or 'heavy' ales, normally dark tan in colour and with a touch of caramel sweetness.

Despite the depressing effect the high taxes of the First World War and after gave to beer strengths in Britain, most, perhaps all, brewers in the 1920s and 1930s still made a strong ale, even if it had to be sold at twice the price or more of standard draught beer. Some brewed two strong beers; Steward & Patteson of Norwich introduced BK Stingo at 1070 OG in 1922 and Norfolk Nips barley wine at 1083 OG in 1929.

But perhaps the heyday of barley wines was, oddly, the 1950s and 1960s, when in a reaction to the austerity of the Second World War, brewers began to introduce new, often pale-coloured very strong beers.

One of the first was Gold Label 'sparkling barley wine', 10.9 per cent abv, from Tennants of Sheffield, which came out in 1951 to sit alongside its darker Tennants' No 1 barley wine and which entered the Guinness Book of Records as the strongest regularly-brewed, nationally distributed beer in Britain.

When Tennants was acquired by Whitbread in 1961, Gold Label, sold in nips, was advertised as 'strong as a double Scotch and half the price', another old beer slogan that would not be allowed today. After a peripatetic existence, including being brewed in Luton at one point, Gold Label is still sold today.

A survey in 1956 found almost seventy different barley wines and strong ales being brewed in Britain, including Kentish Fire from Thomson & Wotton in Ramsgate; Dragon's Blood from Flowers of Luton and Stratford-upon-Avon; and Guards Ale from Hammonds. Several were available on draught, including Barclay Perkins' Winter Brew in London, Adnam's Tally Ho in Suffolk and William Younger's No 1 Strong Scotch Ale in Scotland. By 1972, however, after the brewery take-overs of the 1960s, Frank Baillie could record only forty very strong ales still being brewed, not counting the national brews such as Whitbread's Final Selection (originally Chairman's Selection, since it had, literally, been selected by the company chairman from a choice of beers presented to him by his brewers in the boardroom) and Watney's Export Gold, another pale barley wine.

This fall in numbers was despite the arrival of a couple of classics in the intervening decade and a half. Traquair House Ale, from the Scottish stately home of the same name, where the old family brewhouse reopened in 1965 with a 1075 OG, 7 per cent abv sweetish brew; and Thomas Hardy's Ale, an 1120 OG, 11.7 per cent abv bottle-conditioned beer originally made as a one-off by the Dorchester brewer Eldridge Pope, but subsequently carried on as a yearly event. One rare survivor was Greene King Strong Suffolk from the Bury St Edmunds brewer, at 6 per cent abv not particularly strong, but made from a blend of an aged 12 per cent abv ale called Old 5X, a proper English 'stock' ale stored for at least two years in unlined oak vats covered in Suffolk marl and a 5 per cent abv beer called BPA, or Burton Pale Ale (brewed to a typical Burton Ale recipe including crystal malts, caramel, and Special Brewing Sugar, a dark molasses-type sugar, for colour and extra flavour), in a ratio of just over 80 per cent BPA to just under 20 per cent 5X. Old 5X is not, alas, sold on its own (though lucky visitors to the brewery are sometimes offered a glass), but is also blended into Greene King's 6.9 per cent abv

St Edmund barley wine and with Old Speckled Hen pale ale in bottle to make a stronger beer than the 'ordinary' Hen.

A similar practice was used by Truman, Hanbury & Buxton of London and Burton to make its barley wine. A stock ale was brewed at the company's Burton brewery to an OG of around 1120, matured and then shipped in cask down to Truman's Brick Lane brewery in the East End, where it was blended with a 'runner' ale brewed in Brick Lane at around 1065 OG. The blending rate, at least in the 1960s, according to Derek Prentice, a former Truman's brewer, depended on the final abvs of the constituent brews but aimed at an abv for the bottled product of about 8–9 per cent.

The new brewers of Britain's microbrewery revolution largely ignored barley wines at first, preferring to produce bitters and pale ales. This was mostly because the demand did not seem to be there for very strong draught beers and few had bottling equipment. Even in 1988, the writer Brian Glover found only twenty or so of the 140-odd new small brewers then in existence made a beer that was 1065 OG or above. These included Woodforde's Head Cracker from Norfolk (a link back to Lattimore's) at 1069 OG, Blackout, 1100 OG, from the Big Lamp brewery in Newcastle upon Tyne, and the infamous Roger & Out from the Frog & Parrot brewhouse in Sheffield, at 1125 OG and 16.9 per cent alcohol and sold only in one-third pints, a challenger to the Chancellor's Ale of years past.

The big boost to modern British barley wine production came in 1995, however, when Chris Norman of the then only two years old Cottage brewery in West Lydford, Somerset, won the Champion Beer of Britain award at the Great British Beer Festival with his 1066 OG, 7 per cent abv Norman's Conquest draught strong ale. The resultant boost to sales led to the brewery moving to new premises and twice increasing capacity from ten barrels to thirty and it now supplies more than 1,500 outlets.

Outside Britain, barley wines were uncommon. The Irish brewer, Smithwick's of Kilkenny, made, at least until recently, a beer under the name, though at 4.5 per cent alcohol it was far too weak to be a proper barley wine. The South Australian Brewing Co. of the West End brewery in Adelaide made a 'West End Barley Wine' in the early 1970s, advertised as 'For the spirit drinker who likes the taste of a Good Strong Ale!' In the United States, the Anchor Steam brewery of San Francisco began brewing a barley wine in 1975 called Old Foghorn, inspired by English barley wines, 8.7 per cent abv but more heavily hopped, with hops left in the maturation vessels as the beer ages. Old Foghorn went on itself to inspire a fleet of barley wines from America's new small brewers, including the extremely hoppy Big Foot from Sierra Nevada.

Today, while Bass No 1 can no longer be called Bass, because that trademark now belongs to the multinational brewer AB InBev, Coors, the current owner of the old Bass brewery, still brews No 1 in Burton upon Trent in the former experimental brewery now known as the White Shield brewery. Thomas Hardy ale is still brewed in the West Country, albeit at the O'Hanlon brewery in Devon. Another classic strong mature beer, Gale's Prize Old Ale, perhaps the last authentic aged old ale made in Britain, dark and sour-sweet, has been given a new life after production moved from Horndean, Hampshire to Fuller's brewery in west London.

The beer is kept in vats for at least twelve months before bottling so that the different micro-organisms that supply the complex flavours can do their work properly. Fuller's tankered the last batch of Prize Old Ale to be brewed at Gales' brewery before it closed up to its own brewery in Chiswick to be matured, and it guaranteed the continuance of the original microflora and microfauna that worked on the beer by saving forty hectolitres of the Gales' brewed Prize Old Ale to add to the first batch of Prize Old Ale to be brewed in Fuller's, with forty hectolitres saved from that to help mature the next brew and so on, like a sherry solera. Sadly, the beer is no longer bottle-conditioned as it was at Gales, and nor does it come in cork bottles, but the consensus is that Prize Old Ale is now better than it has been for years, tart as a Belgian lambic ale and marvellous with food.

Fuller's already made a highly regarded strong beer for laying down, Vintage Ale, at 8.5 per cent abv, which first appeared in 1997 as a bottle-conditioned version of its Golden Pride pale barley wine and which has shown that it can easily survive and be excellent drinking for at least ten years. Meanwhile, though strong beers are still not common from Britain's brewers, events such as the Campaign for Real Ale's winter ales festival, which has thrown new attention on old-style brews such as Robinson's 8.5 per cent abv Old Tom, are encouraging small brewers to have a barley wine in the line-up. Modern barley wines include brews such as the Hogs Back brewery of Surrey's well regarded 9 per cent abv A over T, which the brewer insists stands for Aromas over Tongham (its home village) and not how you will fall if you have too much.

12

HERB AND
FLAVOURED ALES

Whether Scurvy-grass, Daucus, Gill, Butler, or Broom,
Or from London, or Southwark, or Lambeth we come;
We humbly implore since the Wine in the Nation,
Has of late so much lost its once great Reputation;
That such Liquor as ours which is genuine and true,
And which all our Masters so carefully brew,
Which all men approve of, tho' many drink Wine,
Yet the good Oyl of Barly there's none will decline:
That we as a body call'd corp'rate may stand,
And a Patent procure from your Seal and your Hand,
That none without Licence, call'd Special, shall fail,
To drink any thing else, but Strong Nappy Brown Ale.

The Bacchanalian Sessions: or The Contention of Liquors, Richard Ames
(1643–1693)

The Dr Butler's Head tavern in Mason's Avenue, near Moorgate in the
City of London, is an oblique reminder that pubs still sold ales flavoured
in the old way, with herbs and plants from fields, woods and moors, for
hundreds of years after hopped beers were first brewed in this country.

'Doctor'William Butler (he failed to qualify as an M.D., though he was
court physician to King James I), who died in 1618, invented a medicinal 'purging' ale containing seven different herbs and roots, described in
1680 as 'an excellent stomack drink' which 'helps digestion, expels wind,
and dissolves congealed phlegm upon the lungs, and is therefore good
against colds, coughs, ptisical and consumptive distempers; and being
drunk in the evening, it moderately fortifies nature, causeth good rest,

and hugely corroborates the brain and memory.' Pubs bearing his image on the signboard, like the one in Mason's Avenue, were advertising that they sold Dr Butler's Ale – there were at least two other Butler's Heads in London, including one in Telegraph Street, the other side of Moorgate, which only closed in the late 1990s.

Eighteenth-century recipes for the doctor's purging ale called for betony (a bitter grassland plant), sage, agrimony (a wayside plant popular in herbal medicine), scurvy-grass, Roman wormwood (less potent than 'regular' wormwood but still bitter), elecampane (a dandelion-like bitter plant still used in herbal cough mixtures) and horseradish to be mixed and put in a bag which should be hung in casks of new ale while they underwent fermentation.

Dr Butler's Ale was still being sold at the Fleece in Leadenhall Market, London around 1718, but the drink seems to have vanished by the mid-1780s. It disappeared as part of a general decline in herb beers evidently caused by the passing of an Act of Parliament in 1711 imposing a one penny a pound tax on hops, at the same time banning the use of 'broom, wormwood, or other bitter ingredient (to serve instead of hops) in brewing or making any ale'. The Act's stated reason for banning bitter herbs from brewing was because 'it had been found by experience that hops used in the making of malt drinks were more wholesome for those that drink the same and of greater advantage to the drink itself than any other bitter ingredient that can be used'. In reality, of course, the ban was to protect the royal revenues by ensuring brewers used taxed hops rather than untaxed herbs.

The only let-out was that the Act allowed retailers to infuse broom and wormwood in ale or beer (the two still being seen as separate drinks, the beer well-hopped, the ale not) 'after it is brewed and tunned, to make it broom or wormwood ale or beer'. The inference is that at this time broom and wormwood were the two most popular flavourings besides hops. Broom, *Cytisus scoparius* (or *Sarothamnus scoparius*), is found everywhere in the British Isles except for Orkney and Shetland and the young green tops of the plant were probably regularly used in season to give a bitter flavour to ale. Among the bitter compounds found in broom is sparteine, a narcotic alkaloid which can cause hallucinations in very large doses and probably caused enhanced merriment even at low doses.

It is notable that many of the herbs once used to flavour ale contain psychotropic or intoxicating ingredients and this is certainly true of wormwood, most famous for being the herb in the original form of absinthe that gave the spirit its notorious hallucinatory effect.

Dr Butler, whose medicinal ale, sold at pubs bearing his head on their sign, contained seven different plants and herbs

Wormwood (*Artemisia absinthium*) is a silver-leaved plant with yellow flowers, around two feet high, found on waste ground. It contains thujone, an addictive narcotic, which will induce hallucinations at high doses, which is why absinthe with wormwood in was banned in France and other countries around the time of the First World War. It also contains absinthin, described by Stephen Harrod Buhner as 'perhaps the bitterest substance known'.

Not much contemporary evidence survives on what herbs were used to flavour and preserve ale in the British Isles before the arrival of hops early in the fifteenth century. There is actually a strong argument for saying no herbs at all were used in much medieval English ale. In Norwich in March 1471 the 'common ale brewers of this citi', who were in competition with the beer brewers and evidently copying their ingredients, were ordered by the mayor and council not to brew 'nowther with hoppes nor gawle [sweet gale or bog myrtle] nor noon other thing … upon peyne of grevous punysshment'. In 1483 the London ale brewers, again trying to maintain the difference between (unhopped) ale and (hopped) beer, persuaded the city authorities to rule that in order for ale to be brewed in 'the good and holesome manner of bruying of ale of old tyme used', no one should 'put in any ale or licour [water] whereof ale shal be made or in the wirkyng and bruying of any maner of ale any hoppes, herbes or other like thing but only licour, malt and yeste'. London and Norwich ale, then at least in the late fifteenth century, seem to have been herb-free.

Not quite sixty years later, in 1542, the writer and physician Andrew Boorde agreed that ale was made of malt and water only and anyone who added 'any other thynge' except 'yest, barme or godesgood [all synonyms for yeast] doth sofysticat theyr ale' – using 'sophisticate' in its original meaning of 'adulterate'.

In continental Northern Europe, in contrast, the use of herbs by medieval brewers is well recorded. This is because from at least the ninth century the state authorities in *bier*-making areas seized the exclusive right to supply herbs to brewers. They used the enforced sale of flavouring and preserving herbs to brewers as a revenue source and a *de facto* tax on brewing. This never happened in the British Isles; in England the authorities found a different way to raise money from the brewers, through 'fines' for allegedly breaking the assize (the regulations covering the brewing and sale of ale), the fines becoming England's own *de facto* local brewing tax.

The herbal mix supplied to brewers in Germany and the Low Countries was known, in a variety of spellings, as *grout*, *gruit* or *grute*, sometimes (in Dutch) *kruyt*. These are all expressions that appear to be connected etymologically with the German and Dutch words meaning herbs, *Kraut* and *kruid*, and, more closely, with words such as grits and groats (*Grütze* in German, *grutten* in Dutch).

The etymology indicates the herbs were probably mixed with ground grain before being sold to the brewers. This was possibly to disguise exactly what plants went into the mixture and prevent anybody duplicating it. The right to supply *gruit* was sometimes 'privatised', sold off by the authorities to individual families, some of whom took the name of their new profession as their family name, giving the surnames Grüter in Germany and de Grutere in Flanders.

The recipe for *gruit* must have varied depending on the area and what plants were available locally. However, the herbs most commonly used are generally accepted to be the moorland bush sweet gale, *Myrica gale*, also known as bog myrtle, *Porst* in German and *pors* in the Scandinavian languages; and yarrow, *Achillea millefolium*, a common grassland weed.

Yarrow has been called 'one of the most widely used herbs in the world', which would be a surprise to most British gardeners, who, if they notice this small, feathery-leaved green plant at all, curse it as an invader in their lawns. For pre-hop brewers it gave bitterness, a preservative effect (through the same antibacterial properties which brought it to the notice of herbal medicine practitioners) and, if the flowering plants were used, strong herby aromas. Its taste is described by one brewer as astringent and vaguely citrusy. It had a reputation in Scandinavia for making ale more potent, perhaps because it is said to contain thujone, like wormwood. Too much yarrow is claimed to cause dizziness and ringing in the ears, 'and even madness'.

Sometimes marsh rosemary or wild rosemary, *Ledum palustre*, which looks and smells rather like the sweet gale plant, was used in *gruit*, probably as a substitute for gale. However, two of the many names given to marsh rosemary in German, *Schweineporst*, 'pigs' gale', and *Falscher Porst*, 'false gale', indicate that it was seen as a poor alternative to true *Porst*. (In Norwegian it was called *Finnmark pors*, gale from Finnmark County, which also appears to be derogatory) This is not surprising; marsh rosemary is said to increase the effect of alcohol and, in large doses, causes headache, vertigo, restlessness, delirium and frenzy.

Modern reproductions of the *gruit* recipe regularly include marsh rosemary or wild rosemary, alongside sweet gale itself and yarrow, but this is almost certainly a mistake – sweet gale and marsh rosemary are rarely found growing in the same regions, and brewers who could get hold of gale would not have used its poorer alternative as well. In Britain it is a rare and possibly introduced plant and unlike gale it was never used by British brewers.

In Ireland bogbean or buckbean, *Menyanthes trifoliata*, was apparently a popular ale flavouring. Bogbean, a bitter-tasting pondside, fen and bog-land plant, is still used in herbal teas and even herbal cigarettes; it is said to stimulate the appetite and cure digestive disorders. It was bitter enough, thanks to the glucoside menyanthin, for nineteenth-century brewers to reckon one ounce was equal to eight ounces of hops.

Arguments continue about the sweetness of hopless ale, even without herbs; yeast does not tackle all the sugars in malt that efficiently, but as it aged the ale would have developed sharp, sour flavours, likely making it refreshing enough without having to add herbs. However, sufficient numbers of medieval and later references do exist to herbs and spices used in ales and beers in the British Isles to say different flavourings were at least sometimes part of the pre-hop tradition with local brewers.

One of the best-known mentions of flavourings for medieval English ale comes in William Langland's long poem *The Vision of Piers Plowman*, written in the late 1300s. In one section, Beton the brewster tempts Glutton away from his journey to church, where he was due to confess his sins: 'I have good ale,' she says, and Glutton, wavering, asks her if she has any 'hot spices' to hand. In the alliterative manner of much medieval and earlier English poetry, Langland wrote out Beton's reply: '"I have peper and piones [peony seeds]," quod she, "and a pound of garlice, A ferthyngworth of fenel-seed for fastyng-dayes."'

Beton's response to Glutton suggests her herbs and spices were added after the ale was brewed, at the time it was served. Pepper, especially 'long pepper', was a spice used in ale and bragget (honeyed ale) until the eighteenth century. Long pepper is made from the tiny berries, which merge to a single, long (compared to 'round' pepper) rod-like structure, that grow on *Piper officinarum* (from India) or *P. retrofractum* (from Indonesia). The flavour of long pepper is described by one writer as hot and warm, with sweet overtones; it contains more of the hot-tasting chemical peperine than common round pepper and others claim it to be stronger and bitterer than the round pepper we are familiar with today. The writer William Harrison in 1577 said that while his wife added 'arras' (either orris-root, the scented roots of various members of the iris family, or orache, *Atriplex patula*, a common British wild herb) and 'baiberries', berries of the bay laurel, to her beer, some 'add so much long peper only but … it is not so good'. Laurel berries were also used in fifteenth-century Dutch *gruit* ales.

Fennel seed was used to treat stomach cramps, which would have been useful if you were fasting and it was listed by the herbalist John Gerard *The Herball or General History of Plants*, published in 1597, as one of the ingredients in sage ale. It was also used in drinks 'to make people lean that are too fat', according to the seventeenth-century herbalist Nicholas Culpepper and, like yarrow, fennel contains small amounts of thujone. Peony seeds were recommended by herbalists as a cure for nightmares and garlic was good for people who had drunk 'corrupt and stinking waters', Culpepper wrote, which might be helpful if the brewster was no good.

As in continental Europe, bog myrtle or sweet gale, *gagellan* in Old English, was added to British ale; this heavily scented heathland shrub grows in wetlands throughout the British Isles. Sweet gale leaves give a strong, spicy, gingery, bitter, balsamic and astringent taste to ale and they will also add some antiseptic protection to the brew. A recipe in

Sweet gale or bog myrtle, one of the most popular pre-hop flavourings for ale

an Anglo-Saxon leechdom, or medical book, for a light drink for lung disease says to boil *gagellan* in wort and ferment it with new yeast, before adding other herbs. These were elecampane, *Inula helenium*, the same bitter plant with antiseptic properties used in Dr Butler's Ale; wormwood; betony; wild celery, *Apium graveolens*; and something called ontre, which may mean radish (adding to the similarity to the doctor's recipe).

In Yorkshire gale ale, leafy branches of bog myrtle were added to the hot wort. Calderbrook, near Littleborough in Lancashire, close to the border with Yorkshire has a pub, the Gale Inn, supposedly named for the plant's use in brewing, though sweet gale apparently no longer grows on the moors in the area and the pub is probably named after the nearby Gale Fell. There are at least three places in England named after bog myrtle or gale: Gailey, Staffordshire, 'grove overgrown with bog myrtle',

Galsworthy, Devon, 'bank or slope with bog myrtle' and Galton, Dorset, 'homestead where bog myrtle grows'.

Celtic herbalists used bog myrtle to treat depression because consuming it calmed the stressed and brought on a good mood. Viking warriors, on the other hand, according to some authorities, consumed large quantities of bog myrtle to bring on hallucinations and, literally, drive themselves berserk before battle. The Tudor cleric William Turner says of bog myrtle that 'it is tried by experience that it is good to be put into beare both by me and by diverse other in Summersetshyre'. However, John Gerard was more wary; he wrote that the fruit of bog myrtle 'is troublesome to the brain; being put into beere or aile while it is in boiling, it maketh the same heady, fit to make a man quickly drunk'.

Another popular herb with English brewers was ground-ivy, *Glechoma hederacea*, which was given the alternative name 'alehoof' because of its use in brewing (and its hoofprint-shaped leaves). It imparts a bitter, very strong, tannic flavour to ale (described by the herbalist and brewer Stephen Harrod Buhner as like black tea), but more importantly it helps fine the drink, clearing new ale overnight, according to Culpepper.

Ground-ivy, with its small, purple-blue flowers is a creeping plant common in woods and hedgerows all over the British Isles. It can be used as a salad herb and even cooked and eaten like spinach. The pre-Norman English cultivated ground-ivy and a recipe in an Anglo-Saxon leechdom distinguishes between the wild and cultivated or garden varieties. Another name for the plant, tunhoof, comes from tun meaning enclosure or garden rather than tun meaning cask. It was steeped in the hot liquor before mashing and it seems to have been a widely used plant in brewing ale, even after the arrival of hops. John Gerard said in 1597 that 'the women of our northern parts, especially Wales and Chesire, do turn Herbe-Alehoof into their ale'.

It was also called Gill-go-over-the-Ground and ale made with it was often called Gill ale, one of the five herb ales, along with Scurvy-grass, Daucus, Butler and Broom, listed by the late seventeenth-century poet Richard Ames in his *The Contention of Liquors*. Gill ale was being advertised on the signboard of the [Red?] Lion pub in Bird-Cage Alley, Southwark around 1722, 'Truly prepared and recommended by famed Doctor Bostock', Bostock being the pub's landlord.

Brewers also used the spicy, clove-scented bitter-tasting roots of common or wood avens or Herb Bennet (also known as colewort, wild rye and clove root), *Geum urbanum*, a common perennial plant whose yellow five-petalled flowers are also found in woodlands and hedgerows around Britain. The plant has antiseptic qualities, useful in helping ale to keep. 'Auence' is mentioned as one of several ingredients in a couple of East Anglian recipes for ale flavourings dated around 1430 from the Paston letters, a rare archive of letters and documents written between 1420 and 1504 by a well-to-do family from Norfolk:

> Pur faire holsom drynk of ale, Recipe sauge, auence, rose maryn, tyme, chopped right smal, and put this and a newe leyd hennes ey [egg] in a bage and hange it in the barell. Item, clowys, maces, and spikenard grounden and put in a bagge and hangen in the barell. And nota that the ey of the henne shal kepe the ale fro sour.

The second and spicier of those two recipes must have been an expensive treat if the spikenard meant to be used was the true 'nard', a pricey perfume made from the Himalayan plant *Nardostachys jatamansi*. However, the recipe writer may have meant ploughman's-spikenard, *Inula conyzae*, an English perennial flowering plant found in scrubland whose roots have a strong, spicy aroma. John Gerard's 1597 recipe for sage ale also mentions spikenard as an ingredient, along with common British plants such as scabious and betony and this must be ploughman's-spikenard.

One plant that does not seem to have been used much in medieval ale is meadowsweet, *Filipendula ulmara*, a two to four-feet-high plant of meadows, fens and stream banks with heads of creamy-white, fragrant flowers. Pollen analysis suggests meadowsweet was a popular ingredient in ale in the Neolithic and Bronze Age periods. Experiments with brewing ale with meadowsweet by the Manchester University archaeologist Merryn Dineley show the plant will preserve the drink for several months. But its name in Old English was *medowyrt*, meadwort, showing it was associated with flavouring mead rather than ale. Gerard recommended meadowsweet as the best 'strowing herb', saying its scent 'makes the heart merrie and joyful and delighteth the senses'. Culpepper suggested putting a leaf of meadowsweet into a cup of claret, saying it gave 'a fine relish to it'. But neither suggested it could be used to flavour ale. It is, incidentally, the plant in which salicyclic acid, the basis for aspirin, was first found, in 1839.

Sometimes intoxicating herbs got into the beer by mistake. In September 1669 the authorities were being warned that a weed or grain growing among the oats and barley in the west of Scotland was making the local ale and beer so intoxicating that a gill, or quarter of a pint, 'will fuddle a man more than a gallon of other drink' and 'the very bread is making people fall asleep'. This weed 'is called roseger or in Latin *lolium*' – in modern English, darnel, *Lolium temulentum*, a wheat-like grassy plant which would malt well, but which was notorious for the strong intoxicating effect it had on those who consumed it.

Early in the seventeenth century, when (hopless) ale and (hopped) beer were still seen as separate drinks, the writer, self-publicist and waterman John Taylor undertook what he called his 'Penyless Pilgrimage' from London to Edinburgh, writing up his experiences in a book published in 1618. Stopping in Manchester, he stayed at the house of a man called John Pinners and recorded with delight that 'there eight several sorts of Ale we had/All able to make one starke drunk or mad'. Taylor was a defender of ale against hopped beer, which even in 1651 he called 'a Dutch boorish liquor … a saucy intruder into this land'. Listing the ales Pinners served, Taylor wrote:

> We had at one time set upon the table
> Good Ale of Hisope, 'twas not Esope fable:
> Then had we Ale of Sage, and Ale of Malt
> And Ale of Woorme-wood, that could make one halt,
> With Ale of Rosemary, and Bettony,
> And two Ales more, or else I needs must lye
> But to conclude this drinking Alye tale
> We had a sort of Ale called scurvy Ale

Observers will spot that Taylor's counting was as bad as his verse, since he tells us they had eight sorts of ale and lists nine, though he names only seven. One was plain malt ale (showing that unherbed ale could be found outside London) and six used named herbs. Looking at each:

Ale of Hisope: hyssop, *Hyssopus officinalis*, an aromatic, astringent, bitter herb, was used as a fining agent as well as a flavouring, like its fellow member of the *Labiatae* family, ground-ivy. It was also an ingredient in a cure for 'ropey' beer (beer suffering from a bacterial infection that left strings of jelly floating through it). In the British Isles hyssop is rare; it was brought here from Southern Europe.

Ale of Sage: sage, *Salvia officinalis*, is another immigrant to the British Isles from Southern Europe. Gerard's sixteenth-century Herball gave the ingredients for sage ale as sage, scabious (unspecified, probably any one of field, small or devil's bit), betony, 'Squinanth' (squinancywort, *Asperula cynanchica*, a relative of woodruff), spikenard and fennel seeds, but also described costmary as 'amongst those herbes wherewith they doe make Sage Ale …' At any rate, 'No man needs to doubt of the wholesomnesse of Sage Ale', Gerard declared. Another contemporary of Taylor said the sage should be 'tund up' (put into the cask) with the ale to release its flavour. Sir Hugh Platt, however, writing in 1609, recommended adding two or three drops of oil of sage to a quart of ale to make the best sage ale. Sage is, like hyssop and ground-ivy, a member of the *Labiatae* family; it has antiseptic qualities, which will help preserve ale. In addition, like several other herbs used in pre-hop brewing, sage contains thujone, which is probably responsible for the belief that sage leaves, flowers and seeds added to a vat of fermenting ale 'greatly increase inebriating quality'.

Ale of Wormwood: there is some debate over whether wormwood is a native to Britain or introduced from Southern Europe. The origin of the Germanic root word for wormwood, *werimuota*, is unknown; folk etymology has turned it into wormwood in English because it is very effective in getting rid of tapeworms and the like. Wormwood has been used to make bitter wine-based drinks since at least Roman times and its name is the origin of the word vermouth. Like yarrow, it is a member of the daisy family and it 'resists putrefaction', according to one writer, which would have helped preserve the ale. A little wormwood goes a long way in making bitter ale. Sir Hugh Platt, who dismissed hops as having only 'weak and feeble virtues' compared to wormwood, advised brewers in 1594 to test the bitterness of their wormwood by make up a decoction of four ounces of hops to nine gallons of water and then a decoction of wormwood leaves. By tasting and comparing the two, the amount of wormwood needed for a brew could be calculated. Dr William Y-Worth (or Yworth) in his *Cerevisiarii Comes or The New and True Art of Brewing*, also praised the plant, saying that hops did not have 'one half the vertues', but warned that 'one handful of Wormwood goes farther than three of other herbs, nay than five of some sort'.

Ale of Rosemary: *Rosmarinus officinalis* is, again, a Mediterranean herb now naturalised in the British Isles. The plant's oils have antioxidant and antiseptic properties, which would help preserve ale if rosemary was added to the wort. It was an ingredient in the Paston family's mid-fifteenth-century ale recipes. However, medieval ale-sellers sometimes merely added rosemary to a pot of ready-to-drink plain ale. In 1364 a London alewife called Alice Caustone was found guilty of deceiving drinkers by serving her ale in 'quart' vessels that had an inch and a half of pitch in the bottom (these must have been leatherjacks, mugs made from leather, which would normally be lined inside with a thin layer of pitch to keep them watertight); the shallowness of the containers was hidden by sprigs of rosemary placed on top of the pitch. The drinkers had to be used to seeing rosemary sprigs in their ale for the deception to have any chance of succeeding.

Ale of Bettony: the flowering spike covered in small magenta flowers and the basal leaves of *Betonica officinalis* or *Stachys officinalis*, were used by herbalists to cure headaches and prevent intoxication. The plant, a member of the dead-nettle family, like ground-ivy and also known as Bishopswort, has a spicy smell and a flavour expressed by the herbalist John Pechey in 1695 as 'hot, dry acrid and bitter' (though Gerard described the taste as 'sweet'). It contains tannins, essential oils, alkaloids and bitter compounds which give betony antiseptic qualities that would help ale to keep; it also has a reputation as a sedative. Betony is still widespread on grassland and heaths in England and Wales.

Scurvy ale: the leaves of scurvy-grass, *Cochlearia officinalis*, a relative of horseradish, are high in vitamin C and the plant, which grows mostly on salt marshes and seaside cliffs, was used by sailors as a treatment for scurvy before its place was taken by citrus fruit. An infusion of scurvy-grass leaves was also used as an end-of-winter tonic, a useful vitamin-dense restorative after months without fresh vegetables. Homemade scurvy-grass ale was probably made by many as a tonic; we know scurvy-grass or 'gittings' was put into the ale drank by the children of the Earl of Bedford at Woburn in Bedfordshire, because in April 1653 the family accounts show that a man called John Morrice was paid 4*d* for gittings for the children's ale. The sharp, pungent aroma and acrid, bitter, salty taste are not liked by everyone and the late seventeenth-century beer writer Thomas Tryon warned that it should never be fermented into beer as this gave 'a very strong, fiery, brimstony spirit'.

Just over seventy years after Taylor's ale-filled stay in Manchester, Tryon, in his *A New Art of Brewing Beer, Ale, and Other Sorts of Liquors*, declared there were 'a great number of brave Herbes and Vegitations that will do the business of brewing, as well as hops, and for many Constitutions much better, for 'tis custom more than their real virtues that renders

Hops of general Use and Esteem'. Tryon went on to list specifically a baker's dozen of dried herbs that could be added to ale, many of which were probably in use for flavouring ale long before hops arrived in Britain. Tryon had two favourite herbs in particular, which he called 'noble' herbs, of 'excellent' use in beer or ale:

Pennyroyal: *Mentha pulegium*, a small-leaved member of the mint family, with a bitter flavour and a pungent odour, which grows wild on the muddy edges of ponds. Tryon said it made 'brave, well-tasted Drink'; today, however, it is regarded as dangerously poisonous, not least because it can induce abortion. It is now an endangered species, known from only a dozen or so places.

Balm or Lemon-Balm: *Melissa officinalis*, another introduced herb from the eastern Mediterranean, and a relative of ground-ivy (as are the mints). It smells (as its alternative name indicates) of lemons. Tryon said it and pennyroyal 'naturally raise and cheer the drooping Spirits', and herbalists use balm to relieve stress, depression and anxiety. The apothecary John Parkinson, writing in 1629, indicated that balm should be 'steeped in Ale' to make 'a Baulme water'. Balm is one of the ingredients in Benedictine liqueur.

Three of Tryon's herbs, wormwood, betony and sage, were also used by Taylor's Manchester brewer, John Pinners. Tryon's other eight top herbs and plants for flavouring beer were mint; 'Tansie'; broom; 'Carduus'; 'Centuary' (centaury); eyebright; dandelion; and 'good hay'.

Mint: for Tryon, could have been any one of the fifteen or thereabouts varieties and hybrids of the plant that grows in Britain. Pre-hop brewers, if they used mint, probably brewed with the 'pleasantly aromatic' water mint, *Mentha aquatica*, a common wetland plant, which does not contain menthol oil; or the almost equally common corn mint, *M. arvensis*; or spearmint, *M. spicata*. They were less likely to use the menthol-flavoured cultivated peppermint, *M. x piperita*, a cross between water mint and spearmint; or garden mint, *M. viridis*. Water mint's scent was described by one writer as 'exactly that of a ropy chimney in a wet summer, where wood fires have been kept in wintertime', while corn mint, which grows, as you could guess, in arable fields, 'has a strong fulsome mixed smell of mellow apples and gingerbread'. The mints contain antioxidants and have antimicrobial qualities, which would help extend the life of mint ale.

Tansy: *Chrysanthemum vulgare* (or *Tanacetum vulgare*), a button-flowered wayside plant, has a taste described by the food writer Roger Phillips as 'strong, pungent and quite disgusting'. The fern-like leaves, smelling of camphor, were once used as a substitute for nutmeg and cinnamon when those spices were hugely expensive. They are very bitter and Tryon warned that 'when you infuse in your Beer or Ale Wormwood, Broom, Tansy, Carduus or any other herb which exceeds in bitterness, you ought not to let them lye in your Wort above half an hour, or if you put in a good quantity, a quarter of an hour will be enough'. Like yarrow and wormwood, two fellow members of the daisy family, tansy leaves contain large amounts of thujone and they also have a moderately high tannin content, while their volatile oils give antibacterial protection. However, it can be poisonous in large quantities and should not be ingested by pregnant women.

Broom: Maude Grieve, author of *A Modern Herbal*, published in 1931, said that shepherds had long known that sheep who ate broom became excited and then stupefied, 'but the intoxicating effects soon pass off'. Broom also contains tannins, which would help to preserve ale and make it taste more astringent.

Carduus: almost certainly meant the yellow-flowered, spiky-leaved, branching-stemmed hairy herb Culpepper called Carduus benedictus, blessed thistle, *Cnicus benedictus*, rather than any of the thistles in the modern botanical family *Carduus*. Three handfuls of dried 'Cardus [sic] Benedictus', meaning the stems and leaves, are among the eleven herbs and spices in a recipe from James Lightbody's *Every Man His Own Gauger* in 1695 for mum, a highly flavoured hopless wheat ale popular in Northern Europe, including Britain, from the fourteenth century to the eighteenth. Mum from 'Hamborough' (Hamburg) was described by one writer around 1720 as 'bitter as gall' and blessed thistle, which contains the bitter compound cnicin, is still used today to make bitter liqueurs. The plant has antiseptic qualities which would help preserve ale; however, large doses irritate the mouth, digestive tract and kidneys and may cause illness. It is a native of the Mediterranean and neighbouring parts of Asia.

Centaury: *Centaurium erythraea*, is a short, pink-flowered, five-petalled member of the gentian family found in grassy heaths and similar dry surroundings. The flowering stems are still used to add bitterness to herbal wines and liqueurs as they contain the bitter compounds gentiopicrin and erythrocentaurin.

Eyebright: *Euphrasia officinalis*, is a semi-parasitic low-growing plant of damp meadows, heaths and woods with a branched stem and small lobed white flowers. It contains tannins and bitter compounds and, as its name suggests, it was regarded by herbalists as very helpful for those with eye problems. Culpepper suggested that 'tunned up with Strong Beer' the juice of eyebright, when drank, has a 'powerful effect to help and restore the sight, decayed through age'.

Dandelion: *Taraxacum officinale*, is a weed loathed by gardeners because of its deep, difficult-to-remove roots. It is still used to make commercial soft drinks, notably dandelion and burdock, and home-made wines. Whole young plants are used, the leaves from older flowers being too harsh, with the main bitter compounds being called taraxacin and taraxacerin. Stephen Harrod Buhner says many herbalists claim dandelion tea has a slight narcotic effect and if this is true of dandelion beer too, this must have added to its attractions. Maude Grieve, in *A Modern Herbal*, said 'work-men in puddling furnaces and potteries in the Midland and Northern counties patronise the herb beers freely, Dandelion Stout ranking as one of the favourites' as a restorative after their hot, thirst-inducing labours. She added that dandelion stout 'is also made in Canada'.

Hay: cut and dried grass was probably originally put into the bottom of the mash tun around the tap to act as a filter to prevent sediment coming out with the wort; farmer-brewers in rural west Wales still used straw or a furze branch for the same purpose up to the early twentieth century. Hay contains coumarin, the glycoside which gives woodruff, *Galium odoratum*, its distinct hay-like flavour. An addition of green essence of woodruff is a feature in the serving of the wheat beer from Berlin, *Berliner Weisse*.

Other herbs and plants mentioned as ingredients in ale in the British Isles include:

Bayberry: otherwise sweet-oak, candleberry or wild myrtle, *Myrica cerifera*, evidently another poor substitute for its relative bog myrtle, being much fiercer in its effects. John Gerard wrote that 'the fruit is trouble-some to the braine being put into beere or ale whilst it is in boyling (which many use to do) it maketh the same headie, fit to make a man quickly drunke.'

Costmary: *Tanacetum balsamita.* As its Latin botanical name implies, this Asian plant is a more balsamic-flavoured relative of tansy. Its popularity as a flavouring ingredient in ale probably only dates from its introduction into Britain as a garden herb in the sixteenth century. John Gerard's *Herball* said that costmary 'is put into Ale to steepe, as also into the barrels and Stands amongst those herbes wherewith they doe make Sage Ale'. The name ultimately derives from the Sanskrit kustha, 'plant used as spice', plus Mary for St Mary; it was also known as alecost. The apothecary John Parkinson in 1629 said putting costmary in ale would 'cause it to have a good rellish, and to be somewhat physicall in the moneth of May'. Thomas Wright's *Dictionary of Obsolete and Provincial English*, published in 1851, said alecost was 'still used in the North' for putting into ale to flavour it, presumably by home-brewers rather than commercial ones.

Heather: both ling (*Calluna vulgaris*) and bell heather (*Erica cinerea*) were used to flavour ale before hops; see chapter 14.

Nettle: *Urtica dioica*, like its relatives the hop and the hemp, has been used for medicine, fibre, dye-making and fertiliser, as well as a beer ingredient and a foodstuff. Stephen Harrod Buhner describes nettle beer as 'one of the sublime herb beers. The taste really is indescribable, being a blend of a number of flavours, a veritable gustatory extravaganza'. I was lucky enough, in about 1996, to have a pint of what must be one of the very few ever commercially-produced draught nettle beers. It was made by one of the former Firkin chain of home-brew pubs in London (England) as a springtime one-off to a recipe supplied, as I recall, by the uncle of the brewer. It was a hop-free beer with a green, herby taste, very pleasant once you accepted it for what it was, but different enough that the bar person insisted anyone trying it for the first time had an initial small glass to see if they wanted to go on for more. Maude Grieve said one of the ingredients in traditionally made nettle beer was clivers, *Galium aparine*, also known as goosegrass.

Mugwort: *Artemisia vulgaris*, is sometimes said to get its name from its use in flavouring ale, but the 'wort' bit means 'plant' and is unconnected with brewing; and the 'mug' bit of mugwort means 'midge', small gnat-like insect, and is unconnected with 'mug', drinking vessel for beer.

However, Maude Grieve in *A Modern Herbal* said it was 'used to a great extent for flavouring beer before the introduction of hops. For this purpose, the plant was gathered when in flower and dried, the fresh herb being considered unsuitable for this object: malt liquor was then boiled with it so as to form a strong decoction, and the liquid thus prepared was added to the beer. Until recent years, it was still used in some parts of the country to flavour the table beer brewed by cottagers.'

Orris root: is made from the rhizome of one or another of several varieties of iris and was used by Elizabethan home brewers to give flavour to ales; orris has a violet scent and a slightly bitter flavour. In Britain the common or flag iris, *Iris germanica*, is an introduced garden species from the Mediterranean, which has now escaped to colonise railway banks and waste ground. Too much orris root can cause nausea and vomiting.

In addition to these regular ale-flavouring herbs and plants, herbalists from at least the Anglo-Saxon years have recommended their patients to drink all sorts of herbs in ale to cure different ailments. Around a hundred known old English 'cures' from around the tenth century involved herbs, roots and spices in ale. Six centuries later Nicholas Culpepper's recommendations for the sick included the juice of clary (*Salvia sclarea*, a close relative of sage) in ale or beer, which he said 'promotes the courses', while John Gerard prescribed the root of comfrey, *Symphytum officinale*, 'made in a posset of ale' for those suffering 'the paine in the back, gotten by any violent motion, such as wrestling, or overmuch use of women'.

While commercial brewers dropped flavouring ingredients other than hops, private brewers continued to use the huge variety of wild ingredients they had always put into their ales. *The London and Country Brewer* says that when hops were dear 'many of the poor People in this Country gather and dry in their Houses' daucus or wild carrot seed from the fields, which gave a 'fine Peach flavour or relish' to their beer.

Others, Ellis said, used 'that wholsome Herb Horehound, which indeed is a fine Bitter and grows on several of our Commons.' This was white horehound, *Marrubium vulgare*, 'extremely bitter' according to Buhner, rather than the nasty-smelling black horehound or Stinking Roger. Horehound is still used in herbal cough mixtures and was sometimes used in a 'beer for coughs'. The juice of horehound, according to Ellis, was also used to spruce up used hops and sell them to the gullible, when dried, as new.

Another herb used to cure coughs, coltsfoot or coughwort, *Tussilago farfara*, is said to have been used in Yorkshire to make cleats ale, cleats being the local name for the plant. However, no proper recipe seems to have survived for it, except the suggestion that nettles, dandelions and hops were also used. Coltsfoot is also known as foalfoot and this was one of the twenty-four ingredients in the 'yarb beer' (herb beer) brewed for the Garland Day celebrations on 29 May every year in Castleton, Derbyshire, in the nineteenth century. This, however, may be 'false colts-foot', *Asarum Europaeum*, otherwise known as wild nard, European wild ginger, and, tellingly, Public House Plant. Other ingredients in Castleton Garland Day beer (which was 'as black as black treacle' and 'good for the blood') included 'Robin-run-i'-t'-hedge' or ground-ivy.

Fruit beers, although much less common than herb beers, were also brewed for centuries. 'Rare' cherry beer was on sale at the Queen's Head, Middle Row, in the City of London in around 1718, presumably brought up from Kent. Elderberry beer is discussed in the 1744 edition of the *London and Country Brewer*. Beer made from the berries of the rowan or mountain ash, *Sorbus aucuparia*, was a Welsh favourite. John Evelyn (1620–1706) wrote in his *Sylva or Discourse on Forest Trees* in 1664: 'Ale and beer brewed with these berries, being ripe, is an incomparable drink, familiar in Wales, where this tree is reputed so sacred, that there is not a churchyard without one of them planted in.'

Ale was also made from the berries of the rowan's relative, the wild service tree, *Sorbus torminalis*. The tree's name is sometimes, wrongly, said to derive from *cervesia*, the Latin for ale; while its alternative name in the south of England, chequer tree, is sometimes supposed to come from it growing in the grounds of pubs called the Chequers; although four or five Chequers pubs in Kent and Sussex do have chequer trees associated with them, this is probably only a coincidence.

Although juniper grows wild in Britain and it is widely used in Scandinavian, especially Norwegian, home brewing traditions as a fla-vouring agent and also in France to brew beer with, British brewers do not seem to have gone for an ingredient more associated in this country with gin. However, one nineteenth-century English writer, John Claudius Loudon, author of the *Arboretum Et Fruticetum Britannicum: Or, The Trees and Shrubs of Britain*, did record that juniper berries:

> are used by the peasants, in some parts of France, to make a kind of
> beer, which is called *genevrette*. For this purpose, they take equal parts
> of barley and juniper berries, and, after boiling the barley about a

quarter of an hour, they throw in the juniper berries. They then pour the whole into a barrel half full of water, and bung it closely for two or three days; after which they give it air to promote fermentation. Some persons add molasses or coarse sugar, to make the liquor stronger. This beer is ready to drink in about a week, and it is bright and sparkling, and powerfully diuretic. Apples or pears, slightly crushed, are sometimes substituted for the barley; but the liquor thus made is apt to turn sour, or become vapid, in a short time.

Spruce beer, made from the fermented sap of the spruce, was on sale at the Angel and Sun in the Strand, London, in 1664. In 1785, the first year of *The Times*, the newspaper carried an advertisement for the New England coffee house in London, run by J. Newman, which offered, alongside Burton ale, wine, rum and brandy, 'American Spruce Beer in the highest Perfection', showing that two years after the end of the War of Independence, someone looks to have been exporting spruce beer from North America to London, presumably to cater for expatriate American drinkers.

Loudon in 1838 gave a recipe for American spruce beer of the sort sold in London, using black spruce (*Picea mariana* – white spruce was never used, he said), quoting the French naturalist Henri-Louis Duhamel du Monceau:

> To make a cask of spruce beer, a boiler is necessary … As soon as the water begins to get hot, a quantity of spruce twigs is put into it, broken into pieces, but tied together into a faggot or bundle, and large enough to measure about 2ft in circumference at the ligature. The water is kept boiling, till the bark separates from the twigs.
>
> While this is doing, a bushel of oats must be roasted, a few at a time, on a large iron stove or hot plate; and about fifteen galettes [flat yeasty cakes], or as many sea biscuits, or if neither of these are to be had, fifteen pounds of bread cut into slices and toasted. As these articles are prepared, they are put into the boiler, where they remain till the spruce fir twigs are well boiled. The spruce branches are then taken out, and the fire extinguished. The oats and the bread fall to the bottom, and the leaves, &c., rise to the top, where they are skimmed off with the scum.
>
> Six pints of molasses, or 12lb. or 15lb. of coarse brown sugar, are then added ; and: the liquor is immediately tunned off into a cask which has contained red wine; or, if it is wished that the spruce beer

should have a fine red colour, five or six pints of wine may be left in the cask. Before the liquor becomes cold, half a pint of yeast is mixed with it …The barrel is then filled up to the bunghole, which is left open to allow it to ferment … If the cask is stopped before the liquor has fermented 24 hours, the spruce beer becomes sharp, like cider; but, if it is suffered to ferment properly, and filled up twice a day, it becomes mild, and agreeable to the palate. It is esteemed very wholesome, and is exceedingly refreshing, especially during summer.

Loudon also indicates that spruce beer was made in Britain, saying: 'The essence of spruce (which is what spruce beer is made from in this country) is obtained by evaporating to the consistence of an extract the water in which the ends of the young branches of black spruce have been boiled.' He adds that (the French naturalists Andre or his son Francois) 'Michaux … states that spruce beer is considered very salutary, and, in long voyages, is found efficacious in preventing attacks of the scurvy'.

Today a small number of British brewers have resurrected the idea of brewing with herbs other than hops, and with fruits. The best-known is Williams Brothers of Alloa, whose Fraoch contains both heather and bog myrtle and who also make an elderberry ale, Ebulum, and a spruce beer, Alba (which takes its name for the Gaelic word for Scotland). Fuller, Smith & Turner in London brews a dark winter ale flavoured with blackberries called Jack Frost. The St Peter's brewery in Suffolk makes an unhopped King Cnut bottled beer at 5 per cent abv, flavoured with nettles and also juniper (a nod, presumably, to the fact that Cnut was Danish). Hall and Woodhouse, the Dorset brewer, also makes a beer flavoured with nettles, Stinger, using 'organic' nettle (are there any other kind?) from a farm run by Hugh Fearnley-Whittingstall, the celebrity chef whose family once ran a brewery in Watford. It also makes Poacher's Choice, a delicious dark beer flavoured with damsons; Golden Champion, made with elderflowers as well as hops; and Golden Glory, made with added peach blossom extract.

13

HONEY BEER

They were drinking iced honey-beer out of tall cut-glass goblets. This had been brought by Popova as a present for Olga – it was the colour of amber and tingled pleasantly on one's tongue. It prompted Pyotr to make some very happy remarks, but it was useless to try to get them in because of Alexei's tiresome and unceasing chatter.

Decadence, Maxim Gorky, 1927

Fermented honey – mead – was the intoxicating drink made thousands of years ago by the pastoral proto-Indo-Europeans, the people who spoke a language that is the ancestor of not just most of the tongues of Europe, but a swath of others across Asia, from Armenian and Persian to Hindi. We know they drank and enjoyed mead because of the wide range of words from the same Indo-European root that cover the meanings mead, honey, drunk/intoxicated and so on that are found in Indo-European languages today from Cork to Calcutta.

In Welsh, for example, *mêl* is 'honey', *medd* (pronounced 'meth') is 'mead' and *meddw* ('methoo') is 'drunk', all derived from proto-Indo-European *medhu*, 'honey' or 'mead', and *meydho*, drunk. (The asterisk indicates these are presumed forms of unrecorded words). In Lithuanian, *medus* is honey and *midus* is mead. In Sanskrit (and Hindi) *mádhu* means 'honey' or 'sweetness', while *mádati* in Sanskrit means 'gets drunk'. In Bengali *mata* means 'to be intoxicated', while 'drunk' in Greek was *methúskein*, from which is derived amethyst, the stone that (supposedly) prevents drunkenness.

Other words across the Indo-European language spectrum meaning mead or honey are *mjöd* in Swedish, *mid* in Old Irish, *medu* in Old Prussian, Old Church Slavonic and Old English, *maddu* in Luwian, a language spoken in Southern Anatolia about 750 BC, *melit* in Hittite, another

Anatolian language, and *mit* in Tocharian B, the vanished Indo-European tongue spoken in what is now Chinese Turkestan until about AD 600.

The sugar in wild honey can turn into alcohol without any human intervention; scientists at the University of Brisbane in Queensland discovered in 1992 that high summer temperatures can cause the nectar of flowering plants to ferment within the blossoms, giving an alcohol content of up to 10 per cent by volume. If foraging bees drink this fermented nectar and carry it back to the hive, the result is 'spiked' honey. Honey from unfermented nectar gathered by bees will also turn into alcohol if the bees cannot keep the temperature and humidity down in their hive.

Discovering hives filled with naturally produced 'mead' is probably how the proto-Indo-Europeans were turned on to this miraculously intoxicating substance seven or eight thousand years ago. Those Indo-Europeans who ceased being pastoralists and settled down as farmers, however, had a new source of intoxicating drink, made from grain and called ale, another ancient word found across Eastern and Northern Europe from the Baltic via the Balkans to Britain. Indeed, there is a hint that the word 'ale' may originally have meant 'mead'. In a glossary of words from the thirteenth century in the now vanished Baltic language Old Prussian, a sister tongue to Latvian and Lithuanian, the Old Prussian *alu* is given as the equivalent of the German *Mete*, mead, while 'beer' in Old Prussian was *piwis*.

After the arrival of ale brewed from grain, however, the drink made from honey continued to be the most prestigious drink, the one consumed by the rich and powerful. The grave from around 520 BC of a Celtic prince found at Hochdorf, near Stuttgart in modern Germany, contained a bronze cauldron that once held around 350 litres (80 gallons) of high-quality mead, a sign of substantial wealth. For those that could not afford mead but wanted some of the prestige associated with this upper-class intoxicant, a cheaper drink was brewed that was a mixture of honey and wheat. Archaeological finds from the Neolithic to the Bronze Age in Scotland suggest that a honey-and-grain alcoholic drink was being consumed in Britain three to six millennia ago. The main flavouring seems to have been meadowsweet, *Filipendula ulmaria*, a marsh, fen and woodland plant whose name means 'mead sweet'. Modern experiments show that meadowsweet has a preservative as well as a flavouring effect, preventing brews going sour for two weeks longer than drinks made without it.

The making of wheat-and-honey ales continued into the Iron Age. Around 320 BC the Greek explorer Pytheas of Massilia (modern Marseilles) came to Britain. His original writings have been lost, but a later Greek writer, Strabo, who died in AD 21, quotes him saying about the natives of Britain that 'where there is grain and even honey, the people get their beverage from them'. Strabo's quote is mildly ambiguous, since it is just possible he is talking about 'Thule', which was further north than the 'Pretannic Islands', or Britain, but given what else we know it seems certain Pytheas, the first literate traveller to reach Britain from the Mediterranean, found the British making ale from grain and honey, 2,300 years ago.

The Celts made their ale from *bracis*, a word which has been identified, based on the Roman writer Pliny the Elder's *Natural History*, from around AD 77, as emmer, a type of bearded wheat. However, it seems more likely, looking at the etymology, that *bracis* actually means 'malt', as in the modern Welsh word for malt, *brag*. (The French word for brewer, *brasseur,* comes from the same root.) From *brag,* or *bracis,* came the name for the honey-and-grain drink: in Old Welsh *bragaut*, in English bragget. But mead remained the most valued locally produced alcoholic drink, twice as expensive as bragget, which was itself twice as expensive as ordinary ale. A Welsh law book of the twelfth century AD, laying down the food tributes due to a king from his subjects, said that alongside flour, meat and butter he should be paid a 'tub' of mead (probably just under six gallons) and if that was not available 'two tubs of bragget or four of ale are paid for one of mead'.

The Saxons, too, seem to have valued bragget more highly than ale. King Ine of Wessex, when he drew up a law code around 693, included in the rent payments due for ten hides of royal land 'twelve ambers of Welsh ale and thirty of clear ale'. The expression 'Welsh ale', *Waelsces aloth*, almost certainly means bragget, which, if it was still even partially made from wheat, would have been noticeably cloudier than 'clear ale' made from barley. (An 'amber', at a later date, anyway, was a measure equal to thirty-two gallons, the same size as the traditional ale barrel.)

Welsh ale (sometimes specifically 'sweet Welsh ale') continued to be listed in English land agreements right through to the twelfth century, when the Abbot of Medeshamstede granted an estate to one Wulfred in return for a rent that included fifteen 'mittan' of clear ale, five 'mittan' of Welsh ale and fifteen of mild ale (newly brewed ale, which would probably still have been cloudy).

Bragget was known to Geoffrey Chaucer, who wrote of Alisoun, the carpenter's wife in the *Miller's Tale*, that 'hire mouth was sweete as braket or the meth' (meth, of course, being mead).

Recipes for bragget have not survived from before the Middle Ages, by which time the drink was being flavoured with spices as well as honey. One fourteenth-century recipe calls for ten gallons of ale, three 'potell' (a pottle was half a gallon) of 'fyne wort', that is, fresh unfermented ale, and three 'quartis' of honey, giving ale and honey in a ratio of around fifteen to one. To this should be added four ounces of cinnamon, four ounces of pepper 'short or long' (long pepper, *Piper officinarum*, is a pungent spice from the Far East), an ounce of cloves, two ounces of 'gingiver' (ginger) and an ounce of galingale, a Chinese plant whose roots have a mild ginger flavour.

Another recipe from 1594 for 'a braggot which is many times mis-taken for a muskadel by the simple sort of people' required fifty-nine gallons of strong new ale, nine gallons of clarified honey (a ratio of six and a half to one) and almost a pound of spices including cinnamon, cloves, ginger, nutmeg, long pepper, liquorice, coriander, cardamom and grains of paradise (hot, pungent seed capsules from a West African shrub of the cardamom family, still used as one of the flavourings in gin). The spices were suspended in a bag inside a hogshead filled with the ale and honey mixture, which would re-ferment and froth over as it worked. The bragget would be ready to drink after three or four months.

Bragget was still being made in 1669 to a recipe that involved boiling the honey with raw ale wort (one pound of honey to every two gallons of ale) and herbs and spices including ginger, cinnamon, cloves, rosemary, thyme, sweet marjoram, mint and sweet-briar, a species of rose with aromatic leaves. But as brewing became more and more the domain of commercial brewers, the use of honey in ale and beer-making withered away. Professional brewers in Britain were actually banned from using honey (or sugar) by a law passed in 1689, a ban repeated in an Act of 1816 to protect government income from the tax on malt.

Even home brewers, while they continued to make mead, seem to have forgotten about bragget by the beginning of the eighteenth cen-tury. A last echo comes in an eighteenth-century recipe for 'Welch ale' (sic), made from pale malt, hops, sugar and grains of paradise again. Perhaps the increased use of hops meant sweet, spiced beer lost its appeal. More likely, pressure from the Revenue, which wanted beers to be made solely from (taxed) malt and (taxed) hops, killed the style off.

One of the rare mentions of 'honey beer' in the nineteenth century comes from a publication called the *Journal of Horticulture and Cottage Gardener* in 1867, which gave a recipe for what was effectively a hopped mead, using 31½lb of honey to 9 gallons of water, and ½lb of hops, boiled for 2½ hours.

Only in the twentieth century did beer made with honey reappear. The Sheffield brewer Hope & Anchor, best known for Jubilee stout, made a bottled Golden Mead Ale in the 1950s, which was popular with hairdressers who washed their clients' hair with it – the beer made the hair especially shiny. The big Norfolk brewer Steward & Patteson, before it disappeared in the 1960s after a takeover by Watney Mann of London, made a bottled Honeysuckle Ale brewed with malt and honey and a bottle label reminiscent of bricks of 'Neapolitan' ice-cream, pink, brown and green, a 1950s British Sunday teatime treat.

Vaux of Sunderland, which had a branch brewery in Sheffield called Ward's, had a success in the 1990s with a honey beer made at Ward's brewery and called Waggle Dance, after the dance bees do to show the rest of the hive where the best flowers are. It was made with half a ton of honey in every 100-barrel batch, or 5oz to the gallon, 2½ teaspoons to the pint, giving it more than 20 per cent honey, less than 80 per cent barley malt. Ward's version used Kent hops, mainly Fuggles. When Vaux and Ward's shut down in 1999 the rights to brew Waggle Dance were acquired by the London brewer Young & Co. of Wandsworth. After Young's brewery closed in 2006, the beer was brewed at Wells' brewery in Bedford, and the name changed to Wells' Waggle Dance.

Vaux was actually beaten to reviving honey beer by the Enville Ales brewery in Stourbridge, in the West Midlands, which was started by Will Constantine-Cort, a beekeeper, in 1993. His first beer, Enville Ale, was made with malt and then given a secondary fermentation with honey to a nineteenth-century recipe from Constantine-Cort's great-great aunt, before being cold-stored (lagered). Other honey beers have now appeared, including Bumble Bee, from the Wentworth brewery in South Yorkshire, BeeWitched from the Wychwood brewery in Oxfordshire and Bumble Ale from the Freeminer brewery in Gloucestershire, both these last two made with Fairtrade honey and Honeydew from Fuller, Smith and Turner in London, made from organic honey and which the brewery recommended serving over ice.

There are also several dark honey beers, including Black Cuillin Dark Ale from the Isle of Skye brewery, made with rolled oats, roasted malt and Scottish honey; Honey Porter from the St Peter's brewery in Suffolk; Honeyed Stout from the Warcop brewery in Gwent, and Old Ember, a 'honey brown ale' from the Highgate brewery in the West Midlands.

France has the most authentically Celtic honey beers, however, with several new small French brewers making *cervoise* (the French word used for unhopped ale, which comes from the Latin *cervesia*, and ultimately from the Celtic *cuirm*) using honey and a mixture of several bittering herbs, in a deliberate imitation of Gaulish brewing methods.

14

HEATHER ALE

From the bonny bells of heather
They brewed a drink longsyne,
Was sweeter far than honey,
Was stronger far than wine

'Heather Ale – A Galloway Legend', Robert Louis Stevenson (1850–1894)

Heather ale, 'the most delicious drink the world has ever known', is a folk tale found throughout Scotland from the Shetlands to Galloway. It was a story once told right around Ireland as well; seventy-five years ago most country folk in Ireland seemed to know about the fabled drink brewed from heather.

The legend's basic theme is almost always the same, whoever is telling it, and wherever it is told. A father and son (or two sons), who are the last survivors of their race, are also the only people left alive who know how to brew the heather ale. They are captured after a battle and ordered to reveal the secret of making the drink, or die. The father says he will disclose the recipe, but only if his son(s) are killed first, because he is afraid his offspring will murder him for divulging the ingredients and methodology of this rare and famous liquor. The son(s) are dispatched into the yonder by their captors and the old man is urged to tell all about heather ale.

But the father laughs at his captors and tells them that they have done what he wanted; weak youth might have given away the secrets of heather ale in return for life, but old age cannot be compelled. The recipe, the old man says, will die with him; he will reveal nothing.

In Scotland the possessors of the secret of heather ale are usually given as the Picts, the mysterious people, possibly Celtic, possibly not, who inhabited the northern half of the country from pre-Roman times until their lands were conquered by the growing kingdom of the Scots under Kenneth mac Alpin around AD 843. The name Pict comes from a Latin word meaning painted or tattooed person and seems to be a translation of the Celtic name for the Picts, *Priten* in Old Welsh. This, too, is derived from a word meaning picture (and is the origin, ultimately, of the name Britain, *Pretanoi* or *Bretanoi* in Greek, the 'land of the tattooed people' – the Welsh for Britain is still *Prydain*).

The earliest dated version of the heather ale story, or at least the first half of it, comes from John Bellenden's translation of Boece's *Scottorum Historiae* of *c.* 1530–33, which says:

> Attoure ina all the desertis and muris [moors] of this realme growis ane herbe, namit hudder [heather], but any seid, richt nutritive baith to beistis and fowlis; specialie to beis. This herbe, in the moneth of July, has ane floure of purple hue, als sweet as huny. The Pichtis maid this herbe, sum time, ane richt delicus and hailsum drink. Nochtheless, the manner of making of it is perist, be exterminioun of the said Pichtis out of Scotland; for they schew nivir the craft of the making of this drink bot to their awin blud.

One typical Scots version of the full story says that the Pictish art of brewing ale from heather 'was muckle sought after by the other folk that lived in the kintry; but they never would let out the secret, but handed it down frae father to son among themselves. Wi' strict instructions frae ane to another never to let onybody ken about it.' After a great battle between the Picts and the Scots 'in which they clean lost the day', only two Picts were left alive, a father and son. The pair was brought in front of the king of the Scots, who told them he would torture them until they confessed the secret of the 'heather yill'. The old man said he could see it was of no use to resist, but he had a request before the king could learn the secret: 'My son ye maun kill Before I will tell How we brew the yill From the heather bell'.

The king, surprised, agreed to kill the lad. But as soon as the son was dead, the father 'started up wi' a great stend, and cried: 'Now do wi' me as you like. My son ye might have forced, for he was but a weak youth, but me you can never force.

> And though you may me kill,
> I will not you tell

A tattooed Pict, as imagined by a seventeenth century English artist. In Scotland the Picts are credited with being the only ones who knew the secret of the 'heather yill'

How we brew the yill
Frae the heather bell!

Another version, from Shetland, puts the incident at the time of the
Norse invasion of those islands in the ninth century, when they were
still inhabited by Picts. This time it is the Vikings who kill all the Picts
except an old man and his son, who are, again, spared so that they can tell
their conquerors the secret of how to brew from heather flowers. Under
torture the father says: 'Kill the lad and then I'll tell you.' But when the
boy is dead, his father tells the invading Norse, triumphantly: 'You can
kill me slow or fast, it is all one. You shall never learn the secrets of our
race from the last of the Picts.'

Around 200 versions of the same story have been collected in Ireland,
identical in their essentials to the story that Robert Louis Stevenson
turned into a poem but with one surprising difference – while in most
Scottish versions the secret was held by the Picts, in almost all the Irish
tales the people who know how to brew heather ale and who refuse to
tell anyone else are the Vikings. In most of the Irish language versions
the heather ale is actually called *an bheóir Lochlannach*, translated as the
Viking beer.

The taste and ingredients of *bheóir Lochlannach* are as much of a mystery today as they were to the ancient Irish. One possible clue is that
in the Irish language versions of the tale the word used for the drink is
one that comes via the Vikings, *beóir*, from the Old Norse *bjorr*, rather
than *cuírm* or *lionn*, the two Irish words for ale. *Beóir* is something of a
'false friend', as linguists say – although it has always been translated as
'beer'; before about AD 1000, the Old Norse *bjorr* and its Old English
equivalent, *beór*, seem to have signified a strong, sweet, honey or honey-
and-fruit drink rather than grain-based beer or ale.

Tenth-century Anglo-Saxon glossaries gave *beór* as the equivalent of
ydromellum in Latin, hydromel, or mead, while *eala* (the root of modern
English 'ale') was *cervisia*, beer. It seems very likely therefore that *bheóir
Lochlannach* was not a beer, or ale, in the modern sense, but a heather-
flavoured mead or something similar, perhaps even a heather-flavoured
cider made from crab-apples.

Another mystery is why, when the Irish told the tale, the people
who held the secret of heather ale changed from the Picts to the
Vikings. The Irish certainly knew who the Picts were; several Pictish
tribes lived in Antrim and Armagh, in Ulster. The Irish called them and
their Scottish brothers and sisters *Cruíthin* – this is simply the Irish or

Q-Celtic version of the British or P-Celtic name for the Picts, *Priten,* with a K sound for the P.

The change in nationality may be because there was no tradition of the Irish Picts being wiped out, while there was a strong folk recollection in Ireland of a massive defeat for the Vikings. Just as many of the Scottish versions mention a last battle between the Picts and Scots, many of the Irish tales about heather ale feature the last big clash involving the Irish and the Vikings, the Battle of Clontarf. This took place just outside Dublin in 1014 and it is traditionally seen as a victory for the Irish under their high king, Brian Boru, over the Viking invaders of Ireland. It was in reality a much more complicated situation, with Brian's army containing his own Viking allies from places such as Limerick as well as Irish warriors from Munster and elsewhere. His opponents, who were fighting to resist the hgh king's domination rather than trying to impose their own, were just as mixed – an alliance of Irishmen from Leinster and Dublin Vikings. But folk tales do not have to reflect real politics and real history.

The first full rendering of the 'classic' Irish version of the tale of heather ale was given by Samuel Morewood in a long book called *A Philosophical and Statistical History … in the Manufacture and Use of Inebriating Liquors*, published in Dublin in 1838. It is almost identical to the story of 'heath ale' (heath meaning ling) recorded by John Locke, writing in the *Ulster Journal of Archaeology* in 1859. Locke said he was told the tale by a peasant living in Cork in 1847 who claimed to be nearly 100 years old and who said he got the story from his grandfather (taking us back to at least the late 1600s).

Locke was told that after the Battle of Clontarf, 'when the native Irish finally crushed the power of the immigrant Vikings' (sic), three surviving Danes, two sons and a father, were captured. The father was ordered by his Irish captors to surrender the secret of making heath ale, which had been 'studiously kept from the natives'. The father refused to talk, saying his sons would kill him if he told the secret. So the Irish put his sons to death, thus removing, they thought, the father's constraint – at which, just as in the Scots stories, the elderly Viking said: 'Now my purpose is accomplished. Youth might have yielded to the fear of death and played the traitor, but age has no such terror,' and he allowed himself to be killed rather than reveal the recipe for heath ale.

Locke gives some details about the drink that are not recorded elsewhere; he said the flavouring for *bheóir Lochlannach* was wood avens or Herb Bennet (*geum urbanum*), called *minarthagh* in Irish. The type of heather used for *bheóir Lochlannach* he said was ling (*Calluna vulgaris*), which is actually known in some parts of Ireland as Viking heather, *fraoch Lochlannach*. *Bheóir Lochlannach*, Locke said, was made from a wort derived from steeping ling in water.

Other tellings of the story from different parts of Ireland sometimes have the old Viking and his (single) son trapped by their pursuers on a cliff top. After the father says he will tell everything if the boy is killed, the son is then thrown over the cliff, whereupon the older Viking laughs at his captors and says they can kill him too, for he is saying nothing. Sometimes he grabs his chief tormentor and pulls him backwards over the cliff with him. A few Irish versions of the tale give tormentil, or bloodroot, *Potentilla tormentilla*, as a flavouring for *bheóir Lochlannach*. Tormentil, a small plant with yellow flowers, a member of the rose family, has bitter-flavoured roots which will cause vomiting if taken to excess that, at the same time, smell pleasantly of roses.

The story in all its versions excites folklorists because of its basic theme, captive cleverly achieves desired death of companion by falsely promising to reveal valuable secret to captors. This is identical to one of the plots found in the Norse Eddas and the Germanic *Niebelungenlied* and turned into opera by the nineteenth-century composer Richard Wagner, except that the secret Attila, the king of the Huns, wanted to get from Gunnar the Nibelung was the whereabouts of the Rhine gold rather than the recipe for a famous beer. Much debate has taken place in folkloric publications about which tale came first, the Rhine gold or the heather ale. Most scholars feel the Vikings told the Gaels the original story and somewhere the real gold of the Nibelungs became the liquid gold of the heather ale.

Rather more interesting to beer drinkers is how much truth there is in the idea that ale was once brewed from heather. There is evidence that brewing with heather may have been taking place in Scotland in the Neolithic period. Drinking vessels discovered during the excavation of a 4,000-year-old settlement on the island of Rhum in 1985 had an organic crust on the inside which contained pollen spores of oats, barley, heather and meadowsweet.

However, this could have been a Neolithic honey-beer, with the heather pollen coming from heather honey rather than heather flowers in the brew.

A couple of thousand years later a drinking vessel was left in a grave of one of the Bronze Age Beaker People at Methilhill, Fife, Scotland. Again, analysis of the spilled contents found Calluna heather pollen with other ingredients suggesting a honey-based brew – meadowsweet (probably for flavouring and preserving), pollen from ribwort plantain and, making up more than half the total, pollen from small-leaved lime, *Tilia cordata*. This last tree grew no closer than 100km (60 miles) south of where the beaker was found, so the lime honey in the Methilhill brew must have been traded from the north of England. The contents of the whole beaker were not analysed when it was found by archaeologists and this too could be a grain-honey beer rather than pure mead, but again it is not clear if the heather was there as an element of the honey in the brew or as a mainstream ingredient.

Heather as an ingredient in ale is apparently found in old Swedish recipes, but not, or hardly at all in Norway, where home brewing is an ancient tradition and it was Norwegian and Danish Vikings who came to the British Isles, rather than Swedes. Hints do exist that heather ale really was made by the Vikings in Ireland and by later brewers as well. Samuel Morewood in 1838 said that 'a few years ago' men digging a watercourse in County Limerick found a mill and 'a portion of brewing materials, together with some cakes of bread and heather, concealed in the position where they were left by the Danes'.

Morewood said that 'it was also stated that a book or manuscript containing the receipt for the making of heather-beer had been found at the same time, but that it was clandestinely taken away'. Alas, this manuscript, if it ever existed, has not been seen since the time of William IV. But what the watercourse digger may have come across was an illegal brewery operated by a rather more modern brewer. The Victorian journalist John Bickerdyke, writing in 1889, said that 'as later as the commencement of this century', around 1801, 'an ale flavoured with heather … was brewed in many parts of Ireland. The practice, it is believed, is now almost if not quite extinct.' The method, Bickerdyke said, was to let the wort drain through heather blossoms placed at the bottom of tubs so that during its passage the wort gains 'a peculiar and agreeable flavour'.

Heather may not just have been adding flavour. The nectar in the heather flowers added extra sugar to a brew and wild yeasts growing on the flowers would have helped with fermentation. But the plant is also 'reputed' to be narcotic, as are several of its relatives in the *Ericaceae* family. In addition, a moss, fungus or 'fog' (fog, sometimes spelt fogg, is the dialect word for moss in Scotland and the north of England) that grows on the heather stems produces a white powder which itself has narcotic and at least mildly hallucinogenic effects.

England had a faint tradition of heather ale brewing, though the legend of the lost recipe is almost completely unknown. John Bickerdyke quoted a manuscript owned by the Duke of Northumberland at

Today Fraoch ale – from the Gaelic word for heather – is brewed again in Scotland, with illustrations on the label taken from Pictish art

Hexham that described a large trough cut from solid rock at the Roman fort at Rudchester, or Vindobala (which he erroneously calls Kutchester) on Hadrian's Wall, a mile west of Heddon. The local Northumbrian peasants, the manuscript said, had a tradition 'that the Romans made a beverage somewhat like beer, of the bells of heather, and that this trough was used in the process of making it'. Since Bickerdyke's time, findings at a Roman fort near the wall, Vindolanda, have shown that the Romans did indeed brew ale at this northern extremity of their empire. However, the Vindobala trough, hewn out of grey sandstone and ten feet long, which was still at Rudchester farm in 1974, has been identified by archaeologists as a sacrificial bath from one of the many temples that once stood around the fort, not a stone mash tun.

In Yorkshire, according to Bickerdyke, home brewers in his time made a beer called 'gale beer' flavoured with 'the blossoms of a species of heather found growing on the moors in that part of the country'. But the main flavouring ingredient in gale ale must have been sweet gale, bog myrtle, *Myrica gale*.

A book called *Sundrie Newe and Artificial Remedies against Famine* described 'A Cheap Liquor for Poore Men when Malt is extream Deare' which involved gathering the flower tops of ling and boiling them in water to make 'a very pleasing & cheape drink'. This, however, sounds more like heather tea than heather ale. The antiquarian Robert Plot said in 1686 that about Shenstone in Staffordshire 'they frequently used

Erica vulgaris [that is, *Calluna vulgaris*], heath or ling instead of hopps to preserve their beer, which gave it no ill taste'. In *Cerevisiarii Comes or The New and True Art of Brewing*, published in 1692, the author, William Y-Worth (or Yworth), said: 'There may also an excellent Drink be made from the tops and flowers of Heath, seasonably gathered and dried, and brewed as you have occasion for it.'

The strongest evidence of an enduring tradition of brewing heather ale comes from Scotland, where the practice seems to have lasted long after the Picts were history. The writer and traveller Thomas Pennant wrote in 1772 that on the Hebridean island of Islay 'ale is frequently made of the young tops of heath, mixing two thirds of that plant with one of malt, sometimes adding hops'. Not quite sixty years later, in 1831, James Logan wrote that:

> in the Highlands it was an almost invariable practice, when brewing, to put a quantity of the green tops of heath in the mash tub, and when the plant is in bloom it adds much to the strength and flavour of the beer. The roots, also, will improve its qualities, for they are of a liquorice sweetness, but their astringency requires them to be used with caution.

As late as 1931, Maude Grieve, writing in *The Modern Herbal*, said that 'In some outlying islands of the Hebrides there is still brewed a drinkable beer by making two thirds Heath tops with one third of malt'.

The Scottish food writer Wilma Paterson recorded in 1979 that she and her family had made 'excellent' heather ale from both ling and its relative, bell heather. Her recipe for heather ale misses out hops, and warns that heather ale 'takes longer to clear than other ales':

Heather Ale
1 gallon of heather tops, cut when in full bloom but not overblown
2lb malt extract
1 ½lb sugar
3 gallons water
1oz dried yeast
The heather tops should be boiled with one gallon of the water for 'nearly an hour', and the strained water then poured onto the malt extract and sugar. Stir, add the rest of the water, and when lukewarm add the yeast. Cover with a cloth and leave to ferment for five or six days. Bottle, adding a teaspoon of sugar to each container, and leave to clear.

It is doubtful that heather ale was produced commercially on any scale but the smallest until the very end of the twentieth century, when the owner of a Glasgow home-brew shop, Bruce Williams, began making Leann Fraoch, Scots Gaelic for heather ale.

Williams claimed that in 1986 a woman gave him a recipe in Gaelic for heather ale that had been handed down through through ten generations, which would take it back to the time of Pennant's trip to Islay. He first brewed what became known, rather tautologically, as Fraoch Heather Ale in 1992 at the West Highland brewery in Taynuilt, Argyll, restricting sales to just six pubs. It took some time to perfect a version of the recipe that was suitable for commercial production, probably because, as Wilma Paterson found, heather ale takes longer to clear than ordinary beer.

Williams's methods eventually included boiling part of the heather tops, mostly purple and white ling carefully washed to remove the fogg or fungus, with a barley-and-wheat mash and then filtering the hot wort through a bed of more washed heather tips. Most of the heather was picked during July and August in the area of Argyllshire between Oban and Connel. The West Highland brewery, which had been started in 1989, closed early in 1995, but before then, in 1993, Williams had transferred production of Fraoch to Maclays, an old-established brewery in Alloa.

In 1997 he opened his own brewery at Strathaven in Lanarkshire, about fifteen miles south-east of Glasgow. The success of Fraoch, on draught and in bottle, inspired Williams to resurrect other old Scots beer recipes, including Grozet, brewed with gooseberries, Ebulum, brewed with elderberries and Scots' Spruce, made with sap extracted from spruce trees. A few years later the brewery moved to Alloa, where it is still based.

15

WOOD-AGED BEERS

'There was a thing here that I never saw. I don't think you've ever seen it either. There were Americans came here and they put whiskey in the beer.' 'No,' I said. 'Oui. My God, yes, that's true.'

Wine of Wyoming, Ernest Hemingway, 1933

Although several important British beer styles, such as porter and India Pale Ale, required ageing in wooden casks or vats, British brewers made big efforts, until very recently, not to let any flavour from the wood get into the beer. Unlike wine makers or distillers, brewers wanted their drink untainted with tannic or vanilla flavours from the oak used for making storage vessels – wood flavours were fine in chardonnay, or scotch, but not in stout or old ale.

Today, however, beers aged to deliberately take flavour from the wood are defining a new and exciting style of beer in Britain. But in past times oak for casks, vats and brewing vessels was sourced from places such as Russia and Poland that were known for growing fine-grained wood that would not impart any flavours to the beer. Casks were lined with 'brewer's pitch'. Vats were scrubbed down so that when stock ales, porters and stouts were being matured in them, no tang of the timber would come through into the beer. As aluminium and steel casks began to replace wooden ones, a protesting group of British consumers formed the Society for the Preservation of Beers from the Wood in 1963, but their objections were more to do with disliking the pressurised, pasteurised beer that frequently came in metal casks, rather than the loss of any real benefits obtainable from wooden ones.

About the only desirable characteristic brewers did want from storing in oak vessels was that brought out by *Brettanomyces* yeast infection. Brett, a different family from the usual *Saccharomyces* brewing yeasts,

The coopers' shop at Benskin's Brewery in Watford in 1890. For most of the history of beer, brewers have tried to keep flavours from the wood out of the drink

gives an earthy, funky aroma to beers and old wooden vessels are often infected with it. Brett flavours develop after three or four months when the standard *Saccharomyces* yeast has done as much as it can to ferment the sugars in the beer and the *Brettanomyces* yeast sneaks up and tackles what sugars are left. They are regarded as essential, as a background, in aged brews such as Guinness Foreign Extra Stout, Belgian lambic and the old-style (and now almost vanished) English stock beers, which were kept for months to mature and from which the Danish biochemist Niels Hjelte Claussen first isolated the yeast in the first decade of the twentieth century.

In wine-making, Brett flavours are regarded as a fault, but beer brewers are (again) beginning deliberately to infect some of their beers with *Brettanomyces*. The bottle-conditioned London Porter from the Meantime brewery in Greenwich, for example, has Brett yeast sourced from the United States added to it during fermentation.

The introduction of wood flavours as a desirable characteristic, in the UK at least, was a serendipitous discovery springing from the wish of the Scotch whisky distiller William Grant in 2002 to add to its range of 'cask reserve' whiskies, all finished off in casks that had previously held other alcoholic drinks, such as sherry or rum. Grant's wanted a beer to fill casks with and enable it to make 'ale cask reserve' whisky once the beer had been emptied out.

Dougal Sharp, then of the Caledonian brewery in Edinburgh, designed a malty, estery, sweet, not very hoppy beer for filling the casks that he and Grant's felt would give a good foundation when those casks were subsequently used for maturing whisky in. The beer was always meant to be thrown away once it had been in the casks long enough for the wood to absorb beer flavours that could then be absorbed by the whisky. But workers at Grant's distillery sampled the beer before it was dumped and liked the oaky, vanilla flavours it had picked up from the new wood so much that instead of disposing of it they started taking it home in lemonade bottles.

When he heard about this, Sharp tried putting the oaky beer into a blind tasting at the brewery, where it scored a consistent nine out of nine with the tasters. The 'tweaked' version of their original brew for Grant's that Dougal and his father Russell launched in 2003 as Innis & Gunn Oak-Aged Beer (Innis and Gunn are names in the Sharp family tree) has been so successful subsequently it has effectively launched a completely new category in the UK marketplace, the first new beer style of the twenty-first century: wood-aged beer. Innis & Gunn has had to learn new tricks with this new category of beer. Each cask produces a slightly different flavour, for example, so that to achieve consistency the beer, after it has been aged for thirty days in the casks, is vatted for another forty-seven days to let the flavours from the different casks marry and mature. Then, immediately after the beer is bottled, the oaky flavours disappear, subdued by the violence of the bottling process, and do not reappear for a month, so every bottle has to be kept at least four weeks before it is released for sale, in order for the proper taste to return.

Subsequently, Innis & Gunn has brought out a number of different versions of cask-aged beer, including one aged sixty days in American oak barrels and then forty-seven days in barrels that had previously contained rum. Again, whisky distillers had been ageing their spirit in 'second-hand' casks for many years, but this was a new development for brewers.

Other small Scots brewers have now brought out beers that have been aged in whisky casks, including Harviestoun, with a brew called Ola Dubh, Gaelic for 'black oil', which is its Engine Oil stout aged in casks formerly used to mature Highland Park single-malt whisky from Orkney. The Brew Dog brewery in Fraserburgh, near Aberdeen, established in March 2007, has been putting its strong Paradox stout in casks that had previously contained whisky from, among other places, Islay distillers such as Caol Ila and Bowmore, with each batch using casks sourced from different distilleries.

As well as flavours, the beer also pulls out alcohol from the casks that had soaked into the staves from the whisky, which is why, for example, Paradox starts out at 8.5 per cent abv and rises to 11 per cent after its time in wood formerly used to mature the whisky. In the nineteenth century, when pub landlords bought whisky by the cask for subsequent retail in their pub, they would extract this alcohol from empty barrels by filling them with a small quantity of water and rolling the casks around the pub yard. This practice, known as 'grogging', has been illegal in Britain since 1898, since the authorities decided that the alcohol liberated from the wooden staves of the cask had not had tax paid on it. Some brewers trying to make beers matured in whisky casks have hit difficulties with Her Majesty's Revenue and Customs, which has told them that because alcohol comes out of the wood into the beer, what they are doing is grogging, and therefore illegal.

One company that had been experimenting with maturing some of its beers in ex-whisky casks was Fuller, Smith & Turner of Chiswick, in London. With Golden Pride in Glenmorangie casks, a mixture of secondary fermentation and leaching out of whisky that had soaked into the wood inside the cask saw the abv of the beer rise from 8.5 per cent to a serious 12.5 per cent; However, with the local revenue and customs people telling Fullers it would be illegal to sell the beer because of the century-old law against grogging, this particular version never reached the buying public. The same was true of Vintage Ale (the version of Golden Pride normally sent out bottle-conditioned) matured in ex-Jim Beam bourbon casks, where the beer saw a similar rise in abv to 11.5 per cent.

However, the brewery eventually found a compromise with the authorities. If it released the whisky cask-matured beer at a lower abv than the beer was when it originally went into the casks – water it down, in other words – then it could put it on sale. The company was thus able to put a version of Golden Pride aged in whisky casks and then reduced in strength to 7.5 per cent abv on sale in the summer of 2008.

While this is likely to give a big fillip to the idea of wood-aged beers in the UK, in the United States brewers have adopted the practice with enormous enthusiasm. A survey by Garrett Oliver, brewmaster at the Brooklyn brewery in New York, of fellow American brewers in 2007 found some 200 or so of the 1,500 craft brewers in the United States made a wood-aged beer of some sort, with a small handful making all-*Brettanomyces* beers; Russian River in California, for example, and its fellow Californian Pizza Port, with Mo'Betta Bretta The range of beers they had aged in oak deliberately to get oak flavours included imperial stout, barley wine, Belgian abbey-style ale, brown ale, red ale, the Scots strong pale ale style Wee Heavy, cherry stout and Belgian golden ale.

Barrels used were mostly Bourbon (by law, Bourbon distillers can only mature their spirit in fresh, unused barrels and thus have a lot of barrels to get rid of once each batch of Bourbon is old enough for bottling), but also red wine (in particular Pinot Noir) and white wine.

Some brewers steamed the casks before filling them to try to steri-lise them, others flushed them with carbon dioxide or sulphur dioxide, but most used them as they came, generally (if they were Bourbon barrels) with a couple of pints of whiskey still inside to help keep the staves moist.

No one method seemed to make much difference to how the beer turned out after its time in the cask, though obviously those beers matured in casks that had Bourbon still in them when filled had more Bourbon character in the final result.

American brewers now hold beer festivals solely dedicated to wood-aged beers and Mr Oliver, whose own brewery made a 10 per cent Bourbon-cask-aged stout called 'Black Ops', declared at a seminar at Thornbridge Hall, Derbyshire in 2007 on wood-aged beers, that wood-ageing has become another flavour tool for modern brewers – not a traditional tool at all, but now an accepted part of the 'creative toolkit'. While deliberate wood ageing had previously been left to the wine makers and distillers, Mr Oliver said they were now being challenged: 'We [brewers] will use barrels in a more interesting way that any of the other drinks disciplines.'

16

LAGER

Suppose we go and try some lager-bier? … It is a new beverage, of German origin … you will not like it for some time, because it is quite different from Barclay and Perkins' beer.

Ten Years in the United States: Being an Englishman's View of Men and Things in the North and South, David W. Mitchell, 1862

If a brewer in Edinburgh had been able to keep the strain of Bavarian bottom-fermenting yeast going that he was sent as a gift in 1835, then Britain might today have an authentic tradition of genuine lager-brewing dating back 170 years. However, he could not and this country missed out on the lager revolution that swept the rest of the world during and after the 1840s and 1850s.

All the same, there were several attempts to brew genuine, authentic lager in the styles of Vienna, Munich and Pilsen in Britain during Queen Victoria's time and if these had taken off more then we might not have had to suffer some of the dreadful attempts at lager beers first seen when a market for the drink finally arrived in this country in the middle of the twentieth century.

The Edinburgh brewer who brewed several times with yeast from Munich in 1835, producing a beer apparently much appreciated by drinkers in the Scottish capital, was John Muir, probably of the Calton Hill brewery, in North Back Canongate. He had been visited in 1833 by Gabriel Sedlmayr II, the twenty-two-year-old son of the owner of the Spaten brewery in Munich, who spent a month at Muir's brewery as part of a 'study tour' of Britain. Sedlmayr's visit also took in a trip to Burton upon Trent, where Bass apparently presented him with a saccharometer, and Glasgow.

The young German brewer, as well as travelling around the different regions of Germany and to Bohemia, Switzerland, Austria, Belgium and the Netherlands studying brewing techniques, visited Britain twice, at least once, in 1837, with his friend Anton Dreher, whose father owned the Klein Schwechat brewery in the suburbs of Vienna. Their journey, which also took in Birmingham, Liverpool, Manchester, Sheffield, Newcastle and Alloa, had a profound influence on the history of beer brewing.

Sedlmayr wanted to improve the Munich style of *lager bier*, literally 'store beer'. This used a variety of yeast that worked best in cold conditions and then sank to the bottom of the fermenting vessel when it had done its work of converting sugar into alcohol, unlike the 'top fermenting' yeasts found at that time almost everywhere else. The Munich brewers stored – lagered – the beer after fermentation in cold conditions for months to ripen and improve. The result was a beer with considerable stability, as well as depth of taste.

Sedlmayr and Dreher picked up an enormous amount of practical information on their 'study trips', including how British brewers used thermometers and saccharometers to track the progress of their brews and how maltsters produced malts that gave the maximum amount of fermentable materials. Not all the brewers they visited were as friendly as Bass and Muir, however, and Sedlmayr and Dreher overcame the reluctance of many of their hosts to divulge company secrets by pinching samples of wort and yeast literally from under their feet. Sedlmayr revealed years later that the pair had walking sticks made 'of lacquered tin, with a valve at the bottom, so that, if one dips the stick in [to the fermenting vessel], it fills up, when taken out the valve closes, and we have the beer in the stick, so we can steal safely'. He added that he and Dreher lived in continual fear of discovery and a beating from their British hosts.

Back home in Munich, Sedlmayr was to use what he had learnt in Britain, together with traditional Bavarian 'decoction' mashing, Bavarian slow-acting bottom-fermenting brewing techniques and cold conditioning, to produce a style of consistent, bright *lager-bier*. This new type of beer would sweep across mainland Europe, carried (literally) by men such as J.C. Jacobsen of Carlsberg in Denmark, who took some of Sedlmayr's yeast home with him to Copenhagen in 1845 to kickstart what became one of the world's biggest lager breweries.

As a reflection of this new beer style, 'Bavarian' became a regular epithet in beer and brewery names outside Bavaria; the Amstel brewery in Amsterdam, for example, was founded in 1870 as the Beiersch Bierbrouwerij De Amstel, *Beiersch* being the Dutch for Bavarian.

Sedlmayr's Munich lager was still dark, like an English brown ale, but Dreher (whose name means 'Tony Turner' in English) was very struck by English pale ales and took back with him the knowledge of how to make English-style pale malts, using coke-fired maltings. This, together with what he learnt from Sedlmayr about bottom-fermenting techniques, would eventually result in the production of a new style of copper-coloured 'Vienna' lager. The success of this beer enabled Dreher to open or acquire breweries around the Austro-Hungarian Empire; in Michelob, Bohemia (a name later 'borrowed' by Adolphus Busch of Anheuser-Busch in the United States), in Budapest and in Trieste. By 1902 the Dreher family firm was the largest under one management in continental Europe.

In Edinburgh, meanwhile, John Muir evidently could not keep the strain of yeast he had been sent by Sedlmayr pure and he soon stopped using it. For more than thirty years British brewers carried on with their top-fermenting ales and stouts, undisturbed by what was happening in the rest of the world. There were occasional sharp digs in the ribs from observers who had seen the advances Bavarian brewers had made. In 1844, for example, Andrew Ure, in his *Dictionary of Arts, Manufactures, and Mines*, drawing on the published works of a famous professor of biochemistry, Julius Liebig in Germany, said:

> The beers of England and France, and the most part of those of Germany, become gradually sour by contact of air. This defect does not belong to the beers of Bavaria, which may be preserved at pleasure in half-full casks, as well as full ones, without alteration in the air. This precious quality must be ascribed to a peculiar process, employed for fermenting the wort, called, in German *untergährung*, or fermentation from below [sic: bottom fermentation is a better translation]; which has solved one of the finest theoretical problems.

British brewers, who confidently believed they were the best in the world, were happy to ignore what was going on outside their shores. In October 1868, however, the *Bradford Daily Telegraph* revealed that 'during the last hot weather the sale of Vienna beer was attempted on a small scale in the City [of London], and it was found to take so with all classes that there are now five establishments where this beverage may be procured in London, viz, three in the City and two in the Strand.'

The Bradford newspaper added that 'when first imported into England, it was though that the Germans resident among us would patronise the favourite drink of the fatherland, they do so but Englishmen seem to like it quite as much as they do, and the quantity consumed is every day increasing.' The writer complained: 'Have our tastes changed or has our beer degenerated in its quality? It is feared that the brewers will have but themselves to thank if there is a material falling off in the quality of malt liquor consumed in England.'

It is sometimes claimed that the Anglo–Bavarian brewery in Shepton Mallet, Wiltshire, founded by William Garton, a Southampton brewer, in 1870, was the first lager brewery in the country, a statement based on the 'Bavarian' part of its name. However, there is no evidence that the brewery ever produced anything other than the standard range of English ales and stouts. Garton invented a method of making invert sugar for brewing and one writer said that his work was designed to produce 'a type of high-quality beer … approximating to that of bottom fermentation beer without the necessity for prolonged storage or lagering'. The name of the brewery, therefore, was evidently meant to show it produced Bavarian-like beers, but with English methods.

Although imports of lager from Copenhagen and Vienna were starting to appear, the first definite recording of lager brewing in England does not occur for another decade, coincidentally in Bradford. The *Brewers' Journal* in 1877 revealed that Joseph Spink and Sons of the Brownroyd brewery, Rose Street, Bradford, were apparently now brewing English lager, adding that it compared 'most favourably with foreign productions'. The experiment did not last, however, for nothing more seems to be heard of Spink's lager.

The next lager brewer in Scotland, forty years on from Muir, was William Younger of Edinburgh, who mashed and fermented their first lager beer in 1879 at the Holyrood brewery in Edinburgh, using yeast imported from the Carlsberg brewery in Copenhagen. The innovation was probably a reaction to the loss of overseas markets for Younger's IPA and similar top-fermented ales to German and other continental lagers. But Younger's stopped brewing lager after a few years, having apparently failed to make any impact.

However, increasing imports of lager into Britain, where it sold at 78s a barrel, more than twice as much as English ale sold for, encouraged entrepreneurs in the early 1880s to start up lager operations here. In County Durham, Knights, Stocks & Co. of Stockton on Tees was brewing 'Tivoli' lager beer, using German brewers. This brought the Tivoli brewery in Berlin down on its neck, and Knights, Stocks were barred in April 1883 from using the Tivoli name.

Britain's first lager-only brewery may have been the Bayerische Lager Beer Brewery Ltd, which was formed in 1881 to acquire for £22,000 in cash and 5,000 shares in the new business the Eltham brewery on Eltham High Street in Kent, a couple of miles from Woolwich and the Thames. The prospectus for the new concern, advertised in *The Times* in September 1881, said that the demand for lager was 'rapidly increasing' and the company believed it could produce lager beer that would 'favourably compare with the choicest productions of the continent' for just 40s a barrel, which could be retailed at 60s a barrel, dramatically undercutting the imported product.

The Bayerische brewery, which took kits name from the German for Bavaria, had 'provisionally secured' as brewer Richard Deeley, son of the former head brewer at Mann, Crossman and Paulin, one of London's leading ale brewers and 'now engaged at one of the largest American lager brewers'. It would be looking at the export and provincial trades, the company said. But 'the principal trade to which immediate attention will be directed will be the supply of Lager beer, on draught and in bottle, to the London and suburban hotels, public-houses and restaurants, the public demand for Lager beer having already become so general as to render its supply a necessary and indispensable adjunct to their trades.'

Investors were promised an 'exceptionally large profit on Lager Beer, as compared with the handsome profit on English beer', 'chiefly owing to the fact that Lager beer is brewed at a much lower gravity, thereby causing a greater saving in the cost of material.' Despite these promises, the concern was not a success, folding by 1888 at the latest. The brewery reopened about 1900 and closed again around 1919–20 – the premises were destroyed by German bombing during the Second World War.

A slightly more successful operation was the Austro-Bavarian Lager Beer and Crystal Ice Company in Tottenham High Road, North London (nods to the homes of both Sedlmayr and Dreher in its name), which was brewing by 1882 with an entirely German staff and backed with German capital. A year later it was reported that 'large quantities of genuine lager beer are sent out for consumption' from the Tottenham brewery.

The brewery's name suggests it was producing only dark and copper-coloured beers; the production in 1842 in the Bohemian town of Plzen (Pilsen in German) of pale, golden lager took many years to catch on even in continental Europe. It was not until 1895, for example, that Sedlmayr's Spaten brewery in Munich brewed its first pale Pilsener-type beer. The Austro-Bavarian brewery was in competition with the growing imports into Britain of German beers. The sale of German light beers, mainly pils-type, in the UK increased five-fold between 1880 and 1895, even though it sold at two to three times the price of English ale. But *Baedeker's Guide to London* in 1894 reported that while genuine Munich beer from the cask was available at the Gambrinus restaurant in Glasshouse Street, Piccadilly Circus, 'English-made Lager-beer is supplied in an establishment in the basement of the Cafe Monico [the French for Munich], Piccadilly Circus, fitted up in the "Old German" style, and in the Tottenham Lager Beer Hall, 395 Strand', supplied, clearly from the Austro-Bavarian brewery. The Tottenham High Road brewery was reformed as the Tottenham Lager Beer brewery in 1886, but went under nine years later, tens of thousands of pounds in debt, having failed to interest sufficient number of English drinkers in the continental brew. It was resurrected in 1896 as the Imperial Lager brewery, but closed finally in 1903.

A far-longer-lasting lager-only brewery financed by British entrepreneurs (though many were of German or Czech extraction), built by Austrians to a continental design and used continental-style decoction mashing and a bottom-fermenting lager yeast, had begun brewing in Wrexham, North Wales, in 1883, two years after the Bayerische Lager Beer brewery Ltd and following more than eighteen months of building work. It was brewing dark Bavarian-style lagers to begin with; apparently the company found the ice machines it had bought to chill the brewery cellars where the beer was left to condition could not do a good enough job to make Pilsen-style beers. It took three years to solve that problem and start producing golden, pils lagers as well.

Even when the technical problems were overcome, the company still struggled and it went into liquidation in 1892. Its assets were sold to Robert Graesser, a German-born industrialist who owned a chemical works near Wrexham. Under his control, the brewery continued, though it laboured to find sales at home and much of the business was in the export trade – 80 per cent of its sales went abroad by the turn of the century.

The lager brewers' problem was that Britain's ale brewers had reacted to the demand for lighter, less alcoholic beers by giving their pale ales and milds lower gravities and serving them quicker after brewing, meaning they were sweeter and less acidic. The *Brewers' Journal* in 1890 declared that 'lager beer in this country has certainly not realised the future prophesied for it some years back. That this is so is in great measure attributable to the competition it at once met at the hands of English brewers, who altered the character of their beers to meet the demands of the times.'

The journalist Alfred Barnard, writing a year earlier, said:

> The cry of sedentary workers … has been of late years for a lighter and less heady beer. The gaseous German Lager has had a fair trial to supply this want, but except for about three weeks in the year, that beer seems ill-adapted to our climate. The English brewers have endeavoured to supply this want by brewing a light sparkling bitter ale, and from the encouragement they have received it is likely the importation of German beer will not increase.

This did not stop at least a dozen other attempts to brew lager in Britain in the years around the end of the nineteenth century and the beginning of the twentieth. They included the English Lager Beer brewery of Batheaston, which hired the Bristol-based brewery architects Charles Johnson & Sons to build it a new brewery in 1891, but closed two years later in 1893. The British Lager Brewery Company was registered at 23/24 Devon Street, Liverpool in 1899, in brewery premises previously occupied by William and John Duck. A surviving bottle label suggests the brewery was exporting its 'Tropical brand' beer to Singapore and Malaya. However, it too quickly closed, in November 1902. Only one of these new operations involved a Continental brewer: the Holsten Brauerei of Hamburg briefly owned a brewery in Wandsworth, South London, from 1902–04.

One lager brewer did find lasting success, however, and it is perhaps no coincidence that it was in Scotland, home to John Muir's first experiments. Hugh Tennent, a member of the family that owned the Wellpark brewery in Glasgow, one of Scotland's biggest beer exporters, had been sent to Germany and Switzerland in the early 1880s to convalesce after a serious illness. He came back with enthusiasm for the lager beers he had tried and doubtless he saw lager brewing in Glasgow as the way to counter the threat to export sales of Tennent's pale ales from foreign lager brewers. In 1884 Hugh, then only twenty-one, took control of Tennent's brewery by buying his older brother's stake. Two Continental brewers, a Dane and a German, were hired, a new German-style lager-brewing plant was installed in the Wellpark buildings and lager brewing for export began in Glasgow in 1885.

Three years later Tennent's was declaring that its lager would 'defy the most delicate palate to detect any difference between it and the best foreign article' – and it was cheaper too. The following year a complete and separate lager brewery was built on the Wellpark site alongside the ale brewery. It opened in 1891 and ran until 1906, when another new brewery 'complete in all details' was opened in the north-east part of the Wellpark site, 'devoted to the manufacture of lager, Munich and Pilsener beers', that is, both amber and light lagers.

Perhaps encouraged by Tennent's example and worried by the increasing loss of export markets to the Continental beer, in 1897 the Burton upon Trent brewer Allsopp & Co. erected a 60,000-barrel lager plant at its Staffordshire home. But sales of lager in the UK remained at less than 1 per cent of total beer sales and Allsopp's lager brewery equipment was eventually, in 1921, transferred from Burton to Arrol's of Alloa in Scotland. By now Scotland was the centre for what little lager brewing there was in the UK: John Jeffrey and Co. of the Heriot brewery in Edinburgh started lager brewing in 1902.

Around the country there were sporadic attempts to brew British lagers, such as 'Anglo Lager' from Mackeson in Hythe, Kent, advertised in 1900 as 'a light and excellent tonic for families'. Largely, however, English brewers stuck to ales. The major exception was Barclay Perkins of the Anchor brewery in Southwark, London, formerly one of the capital's 'big three' porter and stout brewers, which began brewing London Lager in 'light' (Pilsner) and 'dark' (Munich) versions in 1921 and which made one of the few British-brewed lagers available on draught. It was brewed according to proper Continental principles, with a two-week fermentation period and a full four months of cold lagering.

Barclay's brewing books, analysed by the brewing historian Ron Pattinson, show that in 1928, for example, it was brewing an export lager at an original gravity of 1050, a 'Special Dark' lager at 1057 OG and a draught lager at 1044 OG. The export lager used all Kulmbacher malt from Germany, the draught a mixture of Kulmbacher and Taylor's malt from Hertfordshire (Taylor's being a specialist dark malt manufacturer) and the dark lager Kulmbacher, Taylor's, crystal malt and 1.8 per cent roasted barley. Even after ten years of lager sales, though, in 1931, Barclay's felt it necessary to run advertisements showing the 'right' (steep angle) and 'wrong' (ale-style shallow angle) ways to pour bottled lager, to get the right sort of head and in 1935 Barclay's was complaining that half the pubs that served its lager insisted on selling it at the same temperature as English ale, which it gave as the reason why lagers had not taken off in Britain.

Other comparatively big sellers in the tiny British-brewed lager market were Graham's Golden Lager, introduced by Arrol's of Alloa, (by now

Barclay's lager brewhouse at its brewery in Southwark in the 1920s

a subsidiary of Allsopp's of Burton upon Trent) in 1927, which became one of the most widely distributed beers brewed in Scotland within ten years. (The 'Graham' the beer was named after was either Colonel Graham, Allsopp's agent in London, or Willie Graham, town clerk of Alloa, depending on which story you prefer.) In the 1920s lager brewing had begun at the Moss Side brewery in Manchester under the brand name Red Tower and from 1933, when a new German-built lager plant was installed, this concern was known as the Red Tower Lager brewery.

None of these efforts had much impact. In 1948 it was said that only 'small' quantities of lager were brewed in Britain and a year later the writer Maurice Gorham declared: 'Lager is not a very popular drink in pubs, except in fairly high-class saloon bars during very hot weather. One can usually get bottled lager but it is not always iced. A few houses keep it on draught.' Even in 1956 another writer, Andrew Campbell, in a book devoted to British beers, dismissed lager in a few words of exceedingly faint praise: 'The very light mild flavour is popular with the ladies.'

It took a Canadian, E.P. 'Eddie' Taylor, to begin the push that made lager part of the British beer-drinking mainstream. Taylor was chairman of Canadian Breweries, which he had built up to be the biggest brewer in Quebec and Ontario, mainly through the Carling's Black Label lager brand. He believed that Carling (which took its name from a brewery in London, Ontario founded by a Yorkshireman, Thomas Carling, in 1843) would do very well in the British market and signed an agreement in 1953 with a specialist bottled beer brewer, Hope and Anchor Breweries of Sheffield, for it to brew Black Label under licence.

Taylor thought Carling's would sell on its quality alone and it took six or seven years for him to understand that British brewers would not sell someone else's beer in their tied pubs. Realising that the only way to break open the market was to build a pub empire himself and the only way to build a pub empire was to buy other brewers for their tied estates, from early in 1960 Taylor began acquiring British brewing companies. Within a year Taylor's United Breweries had bought nine different UK brewers and acquired a tied estate of 2,000 pubs, at the same time launching draught Black Label. Over the next few years United merged with the big London brewer, Charrington, and then Charrington with the Burton giant, Bass, to form Britain's biggest brewer, Bass Charrington, and guarantee Carling (it eventually dropped the apostrophe and then the 'Black Label') a position as one of Britain's biggest-selling lagers.

The foundation of United Breweries came at a time when demand for lager, albeit still tiny, was growing rapidly. A large part of this increase, according to *The Times* in 1958, was down to 'one of the most successful mixed drinks in recent years, lager and lime-juice, of obscure origin and drunk mostly by the young'. At the Wrexham brewery, owned by Ind Coope & Allsopp from 1949 but still using much of the original plant from 1883, lager was still brewed close to Continental methods; only one week of fermentation but five weeks of lagering and two weeks of chill-proofing at just above freezing point. As sales grew, production was lifted from 480 barrels a week in 1955 to 720 and a new brewhouse was installed in 1958. Very quickly this was seen to be inadequate and a complete new brewery was built, opening in May 1961, which could produce 720 barrels a day – a more than tenfold rise in output in just six years.

At the same time as Wrexham was expanding, Guinness, the stout giant, was also deciding the lager market had great potential as increasing numbers of Britons were exposed to the drink while on holidays abroad. In 1958 the Irish company hired an expert German lager brewer, Dr Hermann Münder of the Dom brewery in Cologne and started to construct a lager brewery at the Great Northern brewery in Dundalk, which it had bought for the purpose.

A flyer for Allsopp's lager, 'suitable for every climate in the world'

Guinness looked at several names for the new beer, before deciding upon Harp – a harp is, of course, the Guinness trademark. Water
from the Mourne Mountains was taken to the brewing research centre
in Weihenstephan, Bavaria for test brews and a cask of yeast from
Weihenstephan was brought back to Dundalk to start the first brew of
Harp in June 1960.

The Irish tests went well enough for Harp to arrive in the UK in April
1961. Guinness had set up a consortium of brewers to sell Harp that
consisted of itself, Scottish & Newcastle in the North, Mitchell & Butler
in the Midlands and Courage (which by now owned Barclay Perkins
and its London lager) in the South, thus ensuring shelf space for the
beer from the start in the consortium's tied houses. After six months
of selling only in North West England, Harp went on national sale in
November 1961. The new beer now needed to be brewed in the UK to
meet demand and other British lagers were axed to make way; Scottish
Brewers, later Scottish & Newcastle, had acquired the Red Tower Lager
brewery (subsequently named the Royal brewery) in Manchester in
1955. It agreed to drop production of a lager there with the curious
name of MY (for McEwan-Younger) to brew Harp instead.

In London, Courage threw the lager production facilities at the old
Barclay Perkins brewery near Southwark Bridge over to Harp. But the
Barclay Perkins brewery was due to close and a new dedicated brewery
was needed. In 1961 work began on building a new brewery at Alton in
Hampshire, where Courage had owned a pale ale brewery since just after
the turn of the century. Within two years, just in time for Beatlemania
(and sex, according to Philip Larkin), the first pint of Alton Harp was
produced. By this time the lager market had doubled in size in three
years, though it still only represented 2 per cent of British beer sales.

The real take-off occurred when the first draught Harp hit the pubs of
Britain in 1965. In Scotland, in three years draught lager captured 20 per
cent of the beer market. A new Harp brewery was opened in Edinburgh in
1970 and brewing of Harp also began at Guinness's London brewery, Park
Royal. Drinkers did not seem to care, that at an OG of 1033, it was weaker
than most continental lagers and weaker than many draught British beers.
The motivation for beer drinking was changing, pushed by everything
from the decline in heavy manual work to the rise in central heating, from
'restoration' to 'refreshment'. Lager, served cold, with more carbon dioxide
'bite', was more 'refreshing' and strength (or flavour) was irrelevant.

In Scotland, meanwhile, the third of the 'big brand' British lagers had
appeared in 1959. After rebuilding the Alloa brewery and incorporating a

Swedish brewhouse, Ind Coope had relaunched Graham's Golden Lager as Skol, named for a Scandinavian expression equivalent to 'Cheers!' (for a while it was known as Graham's Skol Lager). It was part of a grow-ing feeling that lagers, to be successful, had to have at least a vaguely European touch.

The name change was also part of a deliberate pitch for young drink-ers, who were featured in advertising for the brand, something that would not be allowed today. Ind Coope told the *Morning Advertiser* (the trade paper for pubs) that the 'boy and girl' (its own words) in the Skol advertisements, part of 'the biggest advertising campaign Britain has ever seen for any lager' (quite a claim: even in 1960 lager took 19 per cent of all UK beer advertising, despite having only 1 per cent of the market), were 'changing the taste of Britain'. Although Skol eventually faded in the UK, the company Ind Coope grew into, Allied Breweries, set up an international consortium involving breweries from Sweden, Canada and Belgium in 1964 to market and brew Skol abroad. By 1973 it was being brewed in eighteen countries and Skol is still one of the biggest beer brands in Brazil.

Sales of lager in England and Wales were slower to rise than they were in Scotland. Even in 1966 the assistant managing director of Flowers brewery in Stratford upon Avon had written that while 'very light beers of the lager variety' were suited to the climate of the European conti-nent, 'one would not consider lager beers to be particularly well suited to the English weather. It will be interesting to see if the enormous advertising expenditure which is currently being made by several large breweries will be successful in stimulating the popularity of lager.'

But by 1971 lager, both keg and bottled, was taking just under 10 per cent of total beer volumes. A flood of 'Continental-style' lager beers hit the country, though even the ones that claimed a Continental heritage were brewed much weaker than their Continental originals. Whitbread had started brewing a lower-gravity version of the Dutch lager Heineken in 1968, at an OG of 1033 (the same as Harp), much weaker than the 5 per cent abv version of Heineken sold around the world. Within two years this weaker Heineken had 20 per cent of the lager market in England and Wales.

Another national brewer, Watney, signed with the Danish brewer Carlsberg to brew a weaker version of Copenhagen lager, once more at an OG of 1030. It was produced at a new brewery in Northampton, where the London brewer had taken over a local firm, Phipp's, in 1960. The Northampton Carlsberg brewery opened in 1973, by which time lager sales in Britain had increased 50 per cent in two years, despite its high price – Carlsberg, at 1030 OG, sold for 18p, while even the stronger, at an OG of 1037, and heavily-promoted Watney's Red keg bitter was only 14p a pint.

The next four years all saw hot summers, and lager sales continued to rise. By 1976 total lager sales nationally were equal to almost one in four pints, a fantastic boom compared to the one in a hundred pints fifteen years earlier. More than a dozen smaller British brewers, trying to compete with the national brands, were attempting to brew their own 'lager', generally using the wrong sort of equipment and the wrong sort of yeast, and with laughable names: Husky, Schloss, Iceberg, Polar (this last was actually a chilled pale ale introduced by the East Anglian brewer Greene King around 1971 to try to fight chilled lagers, which quickly disappeared).

The low quality of so many small brewers' so-called 'lagers' was an embarrassment to the bigger brewers of what they insisted were 'true' lager beers. Guinness and Bass in 1974 tried to get a definition of 'lager' agreed by the government's food standards committee, but smaller brewers would not accept a statement on lager that ruled out using top-fermenting yeast. However, those brewers not using traditional European methods to brew their lagers were becoming shamed into changing their ways and the 'bastard' lagers gradually disappeared.

With the market flooded by ersatz lagers, literally pale imitations of continental styles, Britain's respectable history of lager brewing was for-gotten and among beer enthusiasts British-brewed lager maintained a dreadful reputation. All the same, by 1989 lager in all its forms, draught, bottled and canned, had finally captured the majority of the UK beer market, with sales of 50.3 per cent by value. Through the 1990s it con-tinued to grow so that at the beginning of the twenty-first century, pale bottom-fermented beer was on the way to becoming two in every three pints of beer drunk in Britain. This was not enough to save Britain's longest-lasting dedicated lager brewery, however. The Wrexham brewery was closed by its then owners, Carlsberg-Tetley, in 2001, victim of the continuing consolidation in the mainstream British brewing industry.

Meanwhile, the 'microbrewery revolution' that had begun around 1976 in Britain ignored lager for what were seen as genuine old British beer styles, such as bitter and porter. Only in 1982 did the first 'microbrewed' lager appear at the Hardington brewery in Somerset, which brewed a 1035 OG 'Lansdorf Lager' and served it via hand-pump at the brewery tap, the Mandeville Arms. However, although the beer was made with pale lager malt and lagered for four weeks, it was brewed with a top-fermenting yeast and a British-style infusion mash, not the decoction mash used by Continental lager brewers. At the Ringwood brewery in Hampshire the same year the small brewery pioneer Peter Austin began making Brauring Lager using bottom-fermenting yeast and served unfiltered and unpasteurised. Unfortunately, the beer would not drop bright and it does not seem to have been in production long.

The need to have different equipment and use different techniques to make authentic lager seems to have stopped any more experiments by Britain's new small brewers for more than a decade. In 1995, however, the first 'big force' in small-operator lager brewing arrived when the Harviestoun brewery in Dollar, Clackmannanshire, then ten years old, launched Schiehallion, a 4.8 per cent abv cask-conditioned draught Bohemian-style lager brewed with Hersbrucker hops from Germany. The beer won the first of a series of gold medals in the speciality beers section of the Campaign for Real Ale's Champion Beer of Britain competition in 1996, thus legitimising lager brewing for the new wave of brewers.

Almost as significantly, also in 1995 the Freedom Brewing Company opened in Parsons Green, London, producing as its main product a premium pilsner-style lager. The brewer was Alistair Hook, one of the few British brewers to have trained at the Weihenstephan brewing university in Bavaria. Freedom later moved to Soho, where, under a new owner, the Brothers Brewing Co., it still brews, though some of its beers are also produced in Abbotts Bromley in Staffordshire. Hook's most important contribution to British lager brewing came in 2000, however, when he opened the Meantime brewery in Greenwich, which was the first new brewery in Britain to specialise in other authentic, unpasteurised Continental beer styles. Among the brews it has produced are a proper Vienna-style lager, a Munich Oktoberfest-style lager and a Franconian-style dark lager.

In 2005 the British cask-conditioned lager scene was given another boost with the launch by the Robert Cain brewery in Liverpool of a cask-conditioned version of its premium lager, a beer already notable for the ninety-day conditioning period it received, far longer than most British lagers ever had. It was also the first lager to be brewed with Maris Otter, the traditional British ale malt. Cain's followed this up in 2007 with the launch of a strong bottled Bock lager, at 8 per cent abv, perhaps the first time this German speciality has been brewed in the UK.

While a number of British microbrewers have tried their hands at lager in the past ten years or so, only a tiny number of small brewers still regularly make cask or bottle-conditioned lagers, including Whitstable in Kent with Bohemian at 5.2 per cent abv; Wylam of Northumberland, with the similarly-named Bohemia at 4.6 per cent abv; the Zerodegrees microbrewery and restaurant in Blackheath, London, which started in 2000 and makes both a pilsener and a black lager; the Brunswick in Derby, with a 5 per cent abv pilsner; Oakleaf brewery of Gosport's marvellously named I Can't Believe It's Not Bitter; the Organic Brewhouse in Cornwall with Charlie's Pride lager at 5.3 per cent abv; and Lager-beer from Woodlands in Shropshire at 4.1 per cent abv.

Only a couple of small British brewers have been brave enough to start up as a lager specialist. The first was Cotswold, of Foscot, Oxfordshire, begun by Richard and Emma Keene in 2005 and producing Premium Cotswold Lager at 5 per cent abv and using Liberty (from America) and Hersbrucker hops and Maris Otter malted barley. The second was the Taddington brewery, based in the former malthouse of Joshua Lingard's brewery at Blackwell Hall, Blackwell, Buxton, Derbyshire, which began in 2008 and which brews Moravka lager to a Czech recipe.

GLOSSARY

Abroad cooper: brewery representative who checked the condition of the beer when it was in the publican's cellars.

Abv: alcohol by volume: the percentage of alcohol in a volume of liquid, the standard modern UK measure of beer strength.

Ale: In references from Saxon times to the end of the seventeenth century, this means a fermented malt liquor made without hops, in strict contrast with beer, which, when the word reached the British Isles in the 1400s, meant a fermented malt liquor flavoured with hops. By the early nineteenth century, ale had become a hopped malt drink. Until the middle of the nineteenth century, however, it generally (but not exclusively) meant a less-hopped drink than beer.

Alehouse: an older name for what later became called the pub.

Attenuation: as beer ferments and sugar is converted into alcohol, the specific gravity (q.v.) of the liquid lowers, a process known as attenuation. Beers where most of the sugar is converted are known as highly attenuated, sweet beers where more of the sugars have survived have low attenuation.

Barley wine: a name that covers a variety of strong beers in different styles barrel: a specific size of cask, thirty-six gallons for the British beer barrel, thirty-two gallons (thirty gallons before 1532) for the ale barrel.

Beer: in references from the fifteenth century onwards, a fermented malt liquor flavoured with hops (q.v.).

Beerhouse: premises licensed to sell beer only, not wine or spirits. Came into being with the 1830 Beerhouse Act. Eventually all beerhouses either closed or acquired full licences.

Bitter: the name first given by the nineteenth-century drinking public to pale ale on draught.

Bottom-fermenting yeast: more accurately, bottom-settling yeast: generally associated with the cool-fermenting yeasts used to make lager beer, although some warm-fermenting ale yeasts can be bottom-settling types.

Brettanomyces: also known as Brett, a type of yeast that will step in when the normal *Saccharomyces* yeast has retired from the scene exhausted, and which is particularly associated with beers stored for a long time in wooden vessels, such as aged stouts (q.v.), old ales (q.v.), stock bitters (q.v.) and Belgian lambic beers.

Brewhouse: the part of a brewery where the mash tun and copper are housed.

Burton ale: a darkish, slightly sweet draught beer, a style developed in Burton upon Trent.

Bushel: a measure of grain, originally a container that would hold exactly eight gallons of water, then the amount of grain that would fit into such a container, generally taken to be around forty-two pounds of malt. (The grain, when measured, would be levelled off with a piece of wood known as a 'strike', hence the pub name Bushel and Strike.)

Butt: a cask with a capacity of 108 gallons (equal to two hogsheads or three barrels), about the biggest that could be easily handled by one (strong) man, and often used in the eighteenth century for maturing beer cask any wooden draught beer container of any size, from pin (q.v.) to tun (q.v.).

Condition: the amount of carbonation in a beer.

Cooper: maker of casks and other brewery vessels out of wood (although a man who specialised in vessels other than casks was known as a back maker).

Copper: the vessel in which the wort (q.v.) was boiled with hops, traditional made of copper, an excellent conductor of heat.

Currency: In this book all currency references before 1971 have been left in pounds, shillings and (old) pence, shortened generally to £ (an L with a line through it, for *libra*, the Latin equivalent), *s* (for *solidus*, a Roman coin) and *d* (for *denarius*, another Roman coin). Thus five pounds two shillings and six (old) pence would be written £5 2s 6d. There were twelve (old) pence to the shilling, and twenty shillings to the pound.

Decoction mashing: the practice of taking away a proportion of the mash, heating it to a high temperature and then adding it back to the rest of the mash to raise the temperature of the whole. A traditional German mashing technique.

Double beer: beer made from wort that has been poured back through the mash to increase its strength by extracting more sugar from the malt.

Entire: a beer made with all the wort collected from a set of mashings on one batch of grain.

Fermentation: the process during which yeast (q.v.) converts sugar into alcohol, changing sweet wort (q.v.) into ale or beer (q.v.).

Fermenting vessel: where fermentation takes place.

Final gravity: the specific gravity (q.v.) of a beer when it has finished fermenting at the brewery. A precise relationship exists between original gravity (q.v.), final gravity and the amount of alcohol in a beer.

Firkin: a nine-gallon cask (equal to a quarter of a barrel).

Gallon: eight pints, 4.54 litres.

Grist: ground malt, ready for mashing.

Guinea: A sum of money equivalent to £1 1s (see currency).

Gyle: (noun) originally freshly-fermenting wort, later a specific brewing batch (as in 'gyle number 42').

Gyle: (verb) to add freshly fermenting wort to a batch of finished beer to raise its condition (q.v.), otherwise known (from the German) as krausening.

Hogshead: a cask of 54 gallons capacity, or 1½ barrels.

Hop: *Humulus lupulus*, a climbing plant grown for the bitter resins found in its strobili or cones, which are boiled with wort (q.v.) and help to preserve the fermented beer, as well as make it bitter and give it flavours that range from orangey through piney to minty, depending on the variety.

Imperial stout: exceptionally strong dark stout, so called from its being sold originally to the court of the Emperor of Russia.

India Pale Ale: name given in Britain (but not India) from around 1837 onwards to the strong stock pale ale originally shipped to the East for expatriate Europeans, which matured fast thanks to its double trip through warm equatorial waters on the way round Africa. IPA became particularly associated with the big Burton upon Trent brewers.

Infusion mash: mashing all the grain at once with hot water, as opposed to the decoction mash (q.v.) system.

Isinglass: the swim bladder of fish, especially the sturgeon, dried and sold to the brewer. He then mixed it with stale beer to turn it into a jelly that will clarify or 'fine' beer when added to a cask, by taking suspended solids with it to the bottom.

Kilderkin: cask of eighteen gallons capacity (half a barrel).

Lager: beer brewed under cool conditions, using a so-called 'bottom- fermenting' yeast (q.v.) and stored for some time to mature, from the German word *Lager*, storeroom. The British equivalent was called stock beer (q.v.).

Liquor: the brewer's name for water.

Malt: grain which has been allowed to start to germinate, to encourage the production of sugars from the starches in each barleycorn or wheat seed, and then dried to stop germination before all the sugar is used up by the growing plant. The amount of drying governs the colour, and in large part the flavour of the malt.

Maltings: the building where malt is made: generally long and thin, with a kiln at one end to dry the malt, in Victorian times several stories high. Some, but not all brewers owned their own maltings.

Mash: mixed grist (q.v.) and liquor (q.v.).

Mashing: mixing the grist (q.v.) with hot liquor (q.v.) to extract the fermentable sugars mash tun: the vessel where mashing takes place. The earliest mash tuns were simple tubs and a wicker basket (known as a strun or huckmuck) was pushed into the middle of the mash (q.v.), so that the sweet wort (q.v.) flowed into the basket to be ladled out into the fermenting vessel (q.v.). Later mash tuns had taps, protected by twigs or straw from blocking up, for the wort to run off through and still later versions had a perforated false floor through which the wort ran to a tap.

Mild: sweetish, often (today) dark beer, generally lightly hopped because it was meant to be served and drunk soon after being brewed.

Milk stout: dark beer brewed with some unfermentable lactic sugar to keep it sweet.

Nip: a bottle containing one third of a pint, usually used for strong beers OG: see original gravity.

Old ale: a name given to any strong aged pale or brown beer.

Original gravity: the specific gravity (q.v.) of wort (q.v.) before fermentation, known as OG. The specific gravity of water is taken to be 1000, and the original gravity of wort, which shows how much fermentable material is dissolved in it, is given in points above 1000, such as 1036, 1047 or 1080. The OG figure gives a guide to the likely alcohol level of the finished beer, with an OG of 1047 meaning a likely final abv (q.v.) of around 4.7 per cent, depending on how well-attenuated (q.v.) the beer is.

Penny: in pre-decimal currency, one 240th of a pound, with twelve pence to the shilling (q.v.). The short form was '*d*', from the Latin *denarius*. See currency.

Pin: a 4½-gallon cask (half a firkin).

Pint: 20 (imperial) fluid ounces, 568ml. There are 8 pints to the gallon.

Porter: originally a strong dark brown bitter beer popular with London's very many street and river porters in the eighteenth century, from whom it derived its name. In its final incarnation, a weak but still dark beer. (Porter, as a well-hopped drink, was always called a 'beer' and never an 'ale').

Present gravity: the specific gravity (q.v.) of a beer in cask or bottle at the point it was measured some time after racking or bottling, which, after secondary fermentation in the cask or bottle had produced more alcohol and thus lowered the specific gravity, will be less than the 'final gravity' (q.v.) at the point the beer left the fermentation vessel.

Pub: short for public house, generally a reference to premises with a full on-licence to sell beer and spirits (unlike a beerhouse), but not offering accommodation (unlike an inn).

Quart: equal to two pints. The standard 'pot' in an inn or pub until the end of the nineteenth century held a quart.

Quarter: a volume measure of malt equal to eight bushels (q.v.). The exact weight of a quarter of malt would vary depending on how dense the malt was and the size of the grains, but it is generally taken as three hundredweight, or 336lb. The capacity of breweries was measured in the number of quarters of malt they could mash at any one time, a quarter of malt producing, very roughly, four barrels (144 gallons) of beer at the 'standard' OG of 1055.

Racking: running the fermented beer off its lees into casks for delivery.

Round: a fermentation vessel.

Secondary fermentation: the fermentation that takes place in the cask after the beer has been racked.

Shilling: in pre-decimal currency, one twentieth of a pound; divided into twelve pence. The short form is '*s*'. See currency.

Small beer: weak beer made, generally, from the last mash of the grain. Sometimes 'entire' small beer would be made by combining all the mashes into one.

Sparging: spraying hot water over the mash tun at the end of mashing to maximise extraction of sugars.

Specific gravity: a measured of the density of a liquid, compared to pure water. With beer, specific gravity falls as fermentation progresses, sugar is used up and alcohol (which is less dense than water) is produced.

Square: a square-shaped fermentation vessel, double-chambered so that excess yeast flows up from the bottom part into the top.

Stock beer: beer brewed for keeping and maturing, the British equivalent (except that it underwent warm conditioning, not cold) to German *Lagerbier*. Stock beer would normally undergo a secondary fermentation involving *Brettanomyces* yeast, (q.v.) which gave it a much-prized flavour.

Stout: originally a slang expression for any strong beer, later specifically a strong version of porter.

Top-fermenting: more accurately, top-settling yeast, yeast since it rises to the top of the fermenting vessel (q.v.) when it has used up all the sugar in the wort (q.v.). Most, but not all, ale yeasts are of the top-settling type.

Tun: a brewery vessel; also, a cask of 240 gallons.

Union system: fermentation method particularly associated with Burton upon Trent in which the excess yeast is separated from the fermenting beer by flowing up a pipe into a trough.

Wort: unfermented beer, the sugary liquid collected from the mash tun.

X: the letter often used by brewers to indicate the strength of their beers and ales; the more Xs, the stronger the beer.

Yeast: the single-celled organism responsible for turning sugar into alcohol. Brewers mostly use the yeast *Saccharomyces cerevisiae*.

Zythophilia: the love of beer, from the Greek zythos, a word for a type of ale.

BIBLIOGRAPHY

Abbott, Harry, *Sonepore Reminiscences: Years 1840-96*, Star Press, Calcutta, 1896

Allen, Alfred Henry, *Allen's Commercial Organic Analysis*, J&A Churchill, London, 1912

Almqvist, Bo, *The Viking Ale and the Rhine Gold, Some notes on an Irish-Scottish folk-legend and a Germanic hero-tale motif*, Arv, 1965: pp.115–135

Amsinck, George Stewart, *Practical Brewings: A Series of 50 Brewings in Extension*, London, 1868

Anon, *The Art of Brewing*, London, c.1840

Anon, *The Brewer's Art,* Whitbread, London, 1948

Anon, *Every Man His Own Brewer*, 1768

Anon, *Guide to Gentlemen and Farmers for Brewing the Finest Malt Liquors*, 1703

Anon, *A Vade Mecum for Malt-Worms/ A Guide for Malt-Worms*, London, c.1718–20

Anon, *Hodgson's India Pale Ale, Notes and Queries,* 7th series, VI, 1888, p.329, p.417

Ashton, John, *Social Life in the Reign of Queen Anne: Taken from Original Sources*, Chatto & Windus, London, 1919

Bailey, R. Douglas, *The Brewer's Analyst: A Systematic Handbook of Analysis Relating to Brewing*, 1907

Baillie, Frank, *The Beer Drinker's Companion*, London, David & Charles, 1974

Barnard, Alfred, *Noted Breweries of Great Britain and Ireland,* vols I–IV, Sir Joseph Causton & Sons, London, 1889–90

Beable, William Henry, *Romance of Great Businesses*, Heath Cranton, 1926

Berkley, Tom, *We Keep a Pub*, Hutchinson, London, 1955

Bickerdyke, John (pseudonym of Charles Henry Cook), *The Curiosities of Ale and Beer*, Swan Sonnenschein, London, 1889

Brande, William, *The Town and Country Brewery Book or, Every Man His Own Brewer*, Dean and Munday, London, c.1830

Brewer's Journal, various

Brown, Pete, *Hops and Glory*, Macmillan, London, 2009

Buhner, Stephen Harrod, *Sacred and Herbal Healing Beers*, Brewers Publications, Colorado, 1998

Bushnan, John Stevenson, *Burton and its Bitter Beer*, WS Orr & Co., London, 1853

Campbell, Andrew, *The Book of Beer*, Dennis Dobson, London, 1956

Chapman, A.C., *Brewing*, 1912

Child, Samuel, *Every Man His Own Brewer, a practical treatise, explaining the art and mystery of brewing porter, ale, twopenny, and table beer*, J. Ridgway, London, 1802

Combrune, Michael, *An Essay on Brewing, with a View of Establishing the Principles of the Art*, London, 1758

Combrune, Michael, *The Theory and Practice of Brewing*, London, 1762

Cooley, Arnold James, *Cyclopaedia of Several Thousand Practical Receipts, and Collateral Information in the Arts, Manufactures and Trades*, London, 1846

Cornell, Martyn, *Beer: The Story of the Pint*, Hodder Headline, London, 2003

Dennison, S.R. and O. McDonagh, *Guinness 1886–1939*, Cork, 1998

Ellis, William, The *London and Country Brewer*, London, 1734

Encyclopedia Britannia, Edinburgh, 1911 edition

Feltham, John, *The Picture of London*, 1802

Gerard, John, *The Herball or General History of Plants*, 1597

Glover, Brian, *New Beer Guide, a guide to Britain's small brewery revolution*, David & Charles, Newton Abbott, 1988

Good Beer Guide 1974–2009, Campaign for Real Ale, St Albans

Gorham, Maurice, *Back to the Local*, London, Percival Marshall, 1949

Gourvish, Terry, *Norfolk Beers from English Barley, a history of Steward & Patteson*, Centre for East Anglian Studies, Norwich, 1987

Gourvish, T.R. and R.G. Wilson, *The British Brewing Industry 1830–1980*, Cambridge University Press, 1994

Grieve, Maude, *A Modern Herbal*, Dover Publications, 1931

Hagen, Anne, *A Handbook of Anglo-Saxon Food and Drink: Processing and Consumption*, Pinner, Anglo-Saxon Books, 1992

Hagen, Anne, *A Second Handbook of Anglo-Saxon Food and Drink: Production and Distribution*, Hockwold-cum-Wilton, Anglo-Saxon Books, 1995

Herbert, James, *The Art of Brewing India Pale Ale and Export Ale, Stock and Mild Ales, Porter and Stout*, Burton upon Trent, 1871

Hofsten, Nils von, *Pors och andra humleersättningar och ölkryddor i äldre tider (Bog Myrtle and Other Substitutes for Hops in Former Times)*, University of Uppsala, 1960

Hooper, Egbert, *The Manual of Brewing Scientific and Technical*, Sheppard and St John, London, 1882

Hornsey, Ian S., *Brewing*, RSC Paperbacks, Cambridge, 1999

Izzard, George, *One for the Road, the autobiography of a London village publican*, Max Parrish, London, 1959

Jackson, Michael, *World Guide to Beer*, Mitchell Beazley, London, 1977

La Pensée, Clive, *The Craft of House Brewing*, Montag Publications, Beverley, 1996

La Pensée, Clive, *The Historical Companion to House Brewing*, Montag Publications, Beverley, 1990

Lewis, R.A. ed., *Pale Ale and Bitter Beer*, Staffordshire County Council Education Department, 1977

Lightbody, James, *The Gauger and Measurer's Companion ...To which is added ...A true method for brewing strong ale in London etc.*, London, 1694

Lynch, P. and J. Vaizey, *Guinness's Brewery in the Irish Economy (1759-1876)*, Cambridge, 1960

Mathias. Peter, *The Brewing Industry in England 1799–1830*, Cambridge, 1959

McDonagh, O., *Origins of Porter, Economic History Review*, 2nd ser., 16, No 3, 1964, pp. 530–35

Molyneux, W., *Burton on Trent, Its History, Its Waters and Its Breweries*, London, 1869

Monckton, H.A., *A History of English Ale and Beer*, Bodley Head, London, 1966

Morewood, Samuel, *A Philosophical and Statistical History of the Inventions and Customs of Ancient and Modern Nations in the Manufacture and Use of Inebriating Liquors*, Dublin, 1838

Nevile, Sir Sydney, *Seventy Rolling Years*, Faber, London, 1958

Nordland, Odd, *Brewing and Beer Traditions in Norway*, Oslo, 1969

Owen, Colin C., *Burton upon Trent, the development of industry*, Phillimore & Co, Chichester, 1978

Owen, Colin C., *The Greatest Brewery in the World, a history of Bass, Ratcliff & Gretton*, Derbyshire Record Society, Chesterfield, 1992

Parry, David Lloyd, *South Yorkshire Stingo, New Ash Green, Brewery History Society*, 1997

Pattinson, Ronald, *Dark Beer*, Amsterdam, 2008

Pattinson, Ronald, *Mild*, Amsterdam, 2007

Patton, Jeffrey, *Additives, Adulterants and Contaminants in Beer*, Patton Publications, Barnstaple, 1989

Pereira, Jonathan, *A treatise on food and diet: with observations on the dietetical regimen suited for disordered states of the digestive organs*, London, 1843

Protz, Roger, *Classic Stout & Porter*, Prion, London, 1997

Pryor, Alan, *Indian Pale Ale: An Icon of Empire*, Commodities of Empire Working Paper No 13, Ferguson Centre for African and Asian Studies, Open University, 2009

Rees, Abraham, *The Cyclopaedia, or, Universal Dictionary of Arts, Sciences and Literature*, Longman, London, 1820

Richardson, John, *Statical Estimates of the Materials for Brewing, or, a treatise on the application and use of the saccharometer*, London, 1784

Richardson, John, *Philosophical Principles of the Science of Brewing*, York, 1784

Roberts, W.H., *The Scottish Ale Brewer*, Oliver & Boyd, Edinburgh, 1837

Sambrook, Pamela, *Country House Brewing in England 1500–1900*, The Hambledon Press, 1996

Seton Karr, W.S. and Hugh Sandeman, *Selections from Calcutta Gazettes 1784–1823*, Calcutta, 1864–69

Stern, Walter M., *The Porters of London*, Longmans, London, 1960

Stopes, Henry, *Malt and Malting, Brewer's Journal*, London, 1885

The Times 1785–1970

Tizard, W.L., *The Theory and Practice of Brewing Illustrated*, London, 1846

Tryon, Thomas, *A New Art of Brewing Beer, Ale, and Other Sorts of Liquors*, London, 1690

Tuck, John, *The Private Brewer's Guide to the Art of Brewing Ale and Porter*, W. Simpkin & R. Marshall, London, 1822

Various, *Burton Pale Ales*: papers presented at a seminar held on 14 July 1990

Various, *Beer in Britain*, The Times Publishing Company, London, 1960

White Horse, *Parson's Green, London*, The White Horse, Parson's Green, 1994

Wahl, Robert and Max Henius, *American handy-book of the brewing, malting and auxiliary trades*, Chicago, 1908

Watkins, George, *The Complete Brewer ... by a Brewer of Extensive Practice*, Dublin, 1766

What's Brewing (newspaper of the Campaign for Real Ale) 1977–2009

Wild, Antony, *The East India Company, Trade and Conquest from 1600*, Harper Collins, 1999

Y-Worth, Dr William, *Cerevisiarii Comes, or the New and True Art of Brewing*, London, 1692

INDEX